Critical Acclaim for
Straight Jacket by Matthew Todd

'This is an essential read for every gay person on the planet.'
Sir Elton John

'Utterly brilliant.'
Owen Jones, *Guardian*

'A sensitive subject, brilliantly and intelligently handled.'
Evan Davis

'This book should have been written a long time ago, but it wasn't . . .
I know it will help other people avoid the mistakes many of us have
made . . . I think everyone, no matter what their background, could,
can, *will* benefit from reading this book. A much-needed and healing
work of tough love, written with love.'
John Grant

'Timely . . . heartbreaking . . . This kind of book is needed.'
Louis Wise, *Sunday Times*

'If only this had been written twenty years ago – I can
only imagine the lives that could have been saved sooner.
This is a hugely important book for *everyone*. It's changed
the way I see myself, other people and the world.'
Paris Lees

'In [his] new book, Matthew Todd reveals the crisis of
shame facing the gay community – and how to solve it.'
Observer

'This powerful book, I believe, will save lives. I'd
like to see every gay man reading this.'
Juno Dawson, *Guardian*

www.penguin.co.uk

'Cannot put it down . . . a book like this is long overdue.'
Charlie Condou

'Part sociological polemic and part self-help book, it zones in
on some of the issues that disproportionately affect the gay
community, from depression and anxiety to drug and alcohol
addiction and body and eating disorders. I found myself both
deeply upset and hugely relieved by its candour. After reading
the book, tender as it is, you can't help but want to share your
own experiences. Consider *Straight Jacket* a call to arms.'
Hugh Montgomery, *the i*

'A superb book . . . Have read it twice now.'
Oliver Thring

'An honest and perceptive book.'
Sunday Express

'Todd doesn't hold back in calling for a shift both outside and inside the
gay community. He calls out hook-up apps such as Grindr, the "mean
girls" persona that so many gay men adopt, and the gay press itself
. . . *Straight Jacket* isn't just a self-help book. It's a resource for anyone
with an interest in knowing what needs to change to bring about real
equality . . . For that, Matthew Todd has another reason to be proud.'
Mobeen Azhar, *Evening Standard*

'An excoriating book, *Straight Jacket: How to be gay and
happy* delves into contemporary gay culture to address
a plethora of issues gay people continue to face.'
Attitude

'It's an important book. I had to read it right through.
It tackles some tough issues and is searingly honest.'
Lorraine Kelly

STRAIGHT JACKET

Overcoming society's legacy of gay shame

MATTHEW TODD

BLACK SWAN

TRANSWORLD PUBLISHERS
61–63 Uxbridge Road, London W5 5SA
www.penguin.co.uk

Transworld is part of the Penguin Random House group of companies
whose addresses can be found at global.penguinrandomhouse.com

First published in Great Britain in 2016 by Bantam Press
an imprint of Transworld Publishers
Black Swan edition published 2018

A CIP catalogue record for this book
is available from the British Library.

ISBN
9780552778404

Typeset in Minion Pro by Thomson Digital Pvt Ltd, Nolda, Delhi.
Printed and bound in Great Britain by Clays Ltd, Elcograf S.p.A.

Penguin Random House is committed to a sustainable
future for our business, our readers and our planet. This book
is made from Forest Stewardship Council® certified paper.

7 9 10 8 6

Although this book includes interviews and references to numerous
real people, some names and identifying features have been
changed in order to preserve their anonymity.

Dedicated to the memory of Mark Houghton, and all those lesbian, gay, bisexual, transgender, queer, questioning or intersex young people whose lives ended too soon, and to their families, with the hope of change

Contents

Part Three: Recovery

'A place where there isn't any trouble . . . Do you suppose there is such a place, Toto? There must be. It's not a place you can get to by a boat or a train. It's far, far away, behind the moon, beyond the rain . . .'

Dorothy Gale,
The Wizard of Oz, 1939

'Expect sarcasm'

Grindr profile, 2015

Foreword
by John Grant

If you're about to start reading this book, I feel very delighted for you, because you are in for a treat. It's a book that should have been written a long time ago, but it wasn't, so here we are at last and it's a great place to be.

Matthew Todd has contributed a great deal to the LGBT community as an obscenely talented man – playwright, comedian, writer, magazine editor (*Attitude*, of course) and gay rights activist. I think *Straight Jacket* is his crowning achievement thus far. Although it's unfortunate that Matthew had to have the experiences that made it possible for him to write it, I'm extremely grateful for the hard-won insights contained in this book and I hope lots of people will read it. I know it will help other people avoid the mistakes many of us have made. For me personally, it's just nice to feel so very understood and it's a relief to hear these words from another gay man.

I feel I should say a few words about my own experience. It took me, has taken me, *is* taking me a very long time to feel comfortable in my skin. I grew up in a small Midwestern town where it was communicated to me at church and school that being gay could only ever possibly lead to Hell and would permanently shut me off from God and the world in general, and that a creature such as I could not expect to have any sort of future. I believed what I was told because at the time I had no reason not to. Why would those I trusted and loved and looked to for protection, and who proclaimed to love me and want only the best for me, tell me things which were not true? I was told and led to believe that any sort of homosexual relationship I ever entered into could not possibly work because such relationships were inferior, sick, perverted and just plain wrong.

Sometimes I hear, and not just from straight people, 'For crying out loud, shut up, get over it, it can't have been that bad, pull yourself together, quit feeling sorry for yourself, quit living in the past, you're an adult . . .' That I am now an adult and therefore responsible for myself and for figuring out how to navigate this world is certainly true. I also know that self-pity has never done anyone any good, and that I must learn to let the past go and live in the moment. However, this deeply ingrained and total rejection of the self has countless negative and long-lasting consequences: in my case, drug, alcohol and sex addiction which ultimately lead to HIV infection. I had already given up the booze and drugs when I became infected through continuing to indulge in destructive behaviour I somehow still believed was normal. The process of overcoming these consequences (minus the HIV, of course) has taken place over the course of many years and I rather doubt it will ever be complete. Who knows?

I think it is quite clear that, as we have entered into an age of ever-increasing tolerance and acceptance towards the LGBT community, the trauma many of us have experienced continues to cause us to project the past on to the present. We have internalized the negative messages we received to such an extent that many of us continue to be unable to accept ourselves (and therefore each other), even though most of the people with whom we come into contact on a daily basis couldn't care less who we're sleeping with and don't pose us any threat. Many of us have suffered from years of post-traumatic stress disorder, every type of addiction known to man, obsession with beauty and success, crippling anxiety disorders, eating disorders, depression and isolation. Perhaps we think that if we admit to these things they would certainly be used against us by those who seek to deny us equality as proof that homosexuality *cannot* 'work' (never mind that all these phenomena are present in every part of every society, regardless of sexual orientation). Maybe we think that, if we are to be accepted, we must be morally beyond reproach, or at least perfect in some sort of way. We can't be gay *and* average or, God forbid, below average. We should be rich and/or beautiful with a perfect body, excel in everything we do, be lousy with talent, have exquisite taste in everything and also impeccable style; we must be either comfortingly masculine or camp in a way that isn't threatening, or is at least amusing; we must make an effort to fit in. I think many of us have become overachievers who are tortured by crippling perfectionism because we think this is what we must do in order to survive.

Of course there are those in the LGBT community who perhaps don't know what the hell I'm talking about, and that is certainly fantastic. But unfortunately there are many gay men and women who know exactly what I'm talking about. *Straight Jacket* is a book about the trauma many have experienced growing up gay, the many ways in which it manifests in daily life and how to begin the process of overcoming it. I think everyone, no matter what their background, could, can, *will* benefit from reading this book. After all, it's a book about understanding ourselves and each other more. There is no 'us and them', either inside or outside the LGBT community. This is a lie we can no longer afford to believe if we hope to conquer the past and live happier, more fulfilled lives.

Prologue

Excerpt (edited for clarity) from 1967 BBC2 documentary Man Alive: *'Consenting Adults Part 1: The Men. Will a change in law save homosexuals from blackmail and fear?'*

The screen shows a suited man, from behind, walking through the West End of London.

Voiceover: Most homosexuals don't live together and don't even live in large cities. They go to the large towns looking for others like themselves: desperately lonely men, scared of discovery; men like this clerk, from a small market town – the sort of man that the present laws seem designed to protect us from. For him, how did it all start?

We see a man sitting with his back to the camera, face hidden.

Man: Well, I met someone in a gents' toilets when I was about fifteen. I had no idea what was going to happen at all. He was in uniform. I just got talking to him and we came out and just walked along, walking and talking. To me, that was something. We eventually went somewhere and things happened – he made love to me and held me and some other things. Then we came out and we talked about films and music, just enjoying friendship, actually, and we arranged to meet a week later. I went home and the next night when I went to bed my mother came into my bedroom and said, 'I hear you've been with a soldier.' I couldn't deny it and she said,

1

'Well tomorrow you better pack your things and go because I don't want anything like that.'

In the morning I asked her if I could stay and she said yes. Eventually the police came to where I worked and they told me I ought to go to the police station and give a statement. I didn't know the person's name or anything. I made a statement and [said] we'd arranged to meet the next week. The police were in the doorways of the shops waiting for him to come but he never came. That was the beginning of it all.

Interviewer: Do you find it very difficult to find and meet homosexuals?

Man: Yes, I do. Very much.

Interviewer: Why?

Man: Well, where can one meet homosexuals in a small town where everybody knows you? Plus the fact there's not many homosexuals in the town where I live. The only places are to go round the toilets and I don't wish that. The only other place is to come to London where you probably meet all kinds of people and that's what I've done. I used to come quite often at weekends.

Interviewer: Where did you used to go to meet other homosexuals?

Man: I tried doing several things actually; perhaps they sound very stupid. I like the theatre, I like the cinema. I used to go, when I arrived in London, to a certain theatre or certain film that I wanted to see and I used to book two seats – quite expensive ones because I like the good things – hoping that I would sell the other ticket just before the performance started. That way I would make sure that there would be somebody that was single sitting next to me at the cinema or the theatre. But in many cases I just lost money because I couldn't sell the tickets . . .

Interviewer: Did you ever manage to sell one to somebody who was single?

Man: Sometimes it was a woman. I lost always, actually.

Interviewer: Have you had any other experiences like this?

Man: I know that I am probably different to a lot of normal other homosexuals; they probably went round to toilets to find somebody to have sexual relations with, but I wanted someone for company. [One day] I went into this toilet, I suppose two or three times over the course of an afternoon, and I came out and somebody, a young person, said they was arresting me for importuning. So they took me to some police station, took my fingerprints and said that I would have to stay there until I appeared in court on Monday. Nobody knew about it at home 'cos they thought I'd come up for a job. I'd never had an experience like it before. I couldn't believe just because I wanted somebody to love me and to have friendship with I had to suffer all this. They put me in a cell and I was there from Saturday afternoon to Monday morning. I never slept, I just sat and cried.

Monday they came and took me to the courts. Just hundreds of people around – I couldn't believe my eyes – I just couldn't believe that I was there. I'd never been in court before so I didn't know what to do or what to say, I didn't even know what was going to happen to me. I asked the detective what I was to say and he told me to plead guilty. So I went to court and I knew this was my chance to say something. They said have I got anything to say and I said 'Yes, I have,' which took me a lot of courage to say. I told them that the reason why was because I was lonely and that was the reason I came to London to meet somebody. I was lucky, they just gave me two years' probation.

Interviewer: Do you think you need help?

Man: Yes, I do. I think everybody that is a homosexual needs help. They need someone – that's what I'm searching for now – I need someone with whom I can share my life. That's all I need. But it seems that it's wrong.

*

It was a truly beautiful afternoon when my friend David married his partner Adrian up on the roof deck of the National Theatre overlooking the Thames. As the glorious sunshine beamed down, it was David's strapping straight brother who got emotional first. Parents on either side, his voice cracked as he toasted 'the best big brother anyone could have', and then tears streamed out in front of the hundred or so jubilant friends and family. I was a mess, obviously.

Earlier we'd watched as they said their vows and then we'd cabbed it over for a joyous party attended by people who had travelled from around the world, including Adrian's native Australia. All of us, to differing degrees, were experiencing something new. The brotherly tears over, David's best schoolfriend got up from his wife and children and, as is customary, rattled off some embarrassing teenage tales. He was followed by Adrian's closest friend, who said, though sad to lose him to the other side of the world, she was overjoyed it was to such a fantastic man. We all blubbed some more.

As I raised my elderflower fizz I looked around at all the smiling faces: David's parents, Adrian's mother and stepfather; children playing on the decking, single people flirting and couples dancing the evening away; straight, gay, differences didn't matter. My mum was there too. My date. Beaming, being given handbag tips by my friend Li, who is Chinese and calls everybody 'darrrling'. She had such a good time she missed her train and had to stay in a hotel. I stopped and thought: we've finally got there.

And it isn't just legal equality. Over the last twenty years I have noticed so many wonderful moments of sheer joy in my friends' lives. Friends' parents making a civil partnership speech where they welcomed their son's partner formally into their family. Another friend, Irish, delighting his Muslim partner (now husband) with a surprise fortieth birthday party where we, his (gay and straight) friends, took over a seaside hotel for the weekend; then a few years later his Muslim relatives joining their civil partnership party. More recently, another young Facebook friend, Matthew, posting a picture of his Christian parents hugging and kissing him in full drag at Belfast's Gay Pride in 2015; he, like many of my friends, living healthily and proudly with HIV. My trans friends finally getting a modicum of the respect they deserve and lesbian women coming to the fore as Ruth Hunt took over Stonewall.

Writing this book in local coffee shops, I often bumped into friends, some single, some in couples, gay men, lesbians, trans, the most exciting thing in their weekend being a Waitrose shop and a trip to the cinema, as other same-sex couples occasionally walked by, hand in hand with their loves. I see young people empowering themselves and having fun, as the pictures of thousands of jubilant, happy people at Brighton Pride 2015 testified. I see more awareness of intersex issues; and young people identifying outside the 'gender binary' gaining more confidence through the connectivity that Facebook and Twitter bring, as well as allowing all young LGBT children to know they are not alone. I see many happy couples. And many happy singles, lots enjoying, safely, the sexual freedom that we have struggled for. A moment at another civil partnership I attended several years ago crystallized the changing times for me – a simple thing: the ten-year-old nephew of one of the grooms tugging at his uncle's sleeve and pleading, 'Can we cut the cake, Uncle Paul?' How amazing. And how right to celebrate everything that has happened. It is gobsmacking. Someone could fill many volumes documenting the gay love and life that is currently flourishing out there in so many different ways. The changes are so positive and so immense that, considered in any depth, they would easily move most of us to tears of joy.

Out on the balcony of David and Adrian's party I glanced over and saw my mum flirting with some older gay men; then I looked back out across the Thames at the twinkling lights of the most gay-friendly city in the world and felt the warmth of the fading sun on my face. I went back in, finished my dessert and then, when no one was looking, ate somebody else's too. And then I went to dance.

Introduction

It was probably coincidence that Robert Goddard killed himself on the same day that the former prime minister Margaret Thatcher died. On 8 April 2013, as we gathered round in the offices of *Attitude* – the UK's bestselling gay magazine, which I edited from 2008 until 2016 – to watch the world's reaction to the passing of the Iron Lady, thirty miles away Rob was reaching the end of his ability to cope.

Rob was the younger brother of *Attitude*'s advertising manager, Andy Goddard. In 2001 Andy travelled the world on an extended honeymoon and Rob stepped in to cover his position. I was deputy editor at the time and I didn't know him well, but I remember we all went to lunch when he joined. He was cocky, bubbly and laughed a lot. He embodied the image of what it meant to be a young gay man at the turn of the millennium: physically fit, athletic, lean, happy, able to camp it up but not taking shit from anyone. He also had that most important thing on the gay scene: sexual currency, as we saw a few years later when someone emailed an explicit picture from his Gaydar profile round the office.

In May 2008, when I had become the editor of *Attitude* and was working more closely with Andy, I asked after Rob from time to time. Andy said he wasn't doing well. He was drinking too much. He couldn't stop taking drugs. He had split from his latest boyfriend. He had suffered a homophobic attack after getting off a bus. He was HIV positive and not coping with it. He had lost his job and moved back in with his parents. Together these things sound like a huge alarm bell, but spread across several years they didn't feel like an emergency. Lots of gay men, like straight people, had transient relationships. Lots of gay men, like straight people, drank a lot and took drugs. Indeed, gay culture seemed to celebrate partying as a central tenet of gay identity and Rob looked very happy in all the Facebook pictures of him out clubbing with his hundreds of friends.

The day after Thatcher's death, Andy called the office to tell us that Rob had done what he'd threatened to do before and taken his own life. He had written notes to his parents and a birthday card to Andy, gone to the seafront where he and his brothers and sister used to play as children, and hanged himself. He was thirty-four years old.

I share Rob's story with you because his experience is not as unusual as any of us would wish. Despite how it may look on the outside, something isn't working. I didn't have to go looking for Rob's story; like so many in this book, his is the story of someone I knew. Despite more LGBT people than ever before, thank goodness, leading happy,

successful lives, it is becoming increasingly clear that a disproportionate number of us are not thriving as we should. Maybe it was
always so. Maybe technology means we are more aware of it now.
Maybe the fight for equality stopped us from seeing it.

But I came to realize it because, despite being a relatively successful
gay man, I have struggled seriously too. When in summer 2010 I
wrote in *Attitude* about my experience, I was overwhelmed by the
response from men up and down the country and further afield –
from Europe, Australia and America – contacting me to say they too
had experienced the pattern of behaviour that I described. In late
2015 Vice's *Chemsex* documentary lifted the lid on one part of the
crisis, but it is one that runs deeper than drugs alone.

How can this be? Haven't we now reached the Promised Land?
It is baffling. I remember just under twenty years ago a quarter of a
million of us celebrated the beginning of changes that would affect
all our lives with the biggest Gay Pride I had attended – not just pride
in our sexuality but equally a celebration of Tony Blair's defeat of the
homophobic Tories and what that would mean for us.

On 5 July 1997, just twenty-three years old, my friends and I
joined the crowds on Clapham Common. Through the haze of
cheap beer and burgers there was a palpable sense of expectation
as we lesbian, gay, bisexual, transgender folk celebrated something
we'd never dared to feel before: hope. Tabs of ecstasy no doubt lifted
some of the crowd, but we were also elevated by relief, as if the steam
had been released from a pressure cooker. On stage, a new thing: an
out-from-the-beginning TV presenter called Graham Norton filmed
a clip for a forthcoming Channel 4 documentary which saw him lead
the entire crowd in a united shout of 'We want equality, Mr Blair!' For
the first time ever we dared to believe we might actually get it.

As our pop heroes Pet Shop Boys took to the stage declaring, 'It's
beautiful to be here!', it felt as though a tanker was slowly beginning
to turn. The tears finally fell as, against the hazy blue of a perfect
London summer evening, Holly Johnson sang 'The Power of Love',
fireworks exploding overhead. As they burst into showers of spar-
kles, it was as if each one was an insult or sneer, a hateful tabloid

headline, a schoolyard punch or kick that we'd all endured, finally breaking apart, burning up, blooming into beautiful, coloured stars and dissipating into nothing but the warmth of the night. I remember crying, not wanting to leave, being led through the beer cans, hugging random strangers as we went. History was being made. The hellish social environment in which every single person on Clapham Common that day had grown up with was shifting. Change was here for us to embrace, knowing that so many people had gone before us who could never have dreamed of the freedoms that were about to be ours.

And indeed, nearly twenty years later, for many of us it is happening. A year after David and Adrian's wedding, the people of Ireland triumphantly disobeyed the Catholic Church and voted for equal marriage, followed swiftly by the Supreme Court of the United States. There are more gay characters on television, Hollywood has a palmful of out gay actors, and more and more schools are addressing homophobic bullying. Everywhere you turn there is progress. There are huge numbers of contented, successful gay people, some in wonderful relationships and marriages, others happily and healthily enjoying a single life. More and more straight people are friends and allies, sexuality is becoming less and less important, and, finally, the rights of transgender people are coming into the spotlight. There is much to celebrate indeed.

But look deeper and there is a problem. Disproportionately high levels of depression, self-harm and suicide; not uncommon problems with emotional intimacy; people keeling over dead in saunas; the highest rates of HIV infection since the epidemic began in the 1980s; and now a small but significant subculture of men who are using, some injecting, seriously dangerous drugs, which, despite accusations of hysteria from the gatekeepers of the gay PR machine, are killing too many people. It is the irony of ironies that the word we chose for ourselves, gay, which originally meant jolly, carefree and happy, has come to describe a group of people who collectively can appear anything but.

I will state here for the first time of many that most gay people are not taking drugs, most gay men are not dependent on alcohol and are neither sex addicts nor bitchy, unhappy miserabilists propping up bars in desperation over their lonely lives. The opposite is true. As I've already said and will say many more times, many, maybe most, of us are leading wonderful and happy, fulfilled lives. But there are patterns that seem disproportionately common and it's time to address them. For although over the last thirty years HIV and AIDS have been considered the number-one problem, the true public health crisis for LGBT people is that of poor mental health, low self-esteem and the damaging ways in which we cope.

At the core of this problem is a shame that has been inflicted upon us so powerfully that those of us whom it affects often do not even realize it. It is a shame with which we were saddled as children, to which we continue to be culturally subjected, and which is magnified by the pinball-machine gay scene and culture that sends some of us spinning from one extreme experience to the next. As therapist and author Joe Kort states so well in his book *10 Smart Things Gay Men Can Do to Improve Their Lives*, what's wrong is not our sexuality itself but our experience of growing up in a society that still does not fully accept that people can be anything other than heterosexual and cisgendered (born into the physical gender you feel you are). It is the damage done to us by growing up strapped inside a cultural straitjacket, a tight-fitting, one-size restraint imposed on us at birth that leaves no room to grow outside its narrow confines. It makes no allowances for the fact that, yes, indeed, some people are different and we deserve – and *need* – to be supported and loved for who we are too.

The time to address these problems is now.

The causes, manifestations and answers to this crisis – and, though I do not wish to sensationalize, my experience makes me believe it is a crisis – are complicated and controversial. But there is a way out of this mess, though there are no easy solutions. By writing this book I hope to provoke a discussion and suggest real change. It is written from my own perspective as a white gay man, though I am fully aware that the issues I raise are pertinent to bisexual men and women, lesbians, transgendered men and women, and those who consider themselves queer, non-binary and/or intersex, as well as to people of all ethnicities and backgrounds. I also know that countless straight people relate to issues discussed here. This book may be relevant to them, but as a gay man I write primarily about the specifics of how it affects us. For the sake of clarity I mostly use the word 'gay'. I've also often used the pronoun 'he', simply for ease.

I have interviewed many people about their experiences – names and details have often been changed, but they are all real and all have agreed to their inclusion. When I mention celebrities I do so only with information already in the public domain. I use people's stories in a non-judgemental way. I'm in no position to judge, as I have done many of the things mentioned myself. I'm grateful to anyone brave or honest enough to share their stories with me and especially respectful of anyone who is in recovery for their problem. I believe they are inspirations to the rest of us, no matter what sexuality, race, religion or gender. Who amongst us has never made mistakes, never told lies, cheated, drunk or eaten too much, smoked, taken drugs, driven too fast, been nasty or selfish or any number of things? All human beings are firmly planted in glass houses. I am also not in denial about the part that the magazine I have edited plays in this story. I'll come to that later.

Straight people, specifically, shouldn't feel smug either. The NHS is weighed down by people, mostly heterosexual, suffering from illnesses that are self-inflicted by behaviour born of medicating painful feelings. It is humanity's story and I've been shocked to see how much confusion, disagreement and ignorance there is about dependency and addiction considering its cost to the world, personal, social and financial. The cause, I believe, of so many of these problems is overpowering, uncomfortable emotions; often shame that is so great it becomes traumatic and unbearable. Regardless of sexuality, childhood trauma seems to manifest in various ways. Sometimes as low self-esteem, depression or anxiety disorders, drink or drug problems, eating disorders, problems with relationships, general irritability or a need to put other people down, or as neediness and 'people-pleasing' where a person puts his or her needs after those of others. Sometimes, apparently for straight men, it emerges as anger and violence. Sometimes it's a mixture, or all, of the above. Sometimes people go off the rails in their twenties but then manage to pull themselves out of the spiral.

Again, there are more straight people than gay with these problems because there are more straight people than gay in the world. The difficulty for LGBT people is that, because of our childhood experience of growing up in shame, we are lucky if we avoid this kind of damage. It is important, though, to understand that most gay people do not go through the extreme things described here. If you are upset by this book, especially if you are young and/or just coming out, know that the future is not written. You do not have to experience the things that I write about in these pages. And if you do experience them, know that they can be overcome. They don't have to be all consuming. You may have a problem but that doesn't mean your life is over, that you cannot get back on track. You totally can.

I want to be clear: this book is about the problems some of us face which I believe we need to do something about. But it is not the entire experience. Again, there are many thriving LGBT+ people of all ages. I was reminded of this at a recent event where I met a male couple who'd been together for decades and who, in their adult lives, had been blissfully happy. It's more common than the media – gay and mainstream – might tell us. Also, as the world changes, far fewer young LGBT+ people will face negatives to the degree I describe. If you are coming out, it's especially important to read books and watch films written specifically to offer positivity. I would recommend Juno Dawson's *This Book Is Gay*, and check out the growing number of young adult books with LGBT+ themes by Patrick Ness, Adam Silvera, David Levithan and others (see the list at the back of this book). Armistead Maupin's *Tales of the City* helped me feel better about myself as I was growing up and there are many titles that will do the same for you. The coming year, 2018, will see the release of the film *Love, Simon*, based on *Simon vs. the Homo Sapiens Agenda* by Becky Albertalli, and there are plenty of other great, inspiring books like it for young LGBT+ people.

Do not use this book to make yourself feel worse, or as 'false evidence' that being gay is a disaster and/or that things can never improve for you. That's not true.

If you relate to this, your head may tell you, 'This book might help other people, but I am more screwed up than he can imagine. I am the *worst*.' If you think that, then we already have something in common – for a long time I thought that too. Trust me when I say it's not true, your head is lying. It is just another thing shame does to us. You *can* deal with it. Turn to pages 349–54 and make use of the helplines and support groups listed there. They are there to help you. **Please use them**. The solution is all in your hands, but no one else can do it for you.

Friends have suggested that the political right may use this book to reinforce their prejudices, but the issues I outline are already in the open. In 2015 the documentary *Chemsex* covered the most urgent and disturbing of the current manifestations of the problems with which we need to deal. It is out there, it is happening, and not facing it is why it has got so bad in the first place.

Lastly, if you are gay and do not recognize yourself in this book then I'm genuinely glad. But know that there are a lot of people who *do* need help. The longer we leave things, the worse they will get. It is not victimological to face these issues; on the contrary, pretending they are not real and doing nothing about them is what traps us in victimhood. Facing them and addressing them is an act of empowerment. Many people, gay and straight, are experiencing these problems. Let's work to help everyone who needs it, now.

I like to think that those men and women who lived before 1967, when male homosexuality was a crime, would be overwhelmed by the progress we've made. But I'm certain they'd want us to live our lives to their greatest potential and not throw away what they could never dream of: the opportunity to like and love not only each other, but, ultimately, ourselves. If we really have the gritty determination that is so popular in the anthems commonly played in gay clubs and homes across the world, then the time has finally arrived to face the storm and find our way out the other side.

Part One

Shame

1

'Gay men don't get old'

'They wear designer sneakers but yours they'll take,
They like party drugs and protein shakes,
They don't care what you're about,
They'll chew you up and spit you out.'

Courtney Act, 'Mean Gays', 2014

KRISTIAN DIGBY COULD have stepped right off the set of *Will &*
Grace. Handsome, urbane, kind, witty and well dressed, he was that
rarest of things: a TV presenter who was out from the beginning of
his career, co-presenting BBC Choice's *That Gay Show* in 2001 and
then moving on to programmes such as BBC1's *To Buy or Not to*
Buy and *Holiday*, where he became the first presenter to cover a 'gay'
travel destination. As his profile grew, Kristian really liked that he
could be, in a small way, something of a role model to gay kids. In
Simon Fanshawe's 2006 documentary *The Trouble With Gay Men*,
a group of young gay teens pointed Kristian out as an inspiration
because, they said, he was 'normal and not camp . . .' We met and
became friends when we first shot him for *Attitude*. The last time
I saw him he was bounding up the stairs at a fundraising event for
the Albert Kennedy Trust, the charity that supports homeless young
LGBT people. For me, that symbolizes who he was.

Kristian was found dead at home on 1 March 2010 after experi-
menting with autoasphyxiation, the practice of starving oneself of

oxygen to heighten sexual pleasure, a sensation apparently more addictive than using cocaine. He had a plastic bin liner over his head and police found a canister of ethyl chloride next to his bed. He was thirty-two.

Three weeks before Kristian's death, Alexander McQueen killed himself. On 11 February 2010, days after the death of his mother and the end of a relationship, the former British Designer of the Year and fashion superstar had written a note that said, 'Look after my dogs, sorry, I love you, Lee' (his real name). In his 2015 biography *Blood Beneath the Skin*, author Andrew Wilson spoke to friends who described Lee's epically low self-esteem, addiction to cocaine, use of crystal meth, body-image issues, eating disorders and erratic relationships, often with rent boys. One person who knew him told how Lee had previously planned to end his life dramatically by, at the close of a catwalk show, rising from the stage in a glass box with a gun and blowing his brains out in front of the cheering crowd. In the event, he took an overdose of pills, before slashing his wrists and hanging himself in his wardrobe. He had previously been diagnosed with mixed anxiety and depressive disorder and had taken overdoses before, in May and July 2009. The coroner found significant levels of cocaine, sleeping pills and tranquillizers in his blood. He was forty years old.

Four months before Alexander McQueen died, on 4 October 2009, Kevin McGee, TV researcher and former civil partner of *Little Britain* star Matt Lucas, also took his own life. Three years after the public saw joyous, celebratory newspaper pictures of Kevin and Matt dressed as pantomime characters and surrounded by celebrities at their themed civil partnership, Kevin posted a status update on his Facebook page that read, 'Kevin McGee thinks death is much better than life'. He then hanged himself in his flat in Edinburgh. Like Kristian, he was thirty-two years old.

At the *Attitude* office we found ourselves publishing one obituary after another. By the time Kristian died, things were starting to feel strange. To lose three high-profile gay men in six months was frightening, like something was wrong, but no one could say what it was.

Nothing linked these deaths . . . And yet somehow they didn't feel like coincidence. But how could that be? To suggest their deaths had anything at all to do with the fact that these men were gay seemed intrinsically homophobic and just, well, wrong.

A few days after Kevin McGee's death, Stephen Gately of Boyzone was also found dead in the flat in Majorca he owned with his civil partner, Andrew Cowles. Stephen was discovered on the sofa the morning after he and Andrew were reportedly accompanied back to their apartment by a man they had met in a local club – something hardly shocking or unusual for many gay couples, or indeed some straight couples. Medical reports eventually showed that Stephen died from pulmonary oedema – fluid on the lungs – after a heart attack brought on by an undiagnosed heart condition that his family said was hereditary. So when Jan Moir wrote in the *Daily Mail* a few days later that Stephen's death was 'sleazy', mentioning a 'dangerous lifestyle' and that the circumstances struck 'another blow to the happy ever after myth of civil partnerships', gay people (and a large number of straight people) took to social media, incandescent with fury. Her comments were homophobic, horribly timed and offensive. I raged myself and went on television to condemn her comments.

But I sensed that people's reaction was about something else too. Perhaps it was because Stephen was the first member of a boy band to come out, or because he seemed a sweet, regular guy; perhaps it was because the *Mail* has a history of homophobia; or perhaps it was because by coming out he'd taken us a step forward and it seemed that Moir was using his death to shove us back.

But I believe the huge reaction to Moir's comments was at least in part because, although they were not relevant to Stephen's death, they touched a nerve.

The truth is that the deaths of Kevin McGee, Alexander McQueen and Kristian Digby were part of a pattern that affects straight people too, but, as painful as it is to acknowledge, seems particularly prevalent amongst LGBT people: depression, anxiety, suicide, use of dangerous drugs and, in the case of some gay and bisexual men, sometimes extreme sexual behaviour.

Most gay people do not do these things and, when they do, for the most part it does not end catastrophically like it did for Kristian, Lee and Kevin. For instance, lots of people will use drugs, such as alcohol and ecstasy, relatively safely. They will have fun. Like everybody else, some of us may find ourselves in a period of difficulty which we get through. But for too many others it has a corrosive effect on their lives.

Some of this was examined in 2015 when Vice released their documentary *Chemsex*, which brought to the surface the problem with specific drugs that has been exploding in London's gay scene over the last ten years; but it did not look at the situation amongst people who do not take drugs.

Reliable studies and stats for LGBT people are notoriously hard to conduct or find. For a long time being gay was considered a mental-health problem in itself. Today, sexual orientation is not monitored by the NHS, meaning we simply do not know if more LGBT people than straight present to the medical services with issues such as depression, or cancer or liver problems as a result of heavy drinking. On top of this, LGBT people, I believe, are still often nervous about disclosing sexuality or gender identity because of the experience we have had.

Some studies do exist, though. In June 2014 Public Health England issued the first of a series of reports which concluded that gay men were disproportionately affected by ill-health in three main areas – mental health; HIV and sexual health; and the use of alcohol, drugs and tobacco. Various other studies in both Britain and the USA* have come to similar conclusions, pointing to higher risks of suicide, suicide ideation (seriously considering killing yourself), self-harm, substance misuse, alcohol abuse and mental disorder amongst LGBT people than the rest of the population. We do not know if more LGBT people actually die from suicide, though a 2013 study by Martin Plöderl *et al.*, 'Suicide Risk and Sexual Orientation', argues that this is the case.

---

*See Bibliography: King *et al.*; Mays and Cochran; Hetrick and Martin, cited in Thompson; Clements-Nolle, Marx and Katz; Hatzenbuehler, Keyes and McLaughlin; Lamis *et al.*; Mathy; and Shields *et al.*

A study (*Part of the Picture, 2009–14*) conducted on behalf of the LGBT Foundation in Manchester found that LGB people used drugs and alcohol at seven times the rate of the general population, and that LGB people were twice as likely to binge-drink as the general population. And in 2015 the UK's leading LGBT mental-health charity PACE[*] published the results of its five-year RaRE (Risk and Resilience Explored) study, which showed, amongst other things, higher levels of self-harm and suicide amongst LGBT than other people, and a greater incidence of body disorders in gay/bi men.

Culturally, homosexuality and misery have been linked so tightly over the years that they have become an offensive cliché to the point where any discussion of problems is dismissed as homophobia. In reality, it's hard to find many famous gay people, from the 1960s through to the modern day, who have not had experience of severe depression, anxiety, body-image issues, eating disorders, or problematic drug or alcohol use. They stretch from the pre-legalization unhappiness expressed by Kenneth Williams, Larry Grayson and Frankie Howerd; the suicide of Joe Meek; the murder of Joe Orton by Kenneth Halliwell; and the denial of Liberace, who hid his sexuality all his life, and Barry Manilow, who only recently publicly revealed his.

Anxiety and depression have dogged numerous figures in the public eye. Out soccer player Robbie Rogers said his decision to leave British football was, in part, because of the effect on his mental health of the conflict between his sexuality and his sporting career. In March 2016 forty-two-year-old *Prison Break* actor Wentworth Miller wrote of depression that had left him suicidal. He described how, in his search for relief and distraction, he turned to food, to the point that eating became the only thing he could count on to get him through. Will Young has bravely spoken about his mental-health problems and porn addiction, in 2015 telling the *Sunday Times* that his anxiety and self-hatred, born in part of struggling with his sexuality, were so

---

[*] Due to government cuts, PACE shut down as this book went to press.

great he couldn't recognize his own face in the mirror. Also in 2015 our latest young pop hero, twenty-five-year-old Olly Alexander of number-one-selling band Years & Years, told *Attitude* and then, in 2016, the *Guardian* of his serious ongoing struggle with anxiety and depression, for which he has had counselling, therapy and been on 'a cocktail of drugs'.

Drug addiction has affected many of our most famous names, including Elton John, Boy George, Stephen Fry, Rufus Wainwright, Marc Almond, Jimmy Somerville, Andy Bell and Olympian pin-up Matthew Mitcham, who wrote of his crystal-meth addiction in his autobiography. Superstar George Michael's problems have been well documented. In 2007 he pleaded guilty to driving under the influence of drugs after he was found slumped at the wheel of his Range Rover and, three years later, served four weeks in prison after driving, under the influence of cannabis, into a North London shop front. In 2013 he fell out of a vehicle travelling at 70mph on the M1.

Stephen Gately, meanwhile, suffered with depression and an addiction to prescription medication. Alcoholism has famously almost destroyed Michael Barrymore and fashion designer John Galliano, while Tom Ford has also revealed his struggle with drink. In his autobiography, the five times Olympic gold medal-winning swimmer Ian Thorpe describes his problematic relationship with alcohol, which he used to quell suicidal feelings.

Suicide and suicide ideation is so common as to feel almost hackneyed. The first and only British professional footballer to come out, Justin Fashanu, killed himself; bisexual Manic Street Preachers lyricist and guitarist Richey Edwards is believed to have taken his own life; Judas Priest singer Rob Halford went into drug-addiction recovery after the suicide of a boyfriend; and Stephen Fry made a thankfully unsuccessful suicide attempt in 2013. Sports stars Gareth Thomas, Graham Oberee, Donal Og Cusack, referee Nigel Owens and the two rugby players who came out in 2015, Keegan Hirst and Sam Stanley, all said they had contemplated suicide as they wrestled with their sexuality. Our other gay boy-bander, Mark Feehily of Westlife, told *Attitude* that he had seriously considered suicide growing up.

Unhappiness with our bodies and eating disorders are also well represented in our community, with Gok Wan, Elton John and Portia De Rossi all having suffered in this area. Buff *Embarrassing Bodies* presenter Dr Christian Jessen told *Attitude* in 2010, 'I have body issues, absolutely, slight body dysmorphia . . . it's about self-esteem and confidence . . . on a bad day . . . I will look in the mirror and what I see will not be how I am . . . I know it's crazy'.

You will, of course, rightly point out that lots of famous people have these kinds of issues. That's often true, but not in the same proportions as LGBT stars. Similar patterns can be seen in the higher-profile members of the LGBT community. Politician and entrepreneur Ivan Massow has been open about his alcoholism, a previous boyfriend having taken his own life. A former agony uncle of a free gay magazine commited suicide in 2000. Gary Frisch, founder of the once omni-popular website Gaydar, died in 2007 after jumping from his Vauxhall flat high on drugs. BBC Radio 1 DJ Kevin Greening died at the end of December 2007 of a heart attack linked to the ecstasy, cocaine and GHB in his blood after spending the evening at a Recon sex event. In November 2013 Co-op non-executive chairman and Terrence Higgins Trust trustee Reverend Paul Flowers was splashed over the front pages after being filmed trying to buy cocaine and crystal meth and discussing his use of those drugs, ketamine and GHB. In May 2008, Leeds-based *Bent* magazine executive Damian Oldfield was murdered by his sometime partner, Anthony Morley, famous for being the very first winner of Mr Gay UK. As I was writing this, celebrated senior policeman and *Gay Times* cover star Paul Cahill went on trial for possession of MDMA, mephedrone and controlled sedatives. He collapsed for mental-health reasons and the trial was postponed.

Gay culture celebrates gay porn stars as the ultimate jackpot winners of our community, but in reality they aren't very good at staying alive. There have been so many suicides or drug-related deaths of US porn performers in the last decade that I can't list them here. The issue has been the subject of many gay media reports and I have my own experience of it. In 2010, *Attitude* shot a group of ten 'porn stars' for the cover of our annual 'Sex' issue, something I regret. At the shoot I was told of a British performer I knew, and whose name I won't mention, who had killed himself. Two of those we photographed, Arpad Miklos and Erik Rhodes, have since lost their lives. Arpad Miklos died in February 2013, aged thirty-nine, from a drug overdose, with a suicide note left at the scene. Rhodes, a heavy steroid user, died in his sleep from a heart attack in June 2012, aged thirty. He had previously created a blog entitled 'A Romance with Misery' on which he wrote, 'I feel so left out . . . so alone'. His last entry read, 'we all knew this is where I'd end up . . . all the pills in the world can't change the fact that I have lost my passion for almost everything in life and i just don't care anymore . . . and if I'm dead when this is finally read, well just know I was dead when i wrote this . . .'

Another man we once shot for a separate feature before he began appearing in porn, Wilfried Knight, a sweet and gentle guy, took his own life in Vancouver on 5 March 2013, two weeks after his husband had also killed himself due to immigration issues. He is one of many. The most recent at the time of writing has been Christopher Luke McAteer, known as Clay on Corbinfisher.com, who shot himself in the head in April 2015, aged just eighteen. It seems that where people's worth is measured by pec size, deep unhappiness often follows. After Knight's death, well-known porn producer Michael Lucas wrote an open letter in which he stated, 'It's not just porn stars who are killing themselves; about ten guys in my gym alone have recently committed suicide.'

Again, you could reasonably argue that the people who work in and around the gay scene might be more likely to have these issues. Possibly true. But what convinced me to write this book was that I have observed these patterns amongst people I know and have grown up with. When I was a child, the ex-headmaster of a local school was murdered by a rent boy. From the immediate group of friends I had when I was sixteen, two have been sectioned, two have dated men who have killed themselves, and two have severe eating disorders, one of them coming close to suicide. A friend I made at the local gay youth group caught HIV after years of predicting he would, saying things like, 'I'm just a piece of shit, I will definitely get it.' A man I knew as a student I now sometimes see running through the streets of Soho making animal noises or performing in soiled trousers for tourists. Another man I knew from my teens, who struggled to accept his sexuality at the time, told me recently how a few years ago he sat on a rooftop thinking of throwing himself off, and recently became HIV positive after letting 'hundreds and hundreds' of men have condomless sex with him. A successful man I went on a date with in my twenties hanged himself after the end of a subsequent relationship. A complicated flatmate of mine died several years ago at the age of thirty-two from AIDS-related problems because he couldn't face taking an HIV test.

Since I started writing this book, more people have approached me for help or given me similar accounts – a friend who disappears for days on end, another who is hooked on drugs, another asking for help for his friend who caught HIV and hepatitis C after getting involved in the 'chemsex' scene. I've lost count of these stories, which are overwhelming in their number and similarity. Low self-esteem, body-image issues, depression and anxiety are the cornerstones of the way these problems manifest. When I began writing in 2011, one man told me of his ex-boyfriend, whose drug use had led to him losing his home. He was living on his friend's sofa, having unsafe sex with large numbers of men and was addicted to crystal meth. He didn't see a reason to live, his friend told me, because, as he put it, 'gay men don't get old'.

I can't be the only person who has had these experiences, but the situation seems to me to be like the boiling-frog experiment. Drop a frog into boiling water and it will react immediately, hopping out as quickly as possible. But put it in a saucepan of cool water and gently heat it up and it won't notice anything is wrong, but will sit there until it boils to death. Written down, these things seem insane; but because they slowly drip-drip into our consciousness we are able to dismiss discussion of them as homophobia or hysteria. Some gay or well-meaning straight commentators are so defensive against any criticism of the way some of us live our lives that they attack discussion of these issues as heteronormative and argue that this is what makes us different.

Over the years some gay artists have tried to ask why things are this way, usually recognizing there is a problem but not understanding why or knowing what the solutions are. (I do not necessarily endorse their work, but merely note them here.)

The first openly gay breakthrough Broadway play, *The Boys in the Band* (1968), was attacked for portraying unhappy gay men. Written by a gay author, it contains the infamous line, 'Show me a happy homosexual and I'll show you a gay corpse.'

The classic 1978 novel *Dancer from the Dance* by Andrew Holleran describes the hedonism of New York and Fire Island and – spoiler – culminates with a main character who, unable to stand the thought of growing old, walks into the sea.

In 1999 Kevin Elyot's hit play *My Night With Reg* suggested gay men have a problem with truth and respect, and in 2007 his television drama *Clapham Junction* bleakly portrayed all the gay characters as self-destructive, self-hating nihilists with no let-up whatsoever.

In 2002 a play at London's Royal Court Theatre, *Fucking Games*, raged at the behaviour of gay men and culminated – spoiler – in one character so full of anger that he intentionally infects another with HIV as a punishment for his promiscuity.

Heroic activist Larry Kramer's seminal novel *Faggots* (1978) and landmark play *The Normal Heart* (1985; recently revived on Broadway and made into an HBO film) suggested gay men were addicted to sex as a reaction to self-loathing. Kramer was attacked for this portrayal, which, he said, was 'the truth' and that he believed gay men 'felt guilty about all the promiscuity and all the partying'.

In 2015 *Queer As Folk* TV writer Russell T. Davies returned with *Cucumber*, the story of the breakdown of a relationship between two fortysomething gay men. Spoiler: one of them is murdered by a man who cannot accept his own sexual feelings for men. Just after it was broadcast I was contacted by a writer pitching a piece about how offensive and unrealistic the storyline was. This was the same week that a twenty-five-year-old, Shane Dunn, was sentenced for slashing the throat of a man in his Kent home with a kitchen knife, after meeting him on the Grindr dating app; both of them had been using crystal meth. Thankfully the injured man survived – despite Dunn only pretending to call an ambulance – after his flatmate returned home and raised the alarm.

A hero of British queer counter-culture, angry performance artist David Hoyle has described the gay scene as 'the biggest suicide cult in history'. One of his most celebrated oeuvres is a song called 'Being gay is a waste of time'. At an event entitled 'Alcohol' at the Royal Festival Hall in 2013, he asked a packed audience, 'Who here truly – truly – believes that their homosexuality isn't a problem?' To nervous laughter, no one raised their hand.

In 2005 my play *Blowing Whistles* was first performed. It is about the breakdown of a relationship through alcohol, drugs and anonymous sex, and it struck a chord, playing several successful runs in London, Australia and the US. Couples sometimes stormed out in the middle of the final scene and some men cried in their seats after the curtain came down, because it touches on the issues that this book is about.

More recently, the 2008 Royal Court play *The Pride* by Alexi Kaye Campbell looked at the issue of sex addiction, while the year before Mike Bartlett's *Cock* had expressed a man's frustration at the apparent futility of being attracted to other men.

There has been lots of discussion but very few answers. This is because it's not our sexuality itself that is the problem. If it were, we might have had that conscious understanding, collectively talked about it and dealt with it. But no: it is the experience we have that causes the problem. The resulting wound does not manifest as a belief that our sexuality is a problem, but simply in us not feeling very good about ourselves – something we think is individual to us and nothing to do with the kind of person we are. Being gay, though, means we have, almost invariably, been shamed growing up. This is the key.

For the gay community this subject has been taboo because it seems to play to a homophobic agenda and, more significantly, because it might collapse our house of cards. Years ago, when my best friend Tim and I, working in student jobs, were asked by our drunken boss if we were 'really happy being gay', we could barely spit the words out quickly enough to reassure him how happy we were and what a stupid, offensive question he'd asked. The fact is, we've been so bullied by heterosexual society that even to admit dissatisfaction is considered anathema to the notion of gay pride, which has compulsively waved its rainbow flag like a deranged Duracell bunny, never able to stop. To ask whether there is a problem is to state that not only does the emperor have no clothes on, but to acknowledge he's off his head in the darkroom, not knowing who he's getting fucked by. The truth of the matter is that it is all too painful. There is a good reason those rooms are dark. It's not other people so many of us don't want to see – it is often ourselves.

The notion of gay pride is good, helpful and meaningful, but proclaiming it parrot fashion does not make it a reality. It's time to go back to basics and examine what's working – and lots is – and what isn't. This isn't about conservatism, heteronormativity or so-called 'slut shaming'. The only thing to be ashamed of is continuing to keep our heads in the sand while too many people lose their health, livelihoods or sanity.

The urgent need to address this situation was brought home to me yet again on an evening in August 2014 when my friend Simon Marks, now training to be a therapist, and I launched a new discussion group called 'A Change of Scene' at Soho's 56 Dean Street, where men can address some of these issues. As we sat outside a coffee shop on Old Compton Street talking about the group, a young man next to us told us he was bisexual and bipolar and needed help. Twenty minutes later another stranger to our right overheard us and told us he thought he may be an alcoholic and he too needed help. In April 2015 our 'Change of Scene' event with the theme of 'Loneliness' saw more than eighty men crammed in, sitting on the floor, on tables, others queuing up the stairs, breaking attendance records for similar events at Dean Street.

This pattern is not restricted to London or the UK. A severe problem with crystal meth has spread from the US to Thailand to Australia, and HIV rates and hepatitis C infection rates seem to be rising across gay communities throughout the Western world. Heroic gay men who responded to the AIDS crisis like no other are losing their lives, such as ACT UP's Spencer Cox, who stopped taking his medication due to a crystal-meth addiction and died in December 2012; or their livelihoods, like Dr Ramon Torres, who lost his job because of use of the same drug. Jay Morris is a twenty-four-year-old Australian recovering crystal-meth addict who began his habit in the UK. His addiction got so bad he was jobless, homeless and became an escort, once having a drug-induced fit in a supermarket. He now runs the Sydney-based group Ice Nation and believes the gay community is bearing the brunt of Australia's crystal-meth problem, fuelled, as it is in the UK, by hook-up apps which enable drugs to be dealt more easily than ever before. It seems that all over the world – even though, for many, things are better than ever, the fight for gay rights is progressing and a happy marriage has become the symbol of contemporary gay success – too many of us are struggling with self-destructive behaviour.

A story that must surely serve as a wake-up call is that of forty-nine-year-old Manhattan therapist Bob Bergeron. Bob was a successful, handsome man. He was excited about a book he was writing called *The Right Side of Forty: the Complete Guide to Happiness for Gay Men at Midlife and Beyond*. He wrote online, 'I've got a concise picture of what being forty is about and it's a great perspective filled with happiness, feeling sexy, possessing comfort relating to other men and taking good care of ourselves.' He gained a publishing deal and was working hard on his book. In a blog entry before his death he wrote about aspiring to look after himself better and to 'stop lying about my age'. In another he made it clear it was important to him to continue being 'a sex object'. His mentor, Stanley Spiegel, was quoted in a *New York Times* article as saying Bob 'still wanted to be sexually attractive . . . for [him] sex was a way to experience power.' On New Year's Eve 2011 Bob took his own life and left a note saying that he was 'done'. Pointing to the title of his book, his note read that 'it was a lie based on bad information'. If an intelligent, attractive therapist like Bob, a man who had an understanding of mental-health issues, felt that his diminishing worth was only that of a sex object, what hope is there for the rest of us?

Indeed it can often seem that there is little hope. I'm sad to say that in December 2015 I noticed the not unusual deaths of several men reported on Facebook. One, though, was the man I'd heard about in 2011 who had told his ex-boyfriend he had no hope because 'gay men don't get old'. His name was Simon Santos. He was a black gay man from Liverpool and he died on 14 December 2015, aged thirty-six, from a heart attack. His ex-boyfriend, Donal Mooney, told me it wasn't the result of one particular shot of crystal meth, but the cumulative effect of lack of self-care, bad diet, unmedicated HIV, varied substance abuse, lack of self-esteem – and lack of support.

But, despite all this, there *is* hope. There are clear reasons why this is happening and they can be addressed. There is another way.

First, though, we need to understand the cultural context in which we all grow up.

2

'I'd Shoot My Son If He Had AIDS Says Vicar!': Roosting Chickens

'We promise an end to the conspiracy of silence . . . Most people know there are such things – "pansies" – mincing, effeminate young men who call themselves "queers" . . . but simple decent folks regard them as freaks and rarities . . .'

Sunday Pictorial exposé 'Evil Men', 1952

'At school our science teacher decided to give us a lesson on AIDS. The teacher referred to homosexuals as "queers" and "evil men" and told us if we became gay we would be "punished in later life" . . . We should be told the facts and left to make up our own minds. I feel a certain respect and understanding for homosexuals and teachers should not express to a class their small-minded, ignorant views.' – Tom Cruise fan, Scotland

Letter to Mizz magazine, May 1987

'Since the passage of the Marriage (Same Sex Couples) Act, the nation has been beset by serious storms and floods . . . The scriptures make it abundantly clear that a Christian nation that abandons its faith and acts contrary to the Gospel will be beset by natural disasters . . .'

David Silvester, UKIP Councillor, 2014

WHAT DOES IT MEAN to be gay? It hasn't yet been scientifically proven one way or another, but I write from the perspective that sexual orientation is set before birth and is not a choice. A small but vocal minority of gay people argue that being gay is something chosen almost as a political act, a protest against society, and for some of the most hard-line lesbian feminists it is a choice explicitly against men. Writer and activist Julie Bindel has said, 'I've met a huge number of lesbians who say, "I don't believe I was born this way", and I believe any woman can be a lesbian and believe we're stopped from feeling sexual attraction to the same sex because of external pressure'. I've also heard a small number of gay men express the view that straight men would be homosexual if they weren't so repressed. This view has fuelled the dated idea that gay men are misogynists who've made the same political choice in reverse – against women – and believe that being gay is somehow superior to being straight.

In my view, both of these assertions are rubbish. I don't consider either men or women, hetero- or homosexuals, to be superior or inferior. Like eye colour, it's just different. If sexuality were a simple matter of choice, then, as I'm single, I'd happily choose a woman as my next partner. Why not? If it were a choice, it would be fun to choose a different type of person next. I'm not looking to make a statement for or against the patriarchy. I'm looking for love and someone to watch *Coronation Street* with. But such a choice isn't open to me. I love and respect women, but I'm not bisexual, or sexually fluid, 'on a spectrum', or someone who falls for 'the person not the gender' (something only non-heterosexual people seem to say). I am a gay man. Like many millions, at ten years of age (and for a good many years after) I would have done *anything* to be like everybody else rather than endure the years of isolation I suffered.

Parts of the gay movement have striven to embolden the 'positive choice' narrative, which is understandable, but which conveniently ignores the fact that many gay people fight their feelings tooth and claw. If it were a choice, then the thousands who attempt so-called 'reparation therapy' would simply choose to be straight.

I'll give you four very recent examples of people who did not make a 'choice' to be gay. A twenty-five-year-old man who contributed his typical story to *Attitude*'s 'Rucomingout' page (linked to website rucomingout.com) in August 2015 described years of covering his room with *FHM* and *Loaded* magazines, talking about girls and cars. 'That's how I spent the majority of my teenage years,' he wrote. 'Trying not only to convince others but myself too that I wasn't gay . . . I'd punish myself again and again for allowing a thought about another guy to enter my head.' Then there was Vito Cammisano, the ex-partner of American footballer Michael Sam, who made a YouTube video in which he described confessing his feelings for boys to a priest when he was in first grade. 'I walked down the aisle and said those Hail Marys *so fast* because I thought I could be forgiven and I wasn't going to be gay . . . I would get so angry at myself, why, why are you like this Vito? This is not right. You're not supposed to be gay . . .' Also in August 2015 rugby player, husband and father of two Keegan Hirst came out. 'By the time I was eighteen, I was in complete denial, hoping it would go away,' he told the *Sunday Mirror*. 'I convinced myself, no way could I be gay, it was inconceivable . . . On the worst days I'd think, "I can't do this, I'd rather be dead than for it all to come out".' Finally, Scottish Conservative leader Ruth Davidson said she struggled to accept she was a lesbian. 'It took time for me to come to some sort of peace with myself about it,' she said in a BBC Radio Scotland interview in 2015. 'It was about the fear and shame and the guilt you feel when you're going through that process, of coming to accept yourself.'

What *is* a major and important political choice, however, is something that not everyone does, even after intellectually accepting that they are gay: coming out, positively identifying as an LGBT person, standing up for who you are and fighting for your rights.

Why would the prospect of being gay be so horrifying to so many people?

In England and Wales, until 1967 (in Scotland until 1980, Northern Ireland 1982 and the Republic of Ireland 1993) male homosexuality was illegal, carrying the threat of imprisonment and a stigma so great that very few dared to come out. People struggled, some living in bohemia or working in safer professions, such as the arts, fashion and hairdressing; but many gay people were married, having illicit homosexual encounters and relationships – if they were lucky. Some older gay people today say they enjoyed the sense of camaraderie and excitement of pre-legalization, but the BBC's archives online show the extreme distress in which many gay men lived before 1967. Suicides were commonplace and I dare say the mental-health problems highlighted in this book were far more prevalent even than they are now.

The Wolfenden Report, which was published in 1957 and ten years later led to the partial decriminalization of homosexual activity, came in the wake of several high-profile cases, including Lord Montagu of Beaulieu, a twenty-eight-year-old peer who was one of three men sent to prison for a gay sexual relationship in 1954. At the end of that year there were 1,069 men in prison in the UK for homosexual sex. When the Sexual Offences Act eventually passed into law in 1967 it decriminalized homosexual activity in private between consenting couples aged twenty-one or over, but a little-known side-effect was that more men were prosecuted for gross indecency in the years that followed – often married men who then killed themselves – as the government sought to send a message that the new 'tolerance' did not mean that anything now went.

In 1969, the same year as the Stonewall bar riots in New York City, the Campaign for Homosexual Equality, Britain's first gay activist group, formed from the Homosexual Law Reform Society of 1964. The first Gay Pride march was staged in 1970 in Highbury Fields and in 1972 the first major Pride rally saw more than a thousand people march from Trafalgar Square to Hyde Park. Also that year, the country's first gay newspaper, *Gay News*, was published. In December 1975 ITV broadcast the groundbreaking film *The Naked Civil Servant* about the life of gay writer Quentin Crisp. Tolerance of gay people was growing, and gay bars and clubs were better attended than ever before.

Then came the 1980s and a calamity that would end the lives of thousands of gay and bisexual men and drastically change the lives of generations. In December 1981 the media reported the first death in the UK from a mysterious illness that had killed several gay and bisexual men in the USA that year. The condition, which seemed to suppress the immune system so that less significant ailments proved fatal, was being referred to as 'Gay Syndrome', 'Gay Cancer' or sometimes GRIDS – Gay Related Immune Deficiency Syndrome. Although at this stage no one understood what it was, in a *Time Out* report a doctor suggested that gay men should cut down on sexual partners.

In June 1982, thirty-seven-year-old House of Commons clerk Terry Higgins collapsed at Heaven nightclub, where he was a part-time bar man, and three weeks later died in hospital from pneumonia. His boyfriend, Rupert Whitaker, and friends set up a charity in his name with the aim of raising £100,000. That same year Boy George, the androgynous front man of a band called Culture Club, became a global superstar, but wasn't yet happy to be known as gay, saying he would rather have a cup of tea than have sex.

Medical ignorance of the habits of gay men prevailed but, whilst it was believed there had been only two confirmed deaths in the UK, in December 1982 *Gay News* warned of 'shocks' to come in the year ahead, noting that a London doctor investigating the health of gay men in the capital reported a large number exhibiting 'swollen glands and general malaise'.

In May 1983 scientists at the Pasteur Institute in France isolated the virus they believed led to AIDS. The British press reported that American sufferers were being treated like 'modern-day lepers'. That same month the UK's bestselling newspaper, the *Sun*, proclaimed 'U.S. GAY BLOOD PLAGUE KILLS THREE IN BRITAIN', stating that six other people were seriously ill with the condition and all but one, a haemophiliac, were homosexuals. The *Sun* reported British doctors criticizing the US blood service, which 'pays gays, junkies and other "less than fit" people to give blood for money'. Slowly, the right-wing media began conveying the message that homosexuality was now a serious threat to mainstream society.

In 1984 Labour's Chris Smith became the first MP to come out as gay, but in the media the tone was hardening. The *Sun* referred to gay people as 'nasty-minded perverts', and when DJ and prime-time comic Kenny Everett's details were found in the diary of a man charged with the murder of four gay men, Everett was forced to acknowledge his sexuality for the first time, describing, in the *Daily Star*, a life of doubt and anxiety. In the *Sunday Mirror*, writer George Gale, under the headline 'GUARDING AGAINST GAY PROPAGANDA', linked homosexuality to paedophilia: 'Just as pederasts flit from boy to boy', he wrote, 'so do homosexuals from one to the other . . .'

The *Mail on Sunday* described the 'awful genesis' of AIDS, seeming to suggest that homosexual sex was itself the cause of the disease. *Him Monthly*, a new, more sexual magazine that had replaced *Gay News*, reported that the Terrence Higgins Trust was working hard just protecting the privacy of AIDS patients, who were subjected 'not only to physical infection but equally to social rejection and isolation'.

Whilst some of the press, such as the *Daily Mirror*, the *Guardian* and *The Times*, tried to report the facts, others used AIDS to beat the left, linking Labour to the group fast becoming public enemy number one. A relentless drip-feed of stories, led by the *Sun* under editor Kelvin MacKenzie, began to portray dangerous gays and lesbians as getting special treatment from councils controlled by Labour, the party of deviance, danger and death. As far as I could see it, MacKenzie seemed to stop at nothing. One example was when the *Sun* published comments from American psychologist Paul Cameron, who said, 'All homosexuals should be exterminated to stop the spread of AIDS. It's time we stopped pussy-footing around'. The *Daily Express* meanwhile featured Tory councillor Bruce Hay suggesting gay people should carry identity cards.

On 25 July 1985 Rock Hudson's publicist announced that the iconic heterosexual movie star was being treated for AIDS and *People* magazine confirmed his homosexuality to the world. When Hudson died on 2 October the condition, for the first time, had a much-loved human face, but although public donations to AIDS charities soared, so did media homophobia. Everyone was under suspicion. Gay celebrities hid. 'Gay? I've never been in love,' said George Michael in the *Daily Star*. The *Mirror*'s speculation that Boy George and Culture Club drummer Jon Moss were lovers was dismissed by their publicist as 'so ridiculous'. Only one high-profile group, Bronski Beat, with lead singer Jimmy Somerville, stood firmly out and unapologetic.

When Stephen Barry, a former valet to Prince Charles, died of AIDS aged thirty-seven in October 1986, Jean Rook of the *Daily Express*, self-proclaimed 'First Lady of Fleet Street', wrote of 'The terrible lesson of Barry's gay life' and how he had died 'a shunned shadow, a hidden Royal Skeleton'. She demanded that the Queen should not be surrounded by 'gay AIDS' and said she would 'never stop condemning the glorification [of] sexual deviants [who] have not merely come out of the cupboard, they have preened and paraded their sexual skills'.

Day after day came attacks on gay people in a propaganda campaign of astonishing intensity. Any opportunity to paint gay men and women as infectious monsters was taken. When public figures were hounded out of the closet – a high-court judge, a member of the secret services, the relative of a celebrity – they would be depicted in cartoons, most often in the *Sun*, as transvestites in make-up, high heels and suspenders. When a deranged gay man horrifically raped and killed a paperboy, the *Sun*'s editorial issued a warning to *all* gay men. 'Homosexuals who say they are normal and society is perverse,' it declaimed, 'are risking a terrible backlash'. By November 1986 even Conservative ministers were apparently expressing concern that the level of homophobia could lead to violence on the streets. The *Sun* seemed to savour the idea of all-out war. 'Some gays are expected to retaliate,' it wrote, 'by spreading the virus to the rest of the community through "revenge sex" with bisexuals.'

Then on 11 December Manchester Police Chief Constable James Anderton made a public speech explicitly condemning 'perverted' homosexuals for spreading AIDS. 'I see ever increasing numbers of them swirling around in a human cesspit of their own making . . .' he boomed. 'I worry intensely about the possibility of whole generations being wiped out and nations decimated'. He said he was speaking as a Christian, as a policeman and as a father. The *Express* topped its front-page report with his line 'GAYS MUST STOP THEIR OBNOXIOUS PRACTICES' and wrote of 'Anderton's Army' of support, offering praise for his 'outburst over degenerates'. The *Sun*'s editorial, 'A plague in our midst', offered 'Three cheers for James Anderton . . . For the first time a major public figure says what the ordinary person is thinking about AIDS . . . Why do they continue to share their beds and defy the warnings of us all?' It suggested Britain needed more men like Anderton and fewer 'gay terrorists holding the decent members of society to ransom'. Days later the media quoted Tory councillor Bill Brownhill saying that, as a cure for AIDS, he would 'gas 90 per cent of queers'. He added that the other 10 per cent were 'genuinely sick and need help'. Asked about his comments later, he said, 'I would shoot them all.'

Brownhill's tactics weren't needed. Gay and bisexual men were falling in growing numbers. Paul O'Grady told me of his experience visiting hospital wards after his cabaret shows as Lily Savage. One teenager, just days from death, told him, 'I've only been with one fella, Lily.' Others weren't so lucky. So powerful was the media hysteria, sometimes even gay people abandoned those suffering. One man, himself now HIV positive, told me of a time in the early days when a man came to his local gay pub with visible Kaposi sarcoma skin cancers, a sure sign of AIDS, and the locals shunned him, stepping away until he left, after which the barman smashed his glass into the bin.

As the country shifted uneasily into 1987, the *Sun* began the year with the story of thirty-seven-year-old Alan Douthwaite from Hartlepool, Cleveland, the first policeman in the UK to die of AIDS, reporting that undertakers had refused to take the 'bachelor's' body from his house; other police eventually had to remove it in plastic sheeting. The *Daily Mirror* had a different take. Albeit in a small single column entitled 'Police honour AIDS victim', it reported that more than thirty colleagues had attended Alan's funeral, led by Commander Gordon Lloyd and Detective Superintendent Paul

Richard. Alan's coffin, with his helmet on top, was carried by six policemen and the paper reported the message on one wreath: 'To a good copper and a best friend. Love Angie'.

But as 1987 progressed it became intolerable to be openly gay in the UK. Gay bashings soared. People retreated into the closet. *Gay Times* reported tragedy after tragedy, such as, for instance, the case of a twenty-three-year-old man who was named in the press after a conviction of gross indecency for cottaging, who then killed himself. The Royal Vauxhall Tavern, a gay club, was raided by police officers wearing rubber gloves. When the telephone in another gay club developed a fault, BT technicians refused to fix it for fear of catching AIDS. After the offices of *Capital Gay* magazine were firebombed, in the House of Commons Tory MP Elaine Kellett-Bowman shrieked, 'Quite right too!' She later spoke in support of the firebombing: 'I am quite prepared to affirm that there should be an intolerance of evil!' Shortly after, Mrs Thatcher awarded her a damehood.

As the *Sun* reported that gay men with AIDS were taking 'cyanide cocktails' and rent boys were rampaging, intent on revenge infections, the hysteria did not just harm gay people. *Gay Times* reported the case of a heterosexual woman suffering with AIDS who was told by her GP that she should cut her wrists, which she did. In October 1987 the *Daily Express* reported the case of a man who, paranoid after sleeping with prostitutes, killed his wife because he believed he had given her AIDS. He made a botched attempt to kill himself, later learning that neither he nor his wife was HIV positive. At his trial he said the coverage of AIDS had warped his mind, and he was given a fifteen-month jail sentence.

Some gay groups, in light of the huge stigma and lack of any effective treatment, advised that people did not test for HIV but practised safe sex with every partner. The *Sun* was apoplectic. Its editorial, headlined 'Gay – and wicked!', said that 'Homosexual organizations are sometimes seen as harmless [but] they can be a force for destructive evil in the land . . . They deserve to be locked away where they can do no more harm'.

And this was not altogether out of the question. Conservative MP Geoffrey Dickens suggested that homosexuality be recriminalized, causing the *News of the World* to publish the results of a survey under the headline 'YOU SAY – OUTLAW GAYS'. It reported that 51 per cent of the public wanted homosexuality to be made an illegal offence again, while 54 per cent wanted people with AIDS to be isolated from society. Given an option of 'in hospitals, islands or camps', 63.8 per cent opted for hospitals, 7.5 per cent for islands and 28.7 per cent camps. Figures published the following year by the British Social Attitudes Survey found that 75 per cent of the population believed homosexual activity was 'always or mostly wrong'. Just 11 per cent believed it was never wrong.

After the government ran its 1987 'Don't die of ignorance' campaign, with billboard and TV ads, and leaflets sent to every home, the *Daily Mail* reported that religious leaders were up in arms, arguing that educating people about safe sex would encourage more 'immorality'. Three weeks later the *Mail* published an article stating that twenty clergymen from the Church of England itself had AIDS and 'at least 400' clergymen supported the Gay Christian movement. Meanwhile, Pope Jean Paul II condemned those Catholic priests who offered comfort to people dying of AIDS. The *Sun* reported comments by a churchman under the headline 'I'D SHOOT MY SON IF HE HAD AIDS SAYS VICAR!'

Sane and compassionate public voices were few and far between, but there were some. In 1987 Princess Diana (as she then was) used her headline-grabbing influence to reach out literally and symbolically to people living with AIDS. Opening the country's first specialist HIV ward, she had herself photographed shaking hands with patients without wearing gloves. This was the first time a public figure showed the world that people with HIV and AIDS were just that: people and not monsters. The images were published around the world, while Conservative MPs and the *Sun* condemned her apparent support of gay people, with John Junor in the *Mail on Sunday* asking if she 'really wanted to go down in history as the patron saint of sodomy'.

On 6 May 1986 the *Sun* had denounced a harmless children's book about a little girl and her two gay fathers called *Jenny Lives with*

Eric and Martin. 'VILE BOOK IN SCHOOLS!' screamed the front-page headline, despite the fact that the book was available in only one teaching resource unit. The following year, during her 1987 conference speech, the prime minister, Margaret Thatcher, delivered her now infamous attack on left-wing councils. She said, 'Children who need to be taught to respect traditional moral values are being taught that they have an inalienable right to be gay.' Also listing attempts to teach kids racial tolerance, she added, 'All of those children are being cheated of a sound start in life. Yes, cheated!'

The Conservative Party turned her words into action. MPs David Wilshire and Dame Jill Knight proposed a new clause to the Local Government Act that would set in law that local authorities 'shall not intentionally promote the teaching in any maintained [i.e. state] school of the acceptability of homosexuality as a pretended family relationship'. Section 28 put a government stamp on the unacceptability of homosexual relationships and in effect stopped teachers from dealing with homophobic bullying or supporting gay or questioning students.

Section 28 would prove to be both rock bottom and a galvanizing turning point. On 27 January 1988 in a Radio 4 interview alongside right-wing journalist Peregrine Worsthorne, actor Ian McKellen stopped talking about 'them' and 'they', and instead said 'me' and 'us', and came out as a gay man. Celebrities Sinéad O'Connor, Robbie Coltrane, the Proclaimers, Billy Bragg and others contributed to an angry anti-Section 28 feature in *NME* and now 'openly' gay Boy George released a protest single, 'No Clause 28'. *Guardian* commentators questioned the logic of such a law. Mass demonstrations took place in Manchester and London, where Michael Cashman, Ian McKellan, actress Sue Johnston and others angrily spoke out. On the eve of the vote in May 1988, lesbians abseiled into the House of Commons and three broke into the BBC news studio and tried to protest on air.

Importantly, a group of figures that included Ian McKellen, Michael Cashman, Lisa Power, comedian Simon Fanshawe, Matthew Parris, critic Nicholas de Jongh and others came together to form a new gay rights lobby group named after the 1969 Stonewall Riots.

Shortly before the Section 28 vote, on 8 March 1988, the *Sun* expressed clearly its view about gay people's position in family life. In a 'rock sensation', it reported that Francis Rossi of Status Quo had said that the day his twenty-year-old son came out to him was the proudest day of his life. He said, 'It took immense courage . . . I love Simon in the same way I love my other sons . . . there is no problem with gays'. The next day, keen to make sure readers hadn't mis-interpreted its intentions, the paper published a cartoon depicting an angry-looking, balding, middle-aged man walking away from his (effeminate) son, who was hanging from a noose, eyes bulging, tongue protruding. Looking up at him was his (effeminate) friend, with the caption, 'I said your dad wouldn't take the news so well, Rodney!'

The message was loud and clear. If you were gay your life was worthless. You were better off dead.

I was fourteen years old then.

I did not have magical earplugs. I was listening and reading, as were all of my generation.

Change slowly came. Peter Tatchell and the direct-action group OutRage! kept the issue of gay rights in the public eye, allowing the more formal lobbyists at Stonewall to target politicians. As more and more of us came out, we showed our families, friends and workmates who gay people really were and public attitudes began to shift.

The Labour Party committed to working with Stonewall, but Conservative MPs fought the progression of gay rights at every turn, including in 1994, when the Commons rejected Edwina Currie's Bill to lower the age of consent for gay men from twenty-one to sixteen, compromising on eighteen instead.

A new confidence emerged. In 1994 *Attitude*, a new, cooler, more fashion-orientated gay magazine was founded. Four years later seminal sitcom *Will & Grace* and TV personalities such as Graham Norton established the gay man as the perfect best friend. Then in 1996 came a monumental breakthrough when scientists discovered that a combination of drugs, if started early enough, could stop the HIV virus from progressing to AIDS.

In 1997 Labour, with a commitment to gay rights, swept to power. The government had to be taken to the European Court of Human Rights before it lifted the Armed Forces ban, but that too fell in 2000, and a year later my friend Tim and I joined Stonewall supporters inside Parliament's Great Hall, jumping to our feet as MPs voted to equalize the age of consent once and for all. Not long afterwards the Adoption and Children Act 2002 made it legal for gay singles or couples to adopt. A year after that – fifteen years after Thatcher had introduced it – the hated Section 28 was scrapped. Protection from discrimination, the Gender Recognition Act for trans people and civil partnerships followed.

Over the nearly twenty years I have spent working at *Attitude*, we have documented the incredible positive changes that have taken place: young people coming out earlier; more frequent and better representation in the media; more schools with policies to deal with homophobic bullying; companies falling over themselves to appear on the Stonewall Employers table of gay-friendly businesses; many happy couples; people living successful lives, some in domestic suburbia, others expressing their radical queer identities in whatever way they choose.

But where are we now? Many of us, usually with more comfortable financial lives, often white, are invested in the finality of this utopian gay ending. Happily, I have met huge numbers of gay people who have good lives and straight people with gay friends who believe that the problems of the past have disappeared. But this isn't the case.

All LGBT adults have had to develop some kind of shield against prejudice, an understanding that some people are stupid – get over it. But we're so conditioned to it we sometimes can barely even see it. Though many of us move to hubs where it's safer, we accept that homophobia is always a possibility. No matter how many parties we go to with our heterosexual friends, we know there might be someone present who is uncomfortable with us. Like the Terminator, we learn to scan new environments for potential threats. Can we be ourselves? Do we have to tone down our mannerisms? Can we mention our partners? Is this bus safe for us? Can I come out in this new job? In public, we know there is always potential to find ourselves verbally or – thankfully rarer – physically attacked, even in the apparently hallowed streets of gay-friendly London. We are self-conscious, always wary of 'micro-aggressions' – a look here, a comment there. Or worse, we know that sometimes people lose their lives for being like us, like sixty-two-year-old Ian Baynham who was kicked to death in London's Trafalgar Square in 2009. His nineteen- and twenty-year-old assailants screamed 'Faggot!' as they knocked him to the ground and stamped on him. They went to prison in 2011 for six and seven years respectively.

When it comes to transgender awareness, Caitlyn Jenner has led a global leap forward, but transgender people continue to suffer even higher levels of these problems than LGB people do; discrimination is still rife at spectacular levels. In 2011, when a Thai airline announced it was hiring transgender staff, comedian Russell Howard's *Good News* programme featured a sketch where beefy men in dresses with their genitals hanging out served drinks to passengers, who reacted by vomiting. When teacher Lucy Meadows announced her transition at the end of 2012, teachers and pupils accepted it but the national press did not. Richard Littlejohn criticized her in the *Daily Mail*, saying 'she's not only in the wrong body, she's in the wrong job'. The press surrounded the school, offering parents payments to make complaints about Ms Meadows and make her life intolerable. She killed herself weeks later, in March 2013, at the age of thirty-two. At her inquest the coroner told the press 'shame on you' and accused the *Daily Mail* of character assassination. Even as I finished this book, at the end of Caitlyn Jenner's sensational year, two trans women, Vicky Thompson, twenty-one, and Joanne Latham, thirty-eight, separately took their own lives after being placed in men's prisons.

Politically, we know that treating LGBT people with full respect is still somehow contentious. In an interview with *Attitude* in 2010,

David Cameron declared his party had changed, yet when push came to shove more than half his MPs voted against same-sex marriage. We are so used to being thrown crumbs that many of us are grateful for this, believing that it is worth celebrating as progress. We watch bemused as a parade of loonies standing for public office suggest insane things such as that we are the cause of bad weather.

Also shocking is the apparently forward-thinking media's continuing treatment of us as not of the same worth as other people. The political fallout over David Cameron's support for same-sex marriage was detailed and raked over with a fine-tooth comb, but how it actually affected those whom it concerned – us – seemed secondary. When Tom Daley announced he was in a relationship with a man in 2014, the no doubt well-intentioned BBC Radio Wales thought it reasonable to pitch the leader of the extremist group Christian Voice, Stephen Green, against former *Attitude* editor Adam Mattera, as if Daley's very right to be who he is was something still up for debate.

The crisis of homophobic bullying in schools is all but ignored in the mainstream media. When eighteen-year-old trainee hairdresser Michael Causer – a slight, seven and a half stone 'sweetheart' who 'wouldn't hurt a fly' – was beaten to death in 2008 after youths found explicit pictures on his phone at a party, the media's reaction was tepid. Most didn't report it. Some did in dribs and drabs. Contrast it to the murder of fellow-Liverpudlian fifteen-year-old Anthony Walker in a horrendous racist attack three years earlier, which rightly rocked the country into countless front pages of soul-searching and outrage.

On television and in films, we are so unused to seeing our lives portrayed honestly that, when a rare specifically gay-themed programme is broadcast, many of us make a point of watching just to see how we come across – often concerned by 'What will straight people think?'

When it comes to religion we live with the perverse satisfaction of uniting the world's major religions: they all believe homosexual relationships are wrong. In 2012 the Pope's representative Archbishop

Antonio Mennini called for alliance between Catholics, Muslims and Jews to oppose gay marriage, and rent-a-gobs speaking in the name of Christianity appeared on television to suggest same-sex marriage would lead to bestiality. We didn't even get Christmas Day off, when the Roman Catholic Archbishop of Westminster, Vincent Nichols, now a cardinal, used his 2012 Christmas Day sermon to launch yet another attack on equal marriage. This pales in comparison with some evangelical churches in the US. Pastor Scott Lively, for example, founded Abiding Truth Ministries as 'the first Christian organization devoted exclusively to opposing homosexuality', and his anti-gay speeches in Uganda fuelled the homophobia that resulted in that country's draconian 2014 Anti-Homosexual Act. In 2015 the media regularly showed images of gay men being thrown off buildings by Isis. In UK-based battles over Christian guesthouses and cake icing, I sometimes detect a sense of warning: 'You should be grateful: we won't make you cakes, but over there they'll kill you!'

You'll also be used to many of the attacks on gay men and women coming from, um, other gay men and women.

We have differing opinions about what it means to be gay, how we should live, but are quick to condemn others as 'giving us a bad name' by either being 'too gay' or, alternatively, 'too straight', calling out the heteronormativity of gay men who are anything less than radical fairies. Some of us are so panicked about being seen as part of a whiny minority that we bristle at anyone who stands up for our rights. On apps we attack other men's effeminacy, race or HIV status in a way that might get us arrested if we were straight. It was embodied for me when I found myself on a radio call-in show arguing with two gay men in succession, one of whom said he was homophobic and didn't like gays, and the other who said marriage should only be for people with real and serious relationships and 'not silly gays'.

We seem collectively confused about who we are. Is it any wonder that many of us struggle to make any sense of our lives at all? Some of us work through the complications and complexities and manage to build happy, healthy, balanced lives, our self-esteem intact, able to love and be loved. It is truly remarkable so many of us emerge unscathed. But for others amongst us everything is definitely not OK. Some of us are adrift, fighting for survival.

I know because I was one of them. While I was living what may have looked from the outside like a successful gay life, there was something wrong with me too.

3

My Share

'The thing I love seeing in you young people is that you are so happy in your own skins. You don't have the self-loathing that the older generation have . . .'

Martin Sherman, author of *Bent*, talking to me and a small group of students after a gay theatre workshop in 2002

CLIMBING THE COLD STAIRS to the sexual-health centre just ten minutes' walk from Victoria – the station that had delivered me to the playground of Central London so many times – for yet another HIV test, I felt like I was going insane. I made a bargain with God: if I could get away with it just one more time I'd be a good gay, move away from the constant string of randoms and hold out for the big relationship I really wanted. I'd made this promise many times before – and yet here I was, anxiously white-knuckling my way through yet another blood test.

This wasn't the way my life was meant to be. Years ago I believed I had joined a special club of sexy, happy, non-stop fabulousness. In reality it was non-stop worry and waiting rooms. By 2000 I'd had so many HIV tests that it sometimes felt that on job applications I should list under hobbies and pastimes 'obsessing about dying of AIDS'.

The confusion I felt was overwhelming. I came from a good family, I had a great job; but my personal life was a disaster. When I wasn't in a terrible relationship, I was boozing and constantly falling into bed

with people who didn't care whether either of us was there, or wrestling with extreme anxiety and the growing awareness that I hated
myself with an intensity that was unbearable.

It all started years before.

I knew I was fucked up by the time I was five years old. It wasn't my
sexuality – I had no awareness of that – but I had an overwhelming
fragility and fear, and an understanding that I wasn't like other
boys. I walked differently, talked differently, behaved differently. My
nervous inability to muster an interest in sport served as a pink flag.
Enthusing about *Mary Poppins* and holding hands with dinner ladies
did the same. Being frequently on the verge of tears attracted hostility.

My childish consciousness slowly started to realize that this way of
being wasn't acceptable. Other boys wondered why I wasn't into football and fighting. Girls wondered why I preferred talking to them.
My parents were generally fantastic. They took my brother and me
to the coast, to the cinema, to theme parks; my father gave up his
time to help with school sports, my mum took us to the theatre. Both
worked as hard as they could to support us. But they too could see
my difference and didn't want me to be hurt by the world, so they
encouraged me to be stronger, more masculine, to kick bullies before
they kicked me, to be something I couldn't be. I learned that being
myself was just not OK.

In my second year of school, aged six, I developed a crush on a boy
a year below me. After a week of gazing at him over the semolina, he
gave me a look that said back off. And so it was, in the dining hall
of Beddington Park Primary School in Croydon, some time in 1979,
that I first consciously felt shame due to my attraction to someone of
the same gender.

I felt as if I was an alien. My self-consciousness got worse. I
believed if people could sense the difference in me I would be hurt,
dead. If I wanted to survive I had to be someone else. The pressure
was immense. It was as if I were wearing a jacket with pockets that
were being loaded with stones. I became clingy, constantly afraid of
abandonment. When a playmate wanted to play with another friend I

pinched and scratched him in panic. His mother rightly complained to mine, adding to my growing shame. When the other boy broke his leg I was overjoyed because I'd have my friend to myself for a week or two. Another realization: that someone else's misfortune could make me feel better.

By the time I was seven more coping mechanisms emerged. I developed immense crushes on any male person who showed me kindness. My eating became erratic. I ate sugary, starchy foods to quell my anxiety, so I put on weight. I tried obsessively to be the best at everything, believing my survival depended on it. A perfectionist, desperate for validation, my hand always shot up first in class, something that was irritating to my schoolmates. During a craze for novelty erasers I had to have more than anyone else, and one day returned from lunch to find the whole lot in a crumbled heap. Immersed in television and film, I lost the ability to differentiate between fantasy and reality, telling schoolfriends that film stars were coming to my birthday party, shamed again when they discovered it was just us and chicken nuggets.

My childhood wasn't all bad by any means. I had friends and lots of fun, but there was no solid ground. Anything could shake my foundations. One night at a kiddie disco a rough-looking boy grabbed me and demanded to know if I was a boy or a girl. I froze, wondering why he was asking me, as I had no idea.

I lived in a constant state of vigilance. Though I couldn't physically defend myself, I could defuse aggression by being quick-witted, often compulsively criticizing before anyone had the chance to land the first blow. Acutely aware of my own flaws, I pounced like a bloodhound on those of others.

Like the majority of the British public, my parents read the *Daily Mail* and, most often, the *Sun* and the *News of the World*. Their discarded copies were left lying around the house, and I read them too. I read headlines and stories about a new disease that had been killing people in America and had now come to Britain. The papers taught me that these people, who were called 'gay' or 'bisexual', were somehow depraved; more than that, they were dangerous.

On a sunny spring day in 1983, standing outside the school hall next to a peeling climbing frame, the biggest realization of my life hit me like the sky crashing down: the way that I was different and these bad words I kept hearing were linked. Gay. Queer. Poof. Pansy. I suddenly understood: *that was me*. That was what *I* was.

I felt a brief flash of excitement at the fact that I'd solved an immense puzzle, but also a dropping in my stomach. How could I be gay? Why was this happening to me? What had I done to deserve this? There were no other gay people in the world that I could see: no friends, no teachers, no one at my church, no one in my family, not on television, in the media, no one writing for the newspapers, no one in the town in which I lived. Being gay was apparently so abhorrent that it could not even be spoken about explicitly for long enough to be condemned. And it was me.

Fighting for survival, I tried to make it go away. If I couldn't feel those gay feelings, maybe it would mean they weren't real. So I sank them, like a murder weapon weighted with stones, to the bottom of my psyche, where they remained, submerged, occasionally rising and falling on powerful currents invisible on the surface, but still shaping all that happened beneath. I shut down, not just sexual feelings but *all* my feelings. I switched off my developing emotional self, believing that feeling anything at all could kill me. I was ten years old.

Sometime in the blur of those years a neighbourhood friend, a year younger than me, kissed me. I resisted, saying it was wrong, and he, like Humphrey Bogart, declared, 'What the hell?' before leaning in again. We did that a few times and then it stopped. Another local friend instigated a fumble between the two of us and a third boy. Then a few days later, to my horror, he screamed across the street that I was a queer.

I became aware that the pleasant physical intimacy I'd felt twice now came with a pay-off of guilt and even more shame. I developed a crush on my best friend, a boy in my class called Ryan. I believed if he would love me, then everything would be all right. He had the power to erase all the pain. Unable to cope with my feelings for him, one day at my house I told him I loved him and that he should tell me he was gay too. He said he wasn't, but I kept on until he said he was. Terrified of the ramifications of what I'd said, back at school I outed him. To cover my tracks I told my parents I'd said I was gay as a double-bluff and my mother told me to 'never say that again'.

By 1985, AIDS hysteria was in full bloom. That was the year that the *Sun* printed: 'The sickest joke among America's 12 million gays goes like this: Son: Mom, I've got good news and bad news. The bad news is I'm gay. The good news is I'm dying.'

I got the terrifying message loud and clear. If my parents knew I was gay they would want me dead. I didn't want to bring shame on my parents so I started to play up, hoping they'd go off me so that if I did kill myself it wouldn't be such a loss for them. I cried myself to sleep, alone in my room, so hard, so many times, that I sometimes forgot what I was crying about.

The following year the *Sun*'s agony aunt ran a special entitled 'My Child Is Gay!' The page's main letter, from the mother of a twenty-three-year-old member of the Royal Navy, was headed: 'I loved him – now I wish he was dead'. She said she wished he'd died in the Falklands War as it would have been an honourable death.

I was going to die either from AIDS or from the homophobic reaction to it. If I could become someone ferocious and larger than life, maybe I could continue to defend myself. I soothed my feelings by eating, getting attention, gossiping, putting enemies down, arguing with friends. I loved the spotlight that performing brought and so I threw myself into school plays. It was about feeling as though I was someone else. My weekends were spent watching movies, obsessing about musicals or trying to make films with friends using video cameras. Fantasy and escapism through entertainment became a bigger and bigger part of my life.

Spending an unhealthy amount of time worrying about myself, I became more and more self-obsessed. That was the answer: I'd be famous and everyone would love me. My need for attention made me like someone who had been dropped in the North Sea and was doing everything they could not to dip under the surface. If I stopped and felt the feelings underneath I would drown. At school I alienated myself, playing up to the camp stereotype and so at least gaining some control over the bullying: causing it, reaffirming it, exploiting it, revelling in it, using it to oppress myself. I was stuck in a cycle of defiantly encouraging others to view me as a freak so that I could still feel in control by feeling unworthy and unwanted. I was doing the best I could.

Debilitating crushes came thick and fast – on schoolfriends, people at the local drama club, performers at stage doors. My mum found me crying one day, brokenhearted, and told me, 'You're too young to be this upset.' I cried even harder. 'You can tell me anything,' she said. But I couldn't. She didn't like gay people; I'd heard her say it. Other family members, neighbours and teachers at school said it too. When a BBC newsreader or presenter wore a red ribbon as a symbol of AIDS awareness, my father angrily spat out the casual tabloid-taught condemnation: 'Why should licence-fee money be spent supporting these perverts?'

Around the age of fourteen my body stopped working and I collapsed. I was diagnosed with glandular fever, unable to get out of bed for weeks. I struggled back to school, completed my GCSEs but became aware that a definitive way of ending the pain was getting closer. I was someone hanging from the roof of a building with my fingers being unpicked one by one.

At fourteen I started obsessively watching the musical *Phantom of the Opera* and whenever I was in London I started buying porn magazines which showed gay sex, something I'd never seen before. It was so intensely powerful that it too blotted out some of the pain. The thrill of porn helped stop me from killing myself, but it also fused the relationship I was developing between sex, emotional pain and shame.

What I craved was love, touch, intimacy, but there were no illicit magazines for that. When friends instigated teenage masturbatory experiences I thought it meant they must be gay too, but I was again knocked down when it became clear they were just horny straight boys starved of females. With a breakdown imminent, I looked up the number of the local boy who had kissed me a few years before and had since moved away. 'Is it a gel?' I heard him ask as he came to the phone. He met me at the local shops but looked as scared as a teenager in 1989 who'd once kissed another boy would.

I was running out of options.

And then, in *Time Out*, I found the number for Gay Switchboard.

'Where do you live, sweetheart?' I bristled at being called sweetheart by a man, but he gave me the number for a group called Croydon Area Gay Youth. I was so shocked to hear that Croydon had any gay people that I almost dropped the phone. I inserted more five-pence pieces and dialled the number. A man answered. I agreed when he suggested we meet up to see whether I'd suit the group. I asked if he would bring someone of my own age.

Uncontactable, in those days before mobile phones, I told my parents I was seeing a friend and I went to meet them: a student called Jeremy, who was caretaking the group, and their then youngest member, a seventeen-year-old called Nat. His face dropped when he saw my chubby self. Jeremy asked if I wanted to come back for a chat at the group's meeting place – the guy who ran it apparently preferred that to going for a coffee. So back on the bus we went, back through the local housing estate, almost back to my home, to where CAGY met every other Friday night: someone's bedsit.

I waited, numb, to have sex with them – not because I wanted to, but the newspapers had told me that's what gays did. But instead Jeremy gave me a cup of tea and asked how I was. They were both gay, they told me. They hadn't had sex with each other, they were friends. They went to gay bars, gay clubs, had gay friends, led gay lives, Nat had been dating someone. To not hear the word 'gay' used to hurt or condemn someone, or adjuncted with 'disgusting', shook me. I felt like a shipwrecked man being rescued by a passing boat and not able to function in the place he longed to be. I wanted to cry, but I couldn't. I wanted to express what I'd been through. I wanted to ask for a hug, but I couldn't. I wanted to ask to be told I was OK, but I couldn't. What I really needed was therapy, but I didn't know it. So I mostly listened. Nat and Jeremy told me I wasn't alone and put on a video of a Gay Pride march and gave me a copy of *Gay Times* to flick through. 'There are thousands of people like us,' they said. 'You are not alone any more. It is going to be all right.'

I told them I didn't want to go to gay clubs or Gay Pride, or read gay magazines, and had no interest in being radical or sleeping around. All I wanted was to find someone to love me. I believed I wasn't like the gays that I'd read about, spreading AIDS and molesting children, or the ones I'd seen on TV – John Inman, Larry Grayson or *'Allo 'Allo*'s Gorden Kaye, apologetic as he was outed by the tabloids. I just wanted a boyfriend. I immediately decided that Nat would be that boyfriend; he was handsome and thickset, but mostly he was just there, in front of me. I started going to the group so I could stalk him.

CAGY lived up to its name. A charming, slightly bizarre cross between a knitting group and a safe house, with perhaps twenty or so people aged from sixteen to thirty (so they said). Most of the members were older. There were younger kids, but they were often too timid to make conversation. On my first visit, one deathly slim, pale sixteen-year-old, who in hindsight must have been anorexic, trembled like a field mouse, barely able to answer whether he wanted a cup of tea. Another seventeen-year-old had driven twenty terrified miles to get there. He twitched as he looked at the windows, asking over and over if we thought his parents or the *News of the World* might have followed him down the M23. It was excruciating to watch. He said he didn't like gay people, 'especially camp ones'. 'Me too,' I gruffly replied.

My breathing would quicken when Nat arrived and I died a little when he left. I obsessively believed I was head over heels in love with him. Once he mentioned he was in a school play the next weekend, so I sniffed out which school it was and went to the opening night, then registered to join its sixth form. A month or so later I plucked up the courage to tell him how I felt, and his gracious and gentle rejection dissipated my crush as quickly as it had appeared.

I came to love CAGY. A year or so later Chaz, the man who ran the group and whose flat we met in, told me that someone from my school had called to join. He described him as being 'a big guy'. Fat, he meant, and I knew immediately who it was. Tim was morbidly obese, loud, over the top and a figure of fun at school. He was picked on but was funny and gave as good as he got. At school on the Monday morning I walked up to him and he ran off in a panic. In time we became close friends and he became a CAGY regular.

In 1990 I was still too scared to go to a gay club. After meetings, members would pile into cars and go to a club called the Palm Beach above an ice rink in Streatham. One night, a load drove past as I cycled out of the housing estate and one of them, a handsome black guy called Rob, waved. I liked him, but someone had warned me that 'he had been to America', which at that time was an unspoken way of saying he was likely to be HIV positive.

I wobbled on my BMX. Rob reached out and his fingers made contact with my hand, leaving a tiny graze. He'd cut me. I tried to look relaxed but started to shake as I cycled home and checked – and yes, *Christ!* I was bleeding. I was *going to die.*

Younger readers may stop and ponder what it felt like to know you could easily catch a virus that would, without fail, kill you. HIV could mean being cast out from your home, fired from your job, disowned by family and friends. Instead of showing compassion for people who needed help, elements of Fleet Street painted gay men as having the intention of crackling AIDS through the air to innocent heterosexual people just for kicks.

So it's not surprising that, in 1990, I was terrified of a scratch and determined the school bullies would not be proved right. I coped alone with a three-month wait for my first HIV test and another neurotic fortnight for the results. It wasn't a nice fourteen weeks.

The second test came a year later, when I met my first boyfriend, and it was for reassurance – though as we both lived at home with our parents, anal sex was not on the table, or in bed or anywhere else for that matter. Just having a kiss and a cuddle meant finding a friend whose sofa we could snog on every time they went to the kitchen to make tea. Considering the media, on the handful of nights we spent together, juggling with machetes would have been more appealing than having anal sex. In truth, it wasn't just the HIV risk; gay sex itself was portrayed as a passport to Armageddon. The thought of it was exciting but also deeply frightening.

Ironically, the real danger my boyfriend was putting himself in was by testing with me. He was twenty-three. I was seventeen – four years under the then homosexual age of consent of twenty-one. That threat clouded our entire relationship. We did the best we could, cuddling at friends' houses, kissing in moonlit hallways of communal flats, but mostly we just sat in his red Fiat holding hands, saying how much we loved each other, releasing every time a car went past in case it was the police. It was difficult to live with – and so was I. Being in an actual relationship brought out a side of me that had been developing under the surface for years and which was, to put it lightly, completely irrational. I was paranoid. A furnace of insecurity raged inside me. I didn't believe he wanted to be with me. I expected him to cheat and dump me. At school I was now presenting myself as above it all, better than other people, but in reality I thought I was unworthy of love. I was rarely at ease and often provoked rows, keen to declare the relationship over just to see if he would want to get back with me. I didn't understand why I was doing it or even that I was doing it. I quizzed him in intricate detail about his past sexual experiences, if he would go back with his girlfriend, if he would find another boyfriend, if he would rather be with the one man he'd slept with before me. I was a nightmare.

Ten months later it ended, as first relationships often do. The catalyst was a night before Christmas with the CAGY boys at the Palm Beach when he was away seeing friends. I'd been nervous of booze before, but that night I got drunk and realized its power. The feelings I'd had for years of not being good enough, not attractive, not likeable, not intelligent, not kind, not funny, not friendly, not part of the gang, not someone who was included or eligible to be part of anything – almost somehow inhuman – dissolved in five Watermelon Bacardi Breezers. Alcohol flipped the switch. As the baseline thumped, Kylie vamped and boys flirted, the aching emptiness disappeared. Suddenly I felt as good as everyone else going wild to the pop music. That night I became part of the gay community for the first time. The disco may have needed me, but I truly needed it more than anything I had before.

With that relationship over, I made a beeline for a handsome new CAGY member and another began. I wasn't very nice to him and it ended two years later. I didn't know what I wanted or didn't want and was all over the place. The relationship I had dreamed about, which was meant to last for ever, had not worked first or second time. When I was dumped from a further flabby three-month fling I felt there was no point in living, and scrambled to find the next man to make that feeling go away.

As I was exposed to the new point of view that gay people were not what the *Sun* had said, I began to realize on an intellectual level that I had been lied to, that it was the newspapers, my family and everyone else who were wrong, not me or my friends. I developed a passion for gay politics that stemmed from the hope that younger people might not have to go through what I had. I went to protests and got involved with their and my own university gay societies. I did work experience for gay rights group Stonewall and was eventually casually employed to answer phones and stuff envelopes. Exposed to gay people, I had the revelation that I was not ashamed but actually proud of my sexuality. Gay Pride Day became the day of the year I most looked forward to, marching in the day and partying at G-A-Y at night.

But my neediness was still there. I realized the suicidal feelings I'd had when I was a teenager were shifting into something different: a belief that the gaping hole in my soul would be filled only by fame or finding The One. I'd go to the Two Brewers in Clapham and stand at the bar, anxiously hoping He would be there. Or to new bars in Soho, like Rupert Street, where everyone seemed better dressed, with better bodies, more money, better flats, better friends, better this, better that, better everything.

On our very first night out on our own in G-A-Y at the London Astoria 2, when I was about twenty-one, Tim and I decided we should try to talk to a group of four slightly older, attractive guys at the bar.

After ten minutes of plucking up courage, we went over and Tim asked if any of them had a light. 'Move on, move on!' they yelled in full-on, snarling, pack mode. 'Ask someone else!' they barked, and we slunk away, shocked. This didn't feel much like the 'gay community' they talked about in the magazines.

I did have some amazing times on the gay scene. I was cheeky and young, rampaging round Soho making the most of being in my twenties and as desirable as I would ever be. But this kind of unfriendly interaction wasn't uncommon. On the gay scene men often had a bark and a bite, and I became apprehensive about talking to them. It felt like if people didn't want to sleep with you, they didn't want to know you. We seemed to communicate only by having sex, and if you weren't worthy of sex then you weren't part of the conversation. The concept of 'the gay world' became a thing. In the gay world, having sex was like shaking hands. In the gay world, it was only about whether every new man was worth going home with. In the gay world, if you were attractive then young people wanted to know you, engage with you, invite you to their parties – and if you weren't, they wouldn't. Sometimes I was the person not allowed into the conversation and sometimes, being young, I got to do the rejecting. In reality, I was doing it too. What you looked like was who you were. There weren't many black or Asian gay men around. Those that liked them were 'dinge queens'. My Chinese friend was ignored or treated as a comic novelty.

My fragile self-esteem wasn't set up to function under these circumstances. But rotten drunk, it was screamingly good fun.

Tim and I made other friends. In our early days at CAGY we had bonded with another newbie, a fifteen-year-old local boy called Lee whose mum had sent him to the group. Lee was skinny, attractive and, as CAGY's then youngest member, thoroughly enjoyed his status as resident 'chicken' and the attention that came with it. One evening, despite his age, a man from the group had gone back to Lee's house, after which he was nicknamed Lego Lee.

Along with other friends we picked up along the way, Tim, Lee and I went to Gay Prides, clubs and parties and looked out for one another. When I was about twenty, Tim and I got jobs in the local cinema and became responsible for the kids' club entertainment. Dressed as nuns, Dracula, Mrs Doubtfire, we would visit Lee behind the till in Superdrug, pleased at the scandal we were bringing to suburbia. We had a ball, me driving up to G-A-Y, where we'd watch Lily Savage or Lulu, and then Kylie in the bigger Astoria next door, before taking our gang of mixed-up boys and girls back to their closeted lives. There was always an understanding that we were there to find the person who would make it all better. On the journey home the sinking loneliness would always flood back in.

In 1996 I got my first proper job as editorial assistant at *Attitude* and life began pulling us in different directions. Lee started going to harder clubs such as Trade, then in 2000 emigrated to Australia, leaving Tim and me stuck together for the next fifteen years.

In the middle of my drunken twenties I met someone at the local gay bar. I was twenty-five, he was twenty-one and I only became interested when he told me how badly he'd been treated by his last boyfriend. Bingo! Someone more vulnerable than me! I could save him! And he'd need me! A few months later I moved out of home and rented a flat in central Croydon. I was starting to think that he could be the mythical One. Then one night he said the L-word and I said it back. And then . . . he shut down and started cheating. We split up and got back together and round it went. I couldn't bear to be with him or without him. It felt like I was addicted to a person and I took him back no matter how badly he treated me. My life started to crumble. I'd find myself crying at work, where I was now deputy editor, end up staggering through busy traffic after dramatic drunken rows, and even turned to my parents, to whom I was out by now. My dad sweetly told me, 'I only know what it's like with girls.'

Eventually I moved to escape my addiction to him, to a flat in Central London, with a flatmate who was a writer at *Attitude*. This was a new chapter. Two single guys in their twenties flatsharing in one of the gayest cities in the world. By this time the internet was a thing and you could meet people off it. Gaydar.co.uk was created and we went nuts for it.

My city life intensified. I was doing what lots of young people were doing: going to bars and clubs, meeting people, going on dates, having a month-long fling every now and then and meeting people online. It seemed like everyone was on Gaydar, and I think I slept with most of them. I say slept, but the internet meant they didn't have to spend the night. Mostly it involved getting them in and out as quickly as possible. It made sense while I continued my hunt for a boyfriend.

My life became a blur. Most nights after work I would go into Soho for a drink either with friends or alone. I expected to meet the love of my life walking down Old Compton Street. I'd go to G-A-Y for a dirt-cheap pint, which became three or four, then to the Shadow Lounge or to Ghetto, a basement bar down an alley next to the Astoria. It wasn't just to meet people. I genuinely loved dancing and was always first on the floor and last off. Going out was addictive – the excitement of getting ready, the bus, the queue, going in, the first drink, enjoying the frisson of friends old and new – it all gave me a buzz.

From the outside, my life looked manageable. I told myself I had a high sex drive, and gay culture suggested the all-you-can-eat buffet was one of the upsides of our sexuality: warriors of sexual freedom, we got to break and make the rules. Our magazines were full of porn, rent boys and saunas. We'd been told gay sex was wrong and we were embarking on a trolley-dash to prove it was right however it came. I was climbing the editorial ladder at *Attitude*, wrote a play that was performed to decent reviews and started a stand-up comedy night which hosted comedians such as Greg Davies and Alan Carr. I also had the healthiest relationship I've ever had with a very sweet man. We had two great years, which gave me a much-needed break from (some) of my craziness, but it became clear we were better suited as friends. All this and I also met my teenage heroes, the Pet Shop Boys, and Boy George, and got to spend a surreal ninety minutes inter-viewing the object of my obsession, Madonna. To the outside world it looked like I was living the gay dream.

But inside my head things were not going well. I felt like I was going mad. Getting up in the morning was difficult. In the shower

I'd feel sick with fear. Work took some edge off. Drinking and having sex masked more – but it was always temporary. The feelings of just not being right always came back. I wasn't having anal sex but the risk of HIV transmission is still there and so, driven by paranoia, testing became another compulsive part of my life. Over the years I was a regular at the city's sexual-health clinics – Mayday Hospital in Croydon, St Barts, the South Westminster Health Centre in Pimlico's Vincent Square and eventually Soho's 56 Dean Street.

At one of my regular HIV tests I tried to talk about it. The health advisor went through the usual questions about what I'd been doing and, after he had reassured me I was at very little risk, I dropped the bombshell.

'I think I'm having too much sex.'

He stared at me like I had just told him I'd buried a body in the garden.

'Excuse me?'

'I'm sleeping with too many people and I want to stop.'

If he'd been chewing gum it would have dropped from his mouth.

'I want to stop but I can't. I get drunk and end up in dodgy situations with people and don't feel great about myself.'

It was a relief to say it out loud. I couldn't tell my GP, but here was a gay man who would know what to do.

'There's nothing wrong with having lots of sex,' he said.

'I know,' I said. 'I'm just uncomfortable with the amount I'm having.'

'Well . . .' he said, 'one of the benefits of being a gay man is we can have as much sex as we want.'

'But this is too much for me.'

He told me I should just enjoy myself. 'Don't feel guilty about it. Be safe and just have fun,' he advised.

Just have fun.

The word that had come to define my existence. I was constantly looking for fun, having fun, advertising for fun, begging for fun, worrying about the fun I'd had, terrified that all that fun had given me a disease or was going to tip me over the edge. Fun was revolving round my head, 24/7. Fun would see me log on to the internet as soon as I got home from work, talking on Gaydar, desperate for a hook-up, whilst keeping myself in the zone by downloading streams of other people having fun. After my last relationship ended, fun had become letting strangers into my house without a second thought. Fun saw me drunkenly texting my friends, begging for sex. Fun saw me putting myself into dangerous and uncomfortable situations. Fun was defining my relationships, dictating how I led my life and leaving me in a state where once again suicide started to look like it might be a way out.

Fun just wasn't fun any more.

Over the years I had counselling through my GP, a woman who told me it was OK to be gay, which was better than nothing; from a nice man at St Barts who tried some CBT that sank like a stone; and from a lovely older gay man who'd had other men present with these issues but couldn't give me the answers I needed.

It wasn't until 2008 that I realized what was going on. I had become the editor of the UK's bestselling gay magazine, my play was being performed to packed houses in London and Sydney, but I could no longer tolerate what was going on in my head. I hadn't had a relationship for three years. I was becoming the kind of gay man I hated as a teenager, a cliché who could not get out of the self-destructive nosedive I was in. My anxiety levels were through the roof. I'd wake up in the night with panic attacks and trouble breathing. I lived with a constant feeling of doom. I was negative about everything. Nothing seemed worth doing. Nobody seemed interesting. Nothing worth getting out of bed for, nobody worth getting into bed for. I wasn't drinking in the way you might think someone with a drink problem would – no mornings, no parks, no blackouts or falling in front of buses – but I was boozing each evening, at the very least with a pint that would turn into three. I was always drunk or hungover, usually at the end of a bar waiting for my life to begin.

My best friend Tim and I rowed constantly, continuing an on-off pattern we'd been in for years. It seemed when he was feeling good, I'd feel bad and when I felt good, he felt bad. Anything would set either of us off. Nothing was working. Everything seemed bleak. All the things that I had been doing to control my feelings – the drink, the men, the apparent success – none of it was making me feel better.

And then something happened for Tim which set off a journey that changed both our lives. He found a solution and shared it with me. I started doing what he was doing, and slowly things began to change for both of us. I realized that many of the problems I had, other gay friends of mine had too. Many of the things I felt, they felt too.

In 2010 I told my colleagues I wanted to write about it in *Attitude*. Supported by the then deputy editor, Daniel Fulvio, in our August 2010 'Issues' issue I wrote a ten-page feature called 'How to Be Gay and Happy'. I wrote that everyone should read a book my therapist had given me: *The Velvet Rage*, by Alan Downs, which for me was the first step to understanding what is going on. We were flooded with letters from readers saying they felt what I described in the article too.

To understand why things are this way for me and so many others, we need to go back to the beginning.

4

Growing Up Gay: the Survival Bond

'People who are homosexual generally start out with a very poor opinion of themselves. How could it be otherwise?'

Terry Sanderson, *How to Be a Happy Homosexual*, 1986

'It felt like it was my dirty little secret . . . it felt like I had chains wrapped round me. I couldn't say anything; I couldn't be who I wanted to be. I felt so alone and trapped in who I was.'

Tom Daley, speaking on *The Jonathan Ross Show*, December 2013

DO YOU REMEMBER WHAT it was like to grow up lesbian, gay, bisexual or transgender? I expect you remember aspects, but I doubt you recall how you lived with it week after week, month after month, year after year in those early days. Until recently, I couldn't remember much of my childhood either.

We don't seem to talk about our childhoods often. When I first met other young gay people we'd discuss how coming out had been, how our parents had reacted and so on – but not what we'd gone through growing up. Even in the *Attitude* office, when the subject of school bullying arose we never lingered on it. None of the mental-health professionals I visited ever suggested exploring whether growing up in a hostile, homophobic society might be linked to the anxiety, low self-esteem and patterns of self-destructive behaviour I was living out. At best, their attitude was, 'You're gay, it's OK, what more is there to say?' But there is a huge amount more to say.

I believe there's a reason we don't wish to think about how our childhood actually *felt*. It's because it was too painful.

Growing up as LGBT, so different, in a culture that has treated us the way I laid out in Chapter 2, bearing the brunt of the HIV/AIDS epidemic, is so emotionally traumatic that our minds can't deal with it. But it isn't just the straightforward active homophobia we face in society that causes the problem. I believe we rationalize and deal with some of that. Unfortunately, the more fundamental damage is begun far earlier and comes from a far more intimate source. Alan Downs discusses it in *The Velvet Rage* and Terry Sanderson also acknowledged it in his seminal book *How to Be a Happy Homosexual* back in 1986. Despite this, it doesn't seem to have been widely accepted.

It is all down to love. Our cynical society isn't comfortable with the concept of love in any serious discourse, but it isn't just wishy-washy greetings-card sentiment: love is fundamentally pivotal to the survival of all human beings.

As Downs explains, when human beings are born they are completely reliant on their parents for a substantially longer period than most species. Newborn babies are entirely vulnerable: they can't feed themselves, walk, talk or crawl, they can't roll over, can't do anything other than communicate when they are happy and content, hungry, unclean, ill or distressed and need to be soothed. We are absolutely dependent on our parents to feed us, keep us safe and provide us with shelter. Without these things, we perish. Francesca D'Amato, a behavioural neuroscientist who is an expert on bonding, says: 'The mother–child bond assures infant survival in terms of protection, nutrition and care'.

Why do our parents give us this care and not just abandon us? It's not simple duty (although there are, of course, major societal pressures to do so); it's because there is an evolved, overwhelming primal bond between parent and child. I call this the *survival bond*, because that is what it is: without this super-powerful bond not only would the survival of individual babies be at risk but also the survival of the species.

You'll know the power of the bond between you and your parents, whether they are alive or dead and however close your relationship is or was. At the simplest level, a comment from your parents hits home like nothing else. Many adults talk of feeling as if they regress to childhood when they go back to their parents for holidays. The bond remains all our lives.

What makes this survival bond so powerful? It begins even before conception. Oxytocin – often called the 'love hormone' or 'cuddle drug' – is involved in sexual attraction, the facilitation of conception and the process of childbirth, helping the cervix contract. Levels of oxytocin peak after giving birth, enabling the mother to bond with the baby and also, according to research by Ruth Feldman at the University of Bar-Ilan in Israel, contributing to the creation of positive parenting traits in both mother and father. All this forges the overwhelming, life-changing feelings of love we've all heard parents express, which come with a desire to do everything they can to protect and nurture their baby.

The baby also does his bit. He instinctively knows he'll die if his parents leave. In her book *The Drama of the Gifted Child*, Alice Miller writes of a newborn baby: 'since their caring is essential for his existence, he does all he can to avoid losing them. From the very first day onward, he will muster all his resources to this end, like a small plant that turns toward the sun in order to survive.' So he is programmed instinctively to work to keep them present by engaging – gurgling and cooing, showing through crying his need to feed, sleep or be changed. He helps sustain the emotional bond between them that is vital to both baby and parents. Parents participate in this bond by picking him up, smiling, touching him, cuddling him and showing affection, reassuring him the survival bond is intact: in short, loving him.

In her book *Why Love Matters: How Affection Shapes a Baby's Brain*, Sue Gerhardt explains exactly why affection is essential. As a child develops his sense of self, his parents help in two major ways: 'mirroring' and 'shaming'. Parents and their babies have a mutually dependent relationship and are finely attuned to each other's emotional state (when it works), each constantly trying to keep the other happy.

The parents 'mirror' their baby's babbling and smiling with their own 'happy faces', reassuring him, smiling back, touching, hugging and kissing him. The baby mirrors them, and back and forth it goes, child and parent(s) working to keep each other happy. Gerhardt says these interactions 'have enormous power in babyhood and toddlerhood because the child is so dependent on the parent for regulation of his states, whether physiological or psychological. Anything that threatens this regulation is very stressful because it puts survival at risk'.

Gerhardt refers to an experiment that shows that the baby knows he has to keep his parents' attention. The YouTube video of the experiment shows a mother making smiley, happy faces at a baby before turning away, then looking back with an emotionless, flat face. In an instant the baby loses his happy expression, looks surprised and confused and tries to restart the positive interaction by waving his arms around. Subconsciously he perceives the survival bond to be under threat and so tries to resume the mirroring to feel secure again. In the experiment, the mother keeps her blank face and the baby looks exceptionally distressed, then bursts into tears. It's upsetting to watch.

Gerhardt writes that not getting positive affirmation from a mother has 'a powerful impact on the growing child'. It causes release of the stress hormone cortisol, which negatively affects the release of the pleasure chemicals dopamine and endorphins. It is so emotionally stressing that it has a negative impact on the child's physical as well as his psychological health. In his book *Magical Beginnings, Enchanted Lives: A Holistic Guide to Pregnancy and Childbirth*, Deepak Chopra discusses how childhood trauma can affect the body's immune response for life. A major study of children who have experienced serious trauma, the ACE study (Adverse Childhood Experiences, acestudy.org) carried out in the USA, found that children who had suffered emotional stress and trauma were seventy to a hundred times more likely to develop diseases such as Crohn's disease, lupus and rheumatoid arthritis as adults. This study is important. We'll come back to it.

The emotional impact is just as powerful. John Bradshaw, the best-selling author of *Healing the Shame That Binds You*, argues that the mirroring from parent to child is fundamental to the child's growing sense of self-worth. He writes:

> We need to know from the beginning that we can trust the world. The world first comes to us in the form of our primary caregivers. We need to know that we can count on someone to be there for us in a humanly predictable manner. If we had a caregiver who was mostly predictable, and who touched us and mirrored all our behaviors, we developed a sense of interpersonal bond, which forms a bridge of empathic mutuality. Such a bridge is crucial for the development of self-worth. The only way a child can develop a sense of self is through a relationship with another. We are 'we' before we are 'I'.

As the child grows, this all-important survival bond evolves but continues to be essential. It changes from being the mechanism that keeps his physical needs met to playing a key part in the process of helping him identify physical and social boundaries and how to relate to other people. Our parents do this by using 'healthy shame' to teach us what is physically safe and socially acceptable.

John Bradshaw states that there are two types of shame – healthy, innate shame and toxic shame. He writes that healthy shame is fundamentally important to childhood development as it helps set boundaries and teaches us to understand that we are not God, but must cope in a world that requires observing rules that enable us to cooperate and live with other people. He says when shame is used healthily it makes us recognize that we are neither perfect nor imperfect, we are just OK. In fact, all human beings are 'perfectly imperfect', meaning that it is totally normal to screw up, to make mistakes, to not always be perfect.

A simple example of how our parents use shame to help set boundaries would be the case of a child getting too close to a living-room fire. His parents teach him this is dangerous by stopping him when he goes near it, using a raised voice and expressing a negative reaction. Intellectually, he might not understand *why* going near the fire is wrong, but he starts to learn that going near it is a threat to the survival bond – and, crucially, that moving away restores it.

> **Action:** Child approaches fire.
> **Parent's reaction:** A negative face, stern comment: 'Don't ever go near the fire!'
> **Result:** Shame.
> **Child's understanding:** 'If I go near the fire I will be shamed. If I stay away from the fire I will be loved.'

When this happens successfully a healthy boundary can be set. The child learns that it's *just the behaviour that is bad*. Go near the fire and there's a threat to the survival bond; move away and it's OK again. This means that his growing sense of self-esteem – the ability to feel good about himself from within – that his parents' love and affection will be fostering is not damaged. He is still a 'good' boy who sometimes does 'bad' things, but he can control whether he does them or not.

The healthy shaming process sets social boundaries as well as physical and stops us from doing socially unacceptable things like going to the toilet in the street or telling your auntie she has a big nose. Unfortunately, though, the shaming process doesn't always work and can do severe damage to a child's sense of self. It relies on a parent making the child understand that when he stops the undesirable behaviour he will be loved and affirmed again. **If a child doesn't get this reassurance, he can go from feeling shamed for a specific, correctable behaviour to feeling shamed about who he fundamentally is. The child's understanding changes from 'I've done something wrong' to 'I am wrong'.**

When this happens the child has been 'toxically' or 'self' shamed.

As you can imagine, the stakes are high and the healthy process can easily go wrong. There is a multitude of reasons why the healthy expression of love and affection that maintains the survival bond may not occur. It relies on the parents being able to express love and affection adequately in the first place, but if they themselves have not received it from their own parents they may not be able to give it adequately to their children. Other factors also come into play. The parents may feel uncomfortable being physically affectionate, they may be depressed, may have their own mental-health issues, may be struggling to find work or be under financial stress, or have problems with drugs or alcohol. They may suffer a bereavement or their partner may walk out on them or cheat on them; there may have been suicides or other things which are considered shameful and have not been talked about, but which linger in the lives of the family. Toxic shame, Bradshaw argues, is inter-generational: it is handed down from parent to child and then to their children. If a parent has toxic shame they will pass it on to their child even if they do not intend to. Bradshaw uses the example of a woman who was in a relationship she didn't want to be in. Even though she didn't vocalize this to her baby, the baby picked up on the negative feelings and shame and grew up shamed himself.

Self-shaming can happen to any child, regardless of sexual orientation, who is overwhelmed with distress or negative messages about himself or herself.

This happens to many children, clearly. But for LGBT people the problem begins when our parents and those around us start to realize we are different. This can be because we, in the case of boys, express an attraction to another boy, or it can be behaviour that society considers to be gender-inappropriate. Although many of us have trouble accepting it (because we have been so savagely shamed for it), there is some evidence of a correlation between gender non-conformity and sexual orientation. Qazi Rahman, senior lecturer in psychiatry at King's College London, is a leading expert on sexual orientation. His research has found that between 50 and 80 per cent of young boys displaying behaviour more commonly associated with girls grew up to be homosexual, and around a third of 'masculine acting' girls became lesbians. In my case, it wasn't an explicit attraction to other boys that first got me labelled as gay, it was because I was behaving in a way that was very different to the other boys.

Many gay people I have spoken to over the years agree that other kids knew we were gay before we did. Most of us weren't explicitly expressing or acting upon a sexual desire for people of the same sex. For us it was pre-sexual. For so many of us, what those kids picked up on was not sexual behaviour but our natural nonconforming gender behaviour.

What we know for sure is that society strongly disapproves of children who do not fit into narrowly defined gender roles. Our parents pick up on the fact that we are different. Their reactions might not always be explicitly judgemental or negative (though they often are), but they send out subtle signals of awareness and/ or disapproval (Alan Downs believes that in the case of gay men this comes mainly from our fathers, but I believe mothers' reactions are equally important). I've seen it myself with the kids in my family. They are gently encouraged to do the things acceptable for their gender. Stepping away from this can be met as subtly as with a show of concern, but the child picks up on it. Remember, because of the survival bond children are critically attuned to the approval of their parents, so the shaming process kicks into action. As we get older it can become more and more explicit.

Many people believe that, because society has moved on, young people are now automatically and easily comfortable with themselves. It is not as simple as that. In July 2015 Twitter users started the hashtag #growingupgay, discussing what it was like to be young and LGBT. These were a few of the tweets:

Being told you're gay and ridiculed for it in school before you even knew you were gay. #growingupgay

When I was 10 I asked my sisters to paint my nails and do my makeup #GrowingUpGay

Weeping on the stairs wearing your mother's wedding dress because you were 'most certainly not allowed outside wearing it' #GrowingUpGay

#GrowingUpGay wanting to play barbies and house but your dad made you play baseball

#growingupgay denying your sexuality for years because society made you look at homosexuality as a sin and something that's inhuman

Not all gay people display this behaviour; for some of us it might be explicitly expressing affection for people of the same gender. Either way, none of it is acceptable to our parents or to society. This is what happens:

Action: Boy is scared of playing football.
Parent's reaction: A negative face, possibly even a condemnatory comment: 'Go and play football – be a man!'
Result: Shame.
Child's understanding: 'I should like football.' Or even worse, 'I should like football because boys like football.' Or 'I'm not acting like a boy.'

In our earlier example of going too close to the fire, the child learns this is a behaviour he can correct easily. But our inherent behaviour – not liking football, or liking Lady Gaga or *Glee*, or whatever it may be – is something we can't change; it's not a choice or a thing we've done, it's a natural part of us, so we can't correct the thing perceived as the problem. It's as if receiving the love of our parents is conditional on changing the colour of our eyes. As children we are not equipped to understand that it is just the actions and beliefs of other human beings – our parents – that are wrong. We internalize the negative feelings and believe that it is *we* that are wrong. What we feel goes from guilt over something we can correct to shame about what we fundamentally are.

We can't change what we are doing wrong because it is *us*.

Confused, we carry on being ourselves and continue being shamed again and again and again. So many aspects of who we are can be met with disapproval – our natural behaviour, our choice of friends, our interest in films or clothes, the way we look or the sound of our voice – that the shame becomes toxic. The cycle continues, and on and on it goes through our entire childhoods. So many of us feel this shame, literally, for years. And over those years the number of shamed behaviours rises. We absorb the messages: don't like the Spice Girls, don't play with dollies, don't play with girls, don't like the theatre, be into football, be more aggressive, don't talk that way, don't walk that way, be tough, fight with boys – all things to which we find it hard to conform. Subconsciously, we feel that all the things that come naturally to us provoke a threat to the survival bond.

Sooner or later, we start having sexual and romantic feelings for members of the same sex – friends, celebrities, whoever – and we learn that those too are wrong. Often we've been told so before we even knew we had them. If we had a choice, we would change. As with all behaviour for which we are shamed, we have a desire to stop it in order to get parental approval back and keep the survival bond strong. But we can't stop this behaviour because it is inside us, inherent, natural, part of who we are.

Instead of understanding that it is one specific stoppable behaviour that is wrong, we come subconsciously to believe that there is something fundamentally wrong with us.

Deep inside, in a way we cannot understand or articulate, we feel we are somehow flawed, bad and unlovable, and that we must fight against who we are to survive.

It is not that to be lesbian, gay, bisexual or transgender is to be inherently flawed, but that society – beginning with our parents – with its rigid rules about sexuality and gender, shames us to the core from the youngest possible age. We are born into a world that does not yet understand that some people are different but that they should still be valued equally and treated with the love and respect that is every human being's birthright.

This is just the beginning.

5

Fight, Flight and Hyper-vigilance

'I am a bag of nerves. I'm a bag of nerves at work, I'm worried all the time: what are people thinking? I'm worried [about] them saying to me "You're a queer."'

Gay man interviewed in the BBC Home Service programme
Male Homosexual, broadcast 5 January 1965

#GrowingUpGay always feeling like I couldn't be myself around anyone, not 100% anyway. Carrying the world on my shoulders

31-year-old Twitter user, UK, 2015

#growingupgay feeling like everyone in class is staring at you when homosexuality was being discussed

Twitter user in his teens, 2015

ALL OVER THE WORLD leading experts on emotional trauma, both gay and straight, acknowledge that the psychological pressure on LGBT children is overwhelming. Iconic author John Bradshaw, in *Healing the Shame That Binds You*, writes that 'there is no group more shamed than LGBT kids'. Pia Mellody, of Arizona's world-renowned treatment centre The Meadows and author of *Facing Codependence*, says that gay people often feel 'shamed by society', while in *The Velvet Rage* Alan Downs describes gay men being 'overwhelmed by shame' and adds '[Childhood] is the start of the journey for gay men and it is by far the most difficult and damaging [part].'

One of the most profound comments comes from Dr Joe Kort, who writes in his book *10 Smart Things Gay Men Can Do to Improve Their Lives* that gay children are subject to 'covert, cultural child abuse'.

Stop and think about that for a moment. This is the truth of our lives. Most of us make it into adulthood, where we are, as Joe says, survivors of abuse. But instead of traditional notions of physical or sexual abuse inflicted by individuals (though that may be part of our stories too), this abuse comes in macro form – from the whole of society, mired in ignorance at best and wilful hatred at worst.

What effect does shame have on people?

Brené Brown, research professor at the University of Houston Graduate College of Social Work, is considered one of the world's leading experts on shame. She told me, 'I'm convinced that the reason most of us revert back to feeling childlike and small when we're in shame is because our brain stores our early shame experiences as trauma, and when it's triggered we return to that place. We don't have the neurobiological research yet to confirm this, but I've coded hundreds of interviews that follow this same pattern. I suspect we'll eventually have the data to support my hypothesis . . . but in the meantime I can say without hesitation that childhood experiences of shame change who we are, how we think about ourselves, and our sense of self-worth'.

Dominic Davies runs London's Pink Therapy, the only LGBT-specific therapy centre in the UK. Amongst the gay clients he sees, he told me, 'Shame's a very core thing for us. Depression and anxiety are still very common themes. It's true that they are for many people, but there's a kind of lens through which depression and anxiety affect us. We view the world differently'.

David Smallwood, author of *Who Says I'm An Addict?* and former therapist at The Priory, then at One40 recovery centre in London's Harley Street, says that, beneath the problems such as low self-esteem, addiction or self-destructive behaviour, it is issues based in shame and anxiety that most of his LGBT patients present with. 'The core issue I see in gay people,' he said, 'and in 99 per cent of people I see with addiction problems regardless of sexuality, is anxiety – and certainly in gay people it's because we're so used to being criticized we become massively hyper-vigilant and that leads to anxiety.'

Anxiety is the state of feeling unsafe, insecure and ill at ease. It often manifests as an inability to relax or properly unwind and calm down, along with a tendency to worry constantly and obsess over every little thing, resulting in thoughts continually turning over in our heads. This has been described as having 'washing machine head' – a mind that never stops turning over and over.

Anxiety is the biggest problem I have faced. From as early as I can remember I have always had a feeling of not being safe, not being like other people, not being part of the group, constantly under threat of being 'found out'. As an adult I've been 'hyper' for much of the time – not able to sit down or relax, always needing the distractions of music, TV, film, the internet. I've had ongoing problems with switching off and getting to sleep. These are things experienced by most of the people I've interviewed for this book and many LGBT people I know.

To understand why anxiety features so heavily in our lives, we need to understand how our 'fight or flight' system works.

The natural state for all animals, including human beings, is one of relaxation, of being in 'at-ease mode'; we feel calm and our blood pressure is normal. But when a threat appears – such as a man coming aggressively towards us wielding a knife – our entire being springs into 'action mode', sending us into a state of hyper-awareness so that we can make the split-second subconscious decision either to attack or to run away: fight or flight. (There are two other parts to the response, freeze and fawn, to which I'll come later.) In action mode we are flooded with adrenaline, giving us the burst of energy we need to fight or flee; our hearts pound, our blood pressure rises, our breathing is fast and shallow, and we feel tense, stressed, unsafe and possibly angry. In other words, we are in a state of heightened anxiety. When the threat passes, the fight or flight response shuts down and we return to our normal state.

The problem is that the fight or flight response cannot differentiate between a real physical threat and one that isn't real but is just perceived in our heads. A man coming towards us with a knife is a threat we can deal with – fight him or get away from him – and the threat passes. But what I believe happens when a child has been self-shamed (for whatever reason: bullied, abused, grown up in poverty, etc.) is that subconsciously he has perceived *himself* as the threat, so the threat is something from which he can never escape: he stays stuck in constant fight or flight mode.

This is what I believe anxiety disorders are: a state of heightened fear of ourselves. Because we've been shamed into believing we ourselves are the threat, we can neither defeat nor move on from the perceived danger, so the fight or flight response never gets the chance to stand down. This means we are in a near-perpetual state of hyper-arousal, with a continual feeling of being unsafe and under threat, always on our guard. **This is what I believe lies at the core of people's emotional problems, including addiction, regardless of the cause.** We spend much of our lives in a state of anxiety, undergoing a kind of post-traumatic stress.

Again, as I've said, this doesn't happen because we are LGBT but because we are toxically shamed for it; and it is also true that not all LGBT people will suffer from anxiety. **But anxiety is one of the core problems for LGBT people because we are taught that being ourselves is wrong and we can do nothing about it.** On top of this, we also face very real threats from people who are antagonistic towards us because (a) they can sense our difference and are homophobic; and (b) they can sense that we feel under threat and anxious, which makes us appear vulnerable, which in turn invites attack.

Not everyone is homophobic, of course, and the world is not 100 per cent safe for anyone, but LGBT people face one more level of danger than straight people do. Some of us had parents who were overtly hostile – from the woman who called her son 'a fucking queer' for playing with a dolly in the supermarket, to parents who have physically attacked their gay children to 'beat it out of them'. We may have faced threats from our schoolmates and even our teachers.

I've been given numerous examples of apparent grown-ups shaming gay children into a state of fear. Martin, now in his mid-thirties, is a man who looks very confident and creative on his Facebook profile. He told me that he was bullied by his stepfather from the age of eight until he went to live with his grandparents when he was fifteen. 'There was a lot of mental and physical abuse,' he said. 'He told me I was an AIDS carrier and that I wasn't normal. It made me feel insecure, paranoid and isolated. A lot of those feelings are still actually with me. I still suffer with anxiety and nerves and low self-esteem.'

Paul, now in his thirties, told me how, when he was eleven, his best friend and her three-year-old sister were at his house when the three-year-old said in front of his family that her father didn't want her 'to play with you any more because you are a queer'. 'Clearly she didn't understand what it meant,' he told me, 'but I remember feeling sick to the stomach. I had a feeling at the time that I liked boys, but was completely in denial, being only eleven. I remember the feeling of hating her dad for saying this to her, but also an intense feeling of shame. The people in the room, my family, laughed because they thought it was funny, but I just wanted to cry and felt that I was the one at fault. I can remember how I felt like it was yesterday – it had a profound impact on me. That intense feeling of public shame. Like my legs had been knocked out from under me, and I was completely alone.'

Another man, Jack, now twenty-nine, described how 'Everyone else seemingly knew I was gay before I even knew what "gay" was. I knew I was different, because people would point it out, but I had no clue *what* was different about me. One of my earliest memories is of an adult calling me a poof. I was about six. It was on the playground. I can't remember who he was, but he was a man, maybe picking up another child. The dinner lady sat me down and explained to me that a poof was a leather couch that you put your feet on. It was sweet of her, but I knew it was an insult. It went on like that the whole time. My mother had to come into school because a teacher that taught me made disparaging remarks and told me to stop acting like a girl. When my mum went in the teacher got really angry, denied it and so my mum came back to me very angry. I felt so embarrassed about it as I didn't understand on a deeper level what it was. I just knew I was in trouble but didn't know why and I just wanted it to go away. I started covering it up. I do not ever remember a day where there wasn't a remark or a look or something made at me. I remember saying to someone when I was about eighteen that I would have just loved to have had a day off. School was really difficult because the boys were relentless . . . At thirteen I went to the head of year, who said if I stopped acting this way then they would stop it. It got to a point where I realized it didn't matter what I said. All the time I was going to teachers and asking for help and not getting any. My mum was coming down constantly, because kids were calling me gay, calling me a girl, throwing food at me on the school bus . . . I'm getting emotional just talking about it now. All these people are treating you so badly, yet it somehow always comes back to it being your fault. The embarrassment got so strong that I stopped telling my parents about it because it was better than re-living it, because it was never going to stop.'

If you come from a culture where homosexuality is even more of a taboo than it is in the UK, the very concept of being gay can seem like an impossibility.

Gan is a gay man from China who lives in the UK. He told me that in China when he was growing up gay people were invisible. 'You don't see them at all,' he said. 'Even gay people themselves often don't really know [they are gay] because it's not considered normal. They believe they are men who just sometimes find men attractive, as you have to marry a woman and procreate. You don't see it in news-papers like here. It used to be considered a mental-health problem. I got constant abuse at school. That was the worst time. People just thought I was flamboyant. I had to keep it secret and it felt shameful. You are told what is right and what is wrong, and I knew this was considered wrong. From a young age you are shamed, and so for the rest of your life you think it is shameful. It's as if even my body rejects it. There's still part of me that feels that, even though I know better and it's bullshit.'

Minhaj is a twenty-seven-year-old Asian man who grew up in a strict, religious Muslim family where gay was never, ever mentioned – if it came up on television, his parents would switch channels in disgust. He said that he had sexual feelings in his teens but didn't act on them until he was twenty-one.

'I spent all that time trapped in a mental closet,' he explained. 'I didn't know any other gay people existed, apart from the TV stereotypes. Any mention of the word at school was used to torment people. Up until about eighteen I still couldn't really put names to all my feelings. I just got weird obsessive crushes on guys that I couldn't talk to anyone about. When I went to uni I was adamant that, despite these feelings, I would eventually get married and have kids, according to my parents' wishes. I couldn't entertain anything different – so I just pushed it down. All the time, though, I was secretly in love with some of my male straight friends and utterly depressed that I would never be able to be with them. I was riddled with low self-esteem and everything about me felt bad. I just felt terrible.'

From an early age we absorb evidence that being ourselves is not 'right', that our innate, unchangeable nature is something that could kill us. We become hyper-aware of our surroundings, continually assessing where we are, questioning whether we are safe, in a constant state of fight or flight and exhibiting the classic symptoms of anxiety – raised blood pressure; fast, shallow breathing; pounding heart. We know that we need to hide from ourselves, because that is where the danger lies.

We live with these scary feelings, not understanding exactly why we have them and then, suddenly – as happened to me at ten years of age – we realize what it is that has made us feel so strange, so unsafe for all this time. We understand that those apparently terrible gay people we have heard so much about – we are one of them. Some of us accept this easily, but many of us do not and perceive it as a terrible, life-threatening flaw. We understand that the problems we have faced are because we are gay. We realize that in order to survive we must not let anyone know our secret. We learn we must suppress ourselves and hide. We want to change but we cannot change – and, with no support or love or help, we turn our fear inwards.

Now it becomes more complicated than just fight or flight: as we can see in animals, the full reaction is 'fight, flight, freeze or fawn' and we may exhibit any of the four of these or all of them. (Remember again, though I'm writing about gay people, this is the experience of any who have been self-shamed as children, not just specifically LGBT people.)

Fight We begin mentally to attack ourselves and anyone else like us, becoming angry and aggressive. Any little thing sets us off, as it connects to the anxious feeling of impending doom and threat that is always just below the surface. This is the 'velvet rage' after which Alan Downs named his book.

Flight We try to run away from our sexuality, from intimate relationships with people, never allowing ourselves to get close to another gay person or to have a loving relationship with someone of the same sex. Sometimes we have relationships and even get married to someone of the opposite sex purely because we think it makes us acceptable.

Freeze We 'play small', trying to shut down and hide ourselves, becoming a wallflower, someone who disappears into the background, is quiet, shy, like an animal trying to camouflage itself so that it is never seen or noticed, or playing dead so that it is not attacked.

Fawn When an animal is under threat, rather than fight, take flight or freeze it may choose to fawn – to submit to the predator and almost beg for mercy. You might have seen your pet dog do this when it rolls over, almost as if conceding that it cannot win the fight and is waving the white flag. I believe human beings do this too – either by 'people-pleasing' or by trying to make others laugh. People-pleasers are those who always put the needs of others first; they do everything they can to help others so that people will like them. You'll also know that many people humiliate themselves, act the clown, send themselves up to make others laugh at them rather than attack them. Without sounding glib, often overweight people do this when they present the 'jolly fat person' persona. I've done it myself, both through being overweight and because I was gay. I believe this is often why people develop overblown, camp personas, and that it's even what drag sometimes is: self-parody as a defence mechanism, saying 'Laugh at me, I'm harmless.' It's seen in a tradition of camp comedy that runs right through Western culture all the way to the present day.

We shut ourselves down. We try to bury the part of ourselves that we understand is not acceptable.

In summary, as self-shamed people we will do anything to bury our real feelings, our real identities, our real selves. We come to learn that if we relax to be who we are, then it may give the game away and open us to attack. This all happens at a pivotal time, when as children we should be doing the very opposite: flourishing, developing, our souls singing and expanding and riding free. Instead we attempt to shut down and, because we cannot pick and choose what we suppress, everything is affected – including, for some of us, our emotional development.

6

Unsafe at School

'It's the plight of individual boys and girls which worries me most. Too often, our children don't get the education they need – the education they deserve ... that opportunity is all too often snatched from them by hard left education authorities and extremist teachers. [Applause] ... Children who need to be taught to respect traditional moral values are being taught that they have an inalienable right to be gay ... All of those children are being cheated of a sound start in life. [Applause]. Yes, cheated. [Applause continues]'

Margaret Thatcher, prime minister,
speech to Conservative Party conference, 9 October 1987

'It's not what they say to me individually that gets at me, it's the constant stream of anti-gay remarks that people don't even know they make. I feel awful all the time. It eats away inside you and sometimes knowing what they'd do to me if they knew makes me lose the ability to breathe.'

Sophie, private secondary school, South East;
from the Stonewall School Report 2012

ON 25 NOVEMBER 2012 Anthony Stubbs, a sixteen-year-old from Leyland in Lancashire, father to a one-month-old baby girl, Lily, disappeared. After a row with his girlfriend, he packed some things into a bag and left the house he shared with her and their daughter. The media helped in the effort to find him. His mum went on *This*

Morning and, on New Year's Day, his girlfriend appeared on the front page of the *Daily Mirror* pleading for him to get in touch.

The police didn't find Anthony's body for two months. He had gone straight from his girlfriend's house to a local woodland, chosen a dense, secluded area and hanged himself with his PlayStation cord.

The media had speculated that he was stressed about being a young father, but in reality Anthony had been struggling to come to terms with his sexuality and was being homophobically bullied because of it. He had taken an overdose the year before and, though at the time he had refused to tell his mum why, he had told a nurse he was 'sick to death of being bullied'.

I went to Leyland to meet Anthony's mother, Denise Machin, at their small house in this tough, working-class area of the north-west, six miles from Preston. She is a single mother and has two other children – three-year-old Oscar and sixteen-year-old Jodie. They have been devastated by Anthony's death.

Denise told me that she had complained to the school when she first realized her son was being bullied, but she didn't think anything was done about it. Denise suggested changing schools, but Anthony didn't want to leave.

'They used to slap him on the way home from school, rip his jumpers,' Denise told me. 'He'd go up to his room crying. The teachers said they couldn't do anything because it was outside of school.' She adds that they would have gone mad if he had been smoking in his school uniform.

Concerned at how distressed he was and the amount of time he was spending in his room, Denise checked Anthony's mobile phone and found explicit texts from men. On his laptop she discovered that he was registered on a dating site with the profile name 'Young, sexy gay' and was talking to, amongst others, a forty-seven-year-old man from Manchester and a thirty-four-year-old teacher from Wales who had sent him porn videos and explicit pictures. 'He knew he was at school,' Denise said, 'because he sent texts saying "Do you want me to fuck you in your school uniform?"'

One of the many distressing elements of this story is that Denise would have supported Anthony if he had come out. He had always been sensitive, caring and sometimes wore foundation, and she told me she had expected that one day 'he would bring a lad home'. He had grown up around her own gay friends and it would have been fine, but she wanted to let him find himself in his own time. After she read the explicit texts she told him it was OK if he was gay or bisexual and that he should just tell his girlfriend, Charlotte, and everything would be OK. Instead he decided to move in with Charlotte and their daughter because it was 'the right thing to do'. Then, towards the end, he came out as bisexual at school, saying he was 'Proud of it!' But this, Denise said, just made the bullying worse.

Anthony didn't take his phone when he left. Denise texted 'Who are you?' to one of the men. 'The reply came back, "You should know, you sucked my dick." She texted him back, 'This is Anthony's mum and he's gone missing and I want to know where he is.' The man did not reply.

After his death Denise found abuse on Anthony's Facebook page. 'It was going "Oh faggot" and all this,' she said. ' "Gay boy, gay boy, shirt lifter", all this to him. "Look at the state of you, you camp fuck". They said "How can a faggot have a baby?" ' The abuse continued even after his body had been found. 'On Ask.fm it was "Oh, your son was a little faggot, I'm glad he hung himself. One less gay in the country." They were saying to Jodie, "Haha, your brother's a faggot," and she was wailing.'

After Anthony's death Denise found a piece of work he wrote for a school assignment. Part of it reads: 'It was my first day at school . . . I wasn't looking forward to it as every other school I've been to I got bullied . . . Two years went by and I was still at the same school. I never missed one day but I did hate every single one of them. I got bullied and tripped up; I even had my money for dinner took of [sic] me. It did upset me but I just dealt with it, what could I do?'

It's a fair question. What can any child who is being bullied for their sexuality or gender orientation do? Bullying in schools is all too common and, whatever the reason for it, it is appalling and can have a devastating impact. Online you will find many incidents of young people, straight as well as gay, taking their lives as a result of it. But homo-, bi- and transphobic bullying presents especially complicated challenges.

Paul Martin, chief executive of Manchester's Lesbian and Gay Foundation, told me, 'Even though we have moved on significantly, even though the world is a different place than it was when we were kids, even though there is some brilliant stuff out there, the reality is that you still have to go through a process to recognize you are different from your peers. Some people are lucky enough to have progressive parents that make it great for them, some people are lucky and in progressive schools or have a fantastic teacher, but the vast majority are not in those places.'

Paul highlights an important aspect that I have already touched upon: it is difficult for a young person to accept their difference, and to complain about it means to acknowledge it and admit it to authority figures. To ask for help for homophobic bullying is to out oneself, not only to others but, crucially, to ourselves – something many children are not ready to do. I wasn't, and though more are perhaps willing to do so today, I don't believe the majority are.

It's my view that suicide by LGBT kids is massively under-reported for this very reason. Growing up, I would see reports in local papers about 'caring, artistic' boys in their early teens who had committed suicide; they were often described as 'passionate about theatre or pop music' and so on, but no one, of course, ever mentioned the word 'gay'. Even today there is very little significant mainstream media coverage of the issue. Whereas we've all seen countless campaigns explicitly, and rightly, against racism, I've never seen any mainstream campaign focus on homophobic bullying in schools. Stonewall's 'Some People Are Gay. Get Over It!' is the closest we have come, but while many schools display those posters, there are also many that do not. I know of teachers, personal friends, who believe putting them up is 'a step too far'.

As a result, these children remain invisible. Thankfully – although tragically – as society grows more tolerant, more parents are stepping forward to tell their stories, like Denise Machin and also Shy Keenan from Colchester, whose fourteen-year-old son, Ayden Olsen, took his own life on 15 March 2013. He was of Japanese and English descent, and left a note outlining years of racist and homophobic abuse. Ayden had come out to his parents and told them he had found somebody he thought he loved but it was not reciprocated. 'We didn't care, we just loved him whatever,' his mother said.

In September of that same year another fourteen-year-old, Elizabeth 'Lizzie' Lowe, took her own life because she was scared of telling her Christian parents she was a lesbian. At her inquest her father, Kevin, said, 'She was more of a tomboy than some of the boys were so it would have been no surprise at all . . . We would have been very supportive.'

These particular young people had accepting parents, but still their children couldn't cope. Why?

Many people do not seem to understand the complications of homophobic bullying and casually lump it in with general bullying. For example, after I wrote an article on the issue in *Attitude* in 2012 I contacted the editor of a leading television news programme to suggest they cover it. He replied that they were already doing a programme on school bullying, implying it all fell under the same umbrella. Even the anti-bullying charities often don't get it. When in 2013 I invited the political party leaders to meet parents of kids who had died as a result of homophobic bullying, Ed Miliband agreed but David Cameron and Nick Clegg declined. Clegg wrote saying that the Coalition government had given an extra £1 million to the charity Beat Bullying, so I called the charity and asked how they dealt with homophobia. They said they'd call me back. They didn't. When I rang again they suggested I call Stonewall – who are a lobbying group, not a support group. In 2015 I attempted to see if Beat Bullying's position had improved, but they had gone into administration. I called another charity, BulliesOut. They seemed like good people doing important work, but didn't appear to me to have much understanding of homophobic bullying. They told me on the phone that they offered a range of workshops but that none of them at that time specifically tackled homophobic bullying. Similarly, it's only in the last few years that ChildLine has started specifically to recognize the needs of LGBT children.

This carries through to schools themselves. While all are required by law to have anti-bullying policies that promote equality, LGBT bullying falls under that umbrella.

Anthony's story, however, shows how complicated the issue of homophobic bullying is. There are several factors that make it different from other types of bullying:

- **Shame** As I've explained in Chapters 4 and 5, often the child is ashamed and scared. Having other people bully them for something they are still coming to terms with amplifies that shame. The Stonewall School Report 2014 showed that 58 per cent of respondents who didn't report homophobic school bullying did not do so because they were 'too embarrassed' and 56 per cent because it was 'not easy to talk about'.

- **Self-acceptance** A key point I want to make in this book is that *accepting you are LGBT is not just difficult because of overt outside influences – it is hard being different.* Being LGBT means you will have a very different life experience from straight people. Perhaps the biggest difference is that you will not be able to have a biological child with the person you love. Then there are the many complexities of being different in a prejudiced world and all the cultural baggage that comes with it: that you are part of a minority group, can face prejudice, can be rejected by religion, you have to come out, etc. The Gay Pride movement has made the mistake of thinking that coming out means a person is automatically proud and strong. Even when parents are comfortable with gay people it does not mean that their kids will easily accept their own difference.

- **Parental difference** A black child being racially bullied will at least receive the message at home that it is fundamentally OK to be who he is. Schools usually reinforce this message. If a black child is being bullied he can go home and tell his parents. He's not outing himself, or saying something to which they could potentially react badly. For LGBT children, to complain is to out oneself. If a child is not yet OK with him- or herself, or not in a home where it is safe to be out to their family, they will likely do anything to avoid this. In a worst-case scenario the child is being homophobically abused/shamed by his parents.

- **Denial potential** If you are black, ginger or overweight, for instance, there is no question of hiding. LGBT children do have that option. Bullying can reinforce both the shame they may already feel and the instinct to try further to shut down what they are.

- **Victim blaming** In general bullying, the onus is on the bully to stop, but in the case of homophobic abuse I've heard many incidents of teachers telling the victim, 'Well if you do act this way/ flaunt it . . .' The child can be made to feel they are somehow responsible. It can reinforce the idea that it is their fault. Those who continue to assert that being gay is a choice feed into this narrative. Even if it were a choice, bullying would still be wrong, but it is really important that school staff understand that, like eye or skin colour, this is something you cannot change. An ex-teacher called Benedict Morrison told me of an incident where a young pupil was so badly beaten he was put in hospital and a teacher told his parents, 'Well he is gay – he is going to have to get used to it.'

- **Section 28** We still live with the ghost of the 1988 legislation that made it illegal for 'any local authority to promote homosexuality', which sent the message that teachers could not stop homophobic bullying. Despite its repeal in 2003 (2000 in Scotland), some teachers, I have been told, still live with the misconception that Section 28 stands. I have heard many instances of headteachers saying parents would not like their school to be explicitly combatting homophobic bullying. A teacher told the 2014 Stonewall Teachers' Report, 'A pupil came to see me to ascertain views on homosexuality. I had to tell them I could not discuss homosexuality and my opinions with them as the school would not like me discussing the topic.'

- **Ignorance** Because there is a lack of understanding on every level of what being LGBT means, teachers can be apprehensive about addressing it. Sometimes there is a belief that to do so is somehow to endorse sexual behaviour. A teacher quoted in Stonewall's 2012 Teachers' Report said, 'Some of my colleagues, although outstanding teachers, aren't great when it comes to gay issues. You can see that they get uncomfortable or giggly. There's never outward prejudice but discomfort, I suppose. There is also loads of misunderstanding when it comes to gay issues.' Another said, 'It is extremely rare for students to be overtly racist or sexist in schools in inner London [but] sadly homophobia is still fairly overt'. I have to say it doesn't help that gay culture is so boundary-less and heavily sexualized. It's only recently that books like James Dawson's *This Book Is Gay* have started to offer age-appropriate resources for even older children.

- **Homophobia** Lots of teachers told the Stonewall Teachers' Report that they didn't think tackling homophobia was appropriate. Many believed the children were too young, others explicitly said they didn't agree with it. One responded, 'I don't wish to'; another, 'I think there are more important issues for teachers to be dealing with. It's the latest issue jumped on by the gay rights mafia and the liberal establishment!' Yet another said, 'This PC agenda about "gay language" is another fad and form of oppression. We should have free speech.' Presumably he doesn't think free speech stretches to the use of racist language. Clearly no teachers would say this about racist bullying.

Paul Martin of Manchester's LGBT Foundation does not see dealing with homophobic bullying as a PC fad. He estimates that over half the people accessing the LGBTF's counselling services in the last year had attempted to take their own lives and he believes there is often a common underlying cause. 'If you scratch the surface with a lot of these guys and girls that come to our services,' he told me, 'often it started at school, when people experienced their first form of rejection. That can quite often be followed up by family and then the general world.'

Kevin is a thirty-seven-year-old man who, like me, grew up in the time of Section 28. He has had extensive therapy as he has battled with addictions, compulsive sexual behaviour and low self-esteem. He told me about his experiences at school and why the homophobic bullying was so damaging.

'Everyone gets bullied at some point,' he said. 'I was bullied because I was from a council estate, and I was bullied for being gay. The stuff about being from a poor family was one thing because we were poor and at least everybody else in my family understood that, but the being gay thing, there wasn't anyone I could speak to about that. My teachers were bullying me as well. I remember we were doing *A Midsummer Night's Dream*. I was about twelve. I was Puck, and being Puck to the best of my abilities, and in front of the entire class, whilst I was stood up, mid-performance, a teacher interrupted me and said, "Do you have to be so queer?" She mocked my voice. When I think now that a teacher could say that to any student, especially in front of a class, it makes me *so* angry. But back then I was just mortified. I felt like I wanted to run out the room, but my legs wouldn't work. I actually apologized. I convinced myself, and it has taken me years to unconvince myself, that I was completely worthless, that I was a freak.'

Kevin tried to kill himself by taking an overdose when he was fourteen. Even then, the cause – his sexuality – was still such a taboo thing that it wasn't talked about.

'I remember things: being in my head of year's office, being in hospital, my mum being angry but at no point asking why I'd done this, and my brother moaning about having to do my paper round, and then it was never really spoken about again.'

When I asked Kevin why he didn't tell his parents he was gay, he said, 'Because I didn't want to end up homeless.'

Since the repeal of Section 28, schools have had a legal obligation to prevent and tackle homophobic bullying, and it is illegal for them to discriminate in any way against a student or member of staff on grounds of sexual orientation, or perceived sexual orientation. Head teachers, assisted by other staff members and governing bodies, are required to implement good behaviour, self-discipline and respect for others; and, under the Single Equality Act 2010 and Public Duty, they have to go beyond non-discrimination and be proactive in advancing equality. Guidance and advice are issued to governing bodies on the identification and prevention of homophobic bullying as part of every school's anti-bullying policy, and the major teachers' unions have all pledged to work towards eradicating it in Britain's schools.

This all sounds great on paper. But what does it mean in practice?

Clearly there are lots of good things happening out there. More and more schools are dealing with homophobia and stamping it out; I'll look at some of these in Chapter 18. The Stonewall Teachers' Report 2014 found that more than 90 per cent of secondary teachers interviewed supported addressing LGBT issues and 97 per cent of those interviewed who had done so would do so again, with 96 per cent saying there were no parental complaints when they did so.

I went to meet Alex Newton, progammes manager at Stonewall.

'There has been some progress,' he said. 'The percentage of secondary schools saying they heard homophobic language "really often" has halved [since Stonewall's 2009 report], but the percentage still hearing it is the same. There's been some progress but that doesn't mean [homophobic bullying is] eradicated. Some teachers might be slightly better at calling out language like "poof" or "faggot" – that doesn't mean it's not a homophobic environment.'

He told me how Liberal Democrat equalities minister Jo Swinson commissioned a literature review and in November 2014, finding there were still issues, the Coalition government made £2 million available to tackle HBT (homo/bi/trans)-phobic bullying, with Stonewall and eight other organizations funded from April 2015 to March 2016 to deliver various programmes in schools.

Alex explained, however, that this figure in itself, quoted in a government press release, has sometimes been interpreted as hard evidence that the problem is diminishing, but it's still quite tricky to tell. 'I don't think I would be comfortable saying homophobic bullying is decreasing,' he said. 'It's a bit early to say things are getting better, especially as the research just covered homophobic rather than biphobic or transphobic bullying. We know these issues are still prevalent and we need to be cautious.' He told me that even on the day I met him he had arrived at work to find three of the usual emails in his inbox from pupils or teachers contacting him for advice about LGBT-phobic bullying.

In 2011 Suran Dickson set up Diversity Role Models (DRM), which works to combat homophobic bullying and takes LGBT people into schools to show kids that gay people aren't anything to be scared of. She is at the coalface of what is happening in our schools. Back then she told me, 'When you start going into schools you realize how huge the problem is. It is immense. To give you an example of the kind of feeling out there, when I begin in a class I always ask "Who here would abandon their friend if they were lesbian, gay or transgender?" and most of them hold their hands up. When I tell them I'm a lesbian, lots of them will pick up their chairs and move away.'

I checked in with DRM again three years later, in summer 2014, and their head of education, Navah Bekhor, said that, whilst things were improving, 'Over 90 per cent of young people we have spoken to in the last few months don't think someone would feel comfortable coming out at school. In some schools, this statistic was 100 per cent . . . Homophobic bullying remains a problem to a greater or lesser extent in all the schools that we have visited. Pupils who disclose their sexuality to us at the end of sessions tell us that they are teased and taunted.' Navah tells me that responses to a survey DRM carried out in a school in Islington included statements from children: 'Gay people should be put in prison for the crime of homosexuality'; 'I would not talk to a gay person'; 'Gay people should die'.

When I spoke to Navah again in 2015 she did think the situation was getting better. DRM have good ongoing relationships with the schools they work with and she has a positive view of how young people's attitudes have evolved. She said that, in her opinion, the majority of young people are reasonable and not prejudiced – *once they are allowed to have a discussion about the subject*. She made the point, though, that it only takes a minority – even one or two – of students who are homophobic to seriously bully a child perceived to be LGBT.

Lots is made of the great work that groups like Diversity Role Models and Stonewall are doing in schools, and rightly so. But this needs to be put in perspective. There are more than 25,000 schools in the UK; in 2015 DRM was working with 130 of them; Stonewall with 1,000; and other charities and groups with small numbers of others. But the majority of schools are left to make their own way, with only the guidance issued to them by the government.

It is in providing this advice that the government has made most strides, but it has still fallen far short of a national policy to tackle the problem, instead leaving it up to individual schools to implement the guidelines as they see fit. As the Conservative government tries to give more power to schools to set their own curriculums, the idea of making them all have the same policy with regard to homophobic bullying 'would go against everything this government is trying to do,' as one person put it, off the record. It's all too easy for schools to set their policy aside rather than putting it into action. One woman who works as a teaching assistant told me, 'It's all very well to have a policy, but if it's stuck on a shelf and no one is making use of it then there's no point.'

The lack of a consistent policy on homosexuality is letting down pupils in another vitally important way too. Schools have a legal obligation to teach about sex in a scientific way in biology lessons, but no more than that. They do not legally have to teach about LGBT people or STIs – including HIV – or, indeed, about condoms and safe sex. Further sex or relationships education is at the school's discretion.

In March 2015 the National AIDS Trust published their *Boys Who Like Boys* report, which surveyed more than a thousand fourteen- to nineteen-year-olds. It found that over a quarter (27 per cent) did not know how HIV was passed on. Almost a third didn't know you can't get HIV from kissing. Nearly three quarters did not know about PEP treatment (a course of medication you can take up to seventy-two hours after exposure to HIV).

A young man called James Hanson said in his response to the survey: 'I was diagnosed with HIV at the age of 18, I knew very little about HIV at that age. I remember very clearly some awful sex ed lessons at school. I was never taught of the love between two men or two women. I was having feelings I didn't know what to do with and I felt so isolated because it was never spoken about. Looking back now, I feel let down.'

A campaign was begun to bring in mandatory sex and relationships education in all schools, with Green MP Caroline Lucas tabling a motion which was backed by many Labour and some Conservative MPs. But in February 2016 the government officially rejected these calls.

Despite all the advances that have been made, the Stonewall Teachers' Report of 2014 found:

- Almost nine in ten secondary-school teachers (86%) and almost half of primary-school teachers (45%) surveyed said pupils in their schools experienced homophobic bullying. The vast majority heard pupils use expressions like 'That's so gay', 'You're so gay'. Two thirds of secondary-school teachers and one third of primary-school teachers heard pupils use terms like 'poof', 'faggot', 'dyke' or 'queer'.

- More than half of secondary-school teachers (55%) and four in ten primary school teachers (42%) said they didn't challenge homophobic language every time they heard it.

- Fewer than half were confident they would have the support of parents in tackling homophobic bullying in schools (46% of secondary-school and 39% of primary-school teachers).

Underlying many of these problems is that staff and governing bodies are largely ignorant of LGBT issues and ill equipped to identify or deal with them. Teacher training courses do not have to cover homo-, bi-, transphobic bullying. The Stonewall Teachers' Report found that only 8 per cent of primary-school teachers and 17 per cent of secondary-school teachers said they had received specific training on tackling homophobic bullying.

Stonewall's School Report from 2012 stated that kids reported that 33 per cent of teachers did not do enough to combat homophobic abuse. One of the biggest points is that the word 'gay' is used casually these days to mean 'bad' or 'lame' or 'defective'. Teacher after teacher expressed the view in Stonewall's study that this usually didn't have specifically homophobic intent. Nor do some academics see it as a problem, saying the meaning of the word 'gay' has now effectively changed. Stonewall take the view it *is* a problem, as do all the teachers that I met while researching this book. Former teacher Benedict Morrison agrees. 'There's a general corrosive use of the word "gay" to mean "substandard", "inadequate", "rubbish",' he told me. 'People dismiss it as trivial, but it is highly problematic as it constructs a culture in which people feel they are entitled to more overt and damaging homophobic views. Kids who may want to identify as gay then find it even more difficult when it [the word itself] is being used to describe inadequacy.'

If anyone is in any doubt, let's change the word. If kids started using the word 'Muslim', or 'black', or 'Jewish' to mean 'bad', 'defective' or 'lame', would we think that was acceptable or that it would not have an effect on those kids, and would teachers tolerate it? Clearly not. There's just no question of it. In the meantime it goes on.

Benedict Morrison described 'horrendous homophobia' in his experience in both state and independent schools. He said that in the former it tended to be overt, but added, 'The stuff I found more frightening, though, was the slightly intellectualized, argued cases in more academic schools. There was a girl that I taught in Year 9 at the time [aged fourteen] who would regularly tell me with a tinge of sadness in her tone that homosexuals should be burned, as if it was an absolute truth. She said, "If ever we get in power they will be." The response from senior managers in the school was that because this was a view that was predicated on a religious belief – she was a Pentecostal Christian – it couldn't be challenged and she had a right to express it.'

Many of you reading this will even have heard homophobic views expressed by teachers – I certainly did when I was at school. One man told me, 'I had a teacher who was always trying to be one of the lads and the cool teacher. One of the ways in which he did this was to call me "gay boy" in front of the other boys, who all laughed. Once on a school trip he would put on effeminate poses and a camp voice when addressing me. At twelve or thirteen years old I thought I would die of shame. I felt embarrassed, miserable and really angry and hurt. Mostly despair, because as an adult he was supposed to protect me from bullies not condone and facilitate it. I think of him and wonder how a person, a teacher, could do that to a young boy.'

Action has been taken in some cases of homophobia in teaching staff. In 2012 a teacher from Brighton was struck off after calling gay people 'poofs' and 'batty boys' and saying 'Don't go into the shower because this group will start bending you over and do you up the ass.' In 2013 Robert Haye, a Seventh Day Adventist, was banned from teaching for two years after telling students that being gay was disgusting and a sin. But these are rare cases and it is likely that there are many more examples of teachers using homophobic language in schools that do not lead to action. The 2015 National AIDS Trust report found that while 99 per cent of its respondents had been bullied by fellow pupils, an alarming 39 per cent had been subjected to bullying by teachers or another adult at school.

It's not just heterosexual teachers who stifle positive representation of gay people in schools. I personally know several teachers who are completely closeted to both staff and pupils in their jobs. A teacher from an independent school in the south-west of England told Stonewall for their Teachers' Report 2009, 'While most of the gay pupils I have known have felt safe coming out in school, all but one of my gay colleagues have concealed their own sexuality for fear of this being used against them by pupils and their parents.'

A Stonewall spokesperson told me, 'YouGov polling shows that more than a third of secondary-school and nearly a third of primary-school teachers hear homophobic language from other school staff. We also know that a majority of teachers don't believe senior staff at school demonstrate clear leadership when tackling homophobic bullying and abuse. Considering these stats it would be unsurprising that teachers lack the confidence to be open about their sexual orientation at work.'

One teacher in the Stonewall Teachers' Report was quoted as saying, 'I am a gay member of staff and the worst place is the staffroom. It is treated as a joke, that is, until someone doesn't like something. I am never expected to object to what is said to me. It is very difficult to be a gay, male teacher in a primary school.'

Another primary-school teacher said, 'I have worked with a gay teacher and staff were more hostile to him than the children were.'

'At one school when I came out I was accused of peddling homosexual propaganda,' says Benedict Morrison. 'I was editing the school magazine and wrote a really sweet article about why we might want to celebrate Gay History Month. We celebrated Black History Month at the school. I talked about how difficult it was for me when I was at school and I hoped, as a teacher, I could help kids have an easier time of it. I had staff phoning me at home telling me this was outrageous, a terrible piece of writing, I couldn't possibly tell parents that there were gay kids at this school. It eventually was published and met with a mix of encouraging support from some parents, old students and some staff, and suspicion from others. The afternoon it was published, six students in the sixth form came out.'

Homophobic bullying does not just damage LGBT children. What is often missed is the effect it has on families.

For the *Attitude* article I wrote in 2012 I met a woman called Mena Houghton, a teaching assistant from Bournemouth. Her son Mark used to be homophobically bullied and beaten up on the way to school. 'I remember asking him if he thought he was perhaps gay,' Mena told me, 'and he said he didn't know.' Along with her husband,

Mena complained to the school but was dismissed as 'an over-protective mother'. When he was fourteen, Mark came home and told his parents that he wanted to kill himself. They got him moved to another school but the bullying continued. Mark had wanted to be a journalist, but now he couldn't wait to leave school.

'I think they were the worst days of his life,' said Mena. 'I've actually got a statement written by him where he says that. The feeling, the way he was made to feel isolated, like a "complete freak". He left school feeling broken and I don't think he ever recovered from that.'

When he left school, Mark started drinking and taking drugs. Mena managed to get him into a rehab, where he got clean and started working at a local gay youth group called Space, which had previously helped him. But seeing that kids were still being bullied in the same way that he had been was too much for Mark – he relapsed and in May 2010 was found dead after an accidental over-dose of heroin.

Mena is strong. She writes to anyone who will listen about homophobic bullying in schools. The strain of losing Mark has devastated her life and she has since separated from her husband.

'My dad used to say when I was young, is it the end of the world?' she said to me. 'No. So we get on with it. And that's how I tended to live. Because I had Mark and Michael, my two boys, I could cope with anything that life threw at me. I've tried to explain it to my other son: I was born with two arms, I'm really grateful that I've still got one arm, but every morning you wake up and you realize you haven't got that other arm. So I tend to put a false arm on . . . eyelashes, make-up . . . but each morning when you get up you're still reminded that your arm is not there. Mark is not there.'

For that *Attitude* article I also went to Cheltenham to meet a very nice, middle-class, middle-aged couple called Roger and Paola Crouch. It was autumn 2011. In early 2010 their fifteen-year-old son Dominic went on a school trip with his classmates. No one knows if he was gay or not, but someone filmed him kissing another boy for a dare and, back at school, as his father Roger put it, Dominic 'went from hero to zero'. He was labelled gay, called the usual names until he could no longer cope. He walked out of school and went to the roof of a local council building, where he spent two hours before throwing himself off. He left several notes, one of which, Roger told me, 'was unequivocal. It said "I've been bullied a lot recently and it's led me to commit suicide".' Roger didn't think Dominic was gay, but was adamant that he should have been allowed to make up his own mind about it in his own time and with support.

Meeting Roger and Paola Crouch was one of the most profound experiences of my time at *Attitude*. I last saw Roger at the Stonewall Awards in November 2011, where he was voted Hero of the Year for all the work he did to draw attention to homophobic bullying. But it was clear when I met him that he could not bear the loss of his son. Several weeks after the Stonewall Awards, Roger hanged himself in his garage.

When I met Denise Machin in January 2014, just days after the anniversary of her son's body being found, she told me of Anthony's girlfriend, Charlotte, who is bringing up her and Anthony's daughter, Lily.

'She is getting on all right now,' Denise says. 'She didn't . . . It hurts her to come up here. She used to come a lot. I said go and do what you've got to do, go and get a boyfriend, move on.'

I asked Denise how she herself was coping.

'I was on anti-sickness tablets and Diazepam when they broke the news [of Anthony's death]. But Jodie, his sister, I had to be strong for her. They were inseparable. She's still not coping now. She won't go to school. I've had police here, and she's a shell of who she was.'

The stories of Anthony, Mark, Dominic and their broken families are a powerful illustration of how destructive this mixture of shame and bullying is, and how vital it is to prevent a new generation suffering in the same way. Some will tell you that this is just a fringe agenda, trying to push extreme left-wing values, as Mrs Thatcher believed, but what we are talking about is, at the most extreme end, preventing the devastation of families.

Not all LGBT children are bullied and, thankfully, not all of those who are feel so bad that they consider suicide. But what about those of us who are overwhelmed and don't take our lives? How do we deal with this complex mixture of pain, shame, feeling different, feeling excited, feeling good, feeling bad, feeling like we have to keep things hidden and under the surface? How do we cope?

Part Two

Escape

7

False Selves and Survival Skills: Chronic Recurrent Humiliation, Distorted Thinking and Addiction

'At some point during school I decided I could either feel hurt or feel nothing. So I opted for nothing. I swapped feelings for achievements, I poured myself into goals and ambitions.'

Writer Juno Dawson,
interviewed on BuzzFeed about her decision
to transition, 24 October 2015

'I just have had a lot of dysfunctional relationships. I've really gone from one cycle to another. I've been stuck in a cycle of being addicted to rejection in some fucked-up way and always choosing someone who is going to reject me . . .'

Olly Alexander, lead singer of Years & Years,
interviewed for the *Downtowner*, March 2015

DESPITE THE UNTOLD MISERY and crime it causes across the world, most of us don't understand what addiction is, what it means to suffer with it and how to manage it. During my own experience I've been staggered to see how much confusion and disagreement there is even amongst medical professionals. For instance, when I saw professional therapists no one ever considered that the repetitive nature of my behaviour might actually constitute an addiction. Even when I was in recovery, at a dinner party a doctor heatedly told me that because I didn't drink in the park or in the morning I didn't have a problem. (I imagine this might have had something to do with the fact that he was taking cocaine that night.) I have heard similar stories from people in recovery time and again.

The traditional understanding – what is called 'the pharmaceutical theory of addiction' – asserts that some drugs are so chemically powerful that anyone who uses them will become hooked. End of. But this doesn't explain why some people use a range of drugs and don't become addicted. Nor does it explain why there seems to be higher rates of addiction amongst LGBT people than amongst the general population.

There is a growing, grassroots, belief that addiction is not simply a problem in itself but rather a symptom of an underlying emotional condition; essentially that addiction is a dysfunctional way of soothing overwhelming distress. Author Johann Hari looks at this in his great 2015 book about the war on drugs, *Chasing the Scream*. He cites the famous rat experiments that were used in the eighties to highlight the dangers of drugs. Those experiments showed a rat alone in a cage being given the option of two bottles, one containing just water, the other a cocaine or heroin solution. The rat consistently chose the drug bottle, again and again until it died. We – society – were told that this was what would happen to us if we used drugs: we wouldn't be able to stop. But a Canadian psychologist called Bruce Alexander thought there was more to it. He wondered why some people became addicted to drugs and others did not. So he built what he called 'Rat Park' – a large, relatively luxurious rat cage, with avenues to explore, wheels and so on, populated with lots of rats. With plenty of space and companions to socialize with, the rats of Rat Park, shockingly, largely didn't use the drug bottles, and those that did consumed just 25 per cent of what single rats in small cages did. Even rats that had previously been in cages on their own gradually reduced their intake of drugs once they were in Rat Park. In Alexander's experiment, no rats died. His study suggested that a major factor in the rats' drug use was that they were relieving the pain of being alone and cooped up in a small cage. They were soothing distress. When they weren't distressed they didn't need the drugs.

This gives us clues as to why people use drugs and alcohol even when it negatively affects their lives – to soothe distress and painful feelings that they cannot manage on their own.

So why do some people experience such distress? It can happen to anyone. Sometimes dependency or addiction can be caused by a single painful event – bereavement, the end of a relationship or the post-traumatic stress of fighting in battle, for instance. Life circumstances, such as living in poverty, can cause ongoing distress, as can loneliness – as was the case with the rats. But why do some people seem positively prone to addictive behaviour regardless of their surroundings?

In his book *Who Says I'm An Addict?*, therapist David Smallwood suggests that addicts are born with greater oversensitivity than others. He believes the 'limbic system', the part of the brain that governs emotions, is naturally more sensitive in some people, causing them to experience feelings more intensely. They are therefore more easily overwhelmed by their feelings and so have a greater need to dull those feelings with drugs or alcohol.

This makes sense. But it does not explain why a relatively higher number of gay people than straight get into problems with, say, drugs.

Clearly, experiencing homophobia in everyday life may cause significant distress. But not everyone experiences ongoing homophobia – far from it – and so that's not the whole story. There is also a growing understanding that experiencing trauma at a young age makes people more likely to display addictive behaviour as adults. One American study looked at children who were in school close to the Twin Towers on 9/11 and found that the greater the trauma they experienced – such as being in fear for their life or knowing someone who died – the greater their subsequent use of alcohol or drugs and the higher the incidence of chaotic behaviour and problems with their studies in adolescence.

Perhaps the most powerful investigation, the ACE (Adverse Childhood Experiences) study carried out by the Centers for Disease Control and Prevention in Atlanta and Kaiser Permanente (a care consortium based in Oakland, California), claims to have found 'staggering proof of the health, social, and economic risks that result from childhood trauma'. Seventeen thousand patients were studied and a strong relationship was found between severe childhood trauma and 'all kinds of addictions including overeating'. The research found that a child with four or more negative childhood experiences (including incest; emotional, physical or sexual abuse; having an addicted or mentally ill parent) was over 1.5 times more likely to become obese, 5 times more likely to become an alcoholic and 46 times more likely to become an intravenous drug user than a child with no negative experiences.

I believe this is why some people feel they have had 'an addictive nature' from birth and others develop addictions in later life. For a person not toxically shamed in childhood it takes a major life trauma – such as fighting in war, or bereavement – to produce such painful feelings that they start relying on drugs or alcohol to cope; but for others who are naturally more sensitive, as David Smallwood suggests, it takes far less: sometimes even just leaving the house or interacting with people can be overwhelming.

So why does childhood trauma make people more likely to have addictions in later life? My instinct is that childhood trauma leads to over-stimulation of the fight or flight reaction and hyper-vigilance, which in turn affects the child's developing limbic system, leaving it and the child permanently more oversensitive and easily overwhelmed. I have no scientific proof of this. Smallwood may well be right that some are naturally more sensitive from birth. It's just my instinct, drawn from my own experience.

Again, it's important to reassert that childhood trauma can affect anyone, regardless of sexuality, and also that the majority of gay people are not what we would call addicts. Go into any recovery meeting across the world and you will meet people of all sexualities who describe low self-esteem, oversensitivity, feelings of not fitting in and of being unable to cope with normal life, all the way from childhood. But specific types of trauma seem to increase the chances of adopting addictive behaviour and developing dependencies. In *Time* magazine, one of the ACE study's founders, Dr Vincent Felitti, discussing what type of childhood trauma did the most damage, said, 'I would have assumed before we looked at it that probably the most destructive problem would be incest – but interestingly it was not, it was co-equal with the others'. Instead, he found 'the one with the slight edge, by 15 per cent over the others, was ***chronic recurrent humiliation***, what we termed as emotional abuse'.

This is a vitally important point: his study found that a child who endures chronic recurrent humiliation is at far more risk of addictive behaviour than a child who has suffered other trauma. Chronic recurrent humiliation is how a great many LGBT people experience childhood. Remember, I assert that we subconsciously perceive that we are fundamentally defective and develop extremely low self-worth, which in turn manifests as depression, suicide ideation and other negative feelings.

When we experience something overwhelmingly distressing – be it a traumatic event or traumatic feelings – we react in one of three ways. We are either overwhelmed and suffer some kind of mental breakdown (or are even driven to suicide), or our mind erases the feeling or makes us do something to distract ourselves from the feeling. I call this 'Shut down, remove or soothe'. You'll see an example of the 'remove' part in people who've been in road accidents or fought in war who can't remember what happened; or when women forget the pain of childbirth; or when adults in therapy suddenly remember experiences of abuse from decades ago that they had completely blocked out.

'Splitting' is a psychological phenomenon where a person compartmentalizes part of their experience which is not acceptable to them. In other words, they deny to themselves that it's true. For example, they might try to dismiss that they have gay sexual impulses and tell themselves it's just a phase, or that the experience wasn't gay because the other person instigated it, or that they weren't a receptive partner. It doesn't happen to everyone, of course; some of us accept the feelings straight away. But not everyone does.

I received a disturbing letter from a man in his mid-twenties, serving time in prison – something he said had ruined his and his family's lives – after he went online to try to prove to himself that the homosexual feelings he was having did not mean he was gay and that maybe he was 'just going through some type of crisis'. Online he started talking to a person who said he was seventeen but turned out actually to be fourteen.

'Even after my trial I struggled to admit to myself that I was gay,' he wrote. 'I even went to mental health because I thought I had gone mad. Then one day I sat down and thought back and sieved through all of my suppressed memories. It all came flooding back to me, memories as far back as high school when I would look at other lads in my year in a way other people didn't . . . when I was asked why I would make up the excuse "Oh, I thought I recognized him from somewhere." I am not making excuses. Choosing to talk to someone on the internet was the biggest mistake of my life.'

It seems shocking that people can feel this way in this day and age, but it shows how unacceptable gay feelings are to some people. We can also 'soothe' our feelings by doing something that distracts us from them. It can be blocking them with drink, drugs, food, sex, shopping, gambling, making ourselves feel better, getting validation, or any number of things. Anything that is powerful enough to change our feelings can do the trick and make us feel better.

A major problem with shutting down or 'disassociating' from our feelings is that **it doesn't just block the bad feelings: it blocks the good ones too**. You can't grow emotionally if you can't fully feel and express your emotions and your authentic self. John Bradshaw, in *Healing the Shame That Binds You*, notes neuroscientists Joseph E. LeDoux, Allan N. Schore and Diana Fosha who:

> have presented compelling evidence that our true sense of self
> is based on our authentic core feelings. Silvan Tompkins has
> shown that our feelings are the primary motivating source in

our lives. Without acknowledging our core feelings, we lose our sense of self. **Our false selves are based on our survival skills** [my emphasis]. Our false selves are like the script for a play. The script tells us what feelings we should have. We have to accept the scripted feelings as authentic.

In other words, when we use outside things to dull painful feelings, it's hard to know what we actually feel at all and who we really are. It is only by experiencing our real, authentic selves and emotions that we learn and grow. If we can't do that, then all our reactions and feelings can become distorted, which I believe often leads to two conditions known as 'codependency' and/or 'counterdependency'.

Codependency is a flawed way of seeing things, and behaviour that is overly dependent on other people and their feelings. People with codependency tend to have low self-esteem, to be over-reliant on other people, and to be unable to stop themselves from being clingy and absorbing other people's feelings; they also have weak boundaries. In other words, codependents need people too much. Often they are overly vulnerable, touchy, fly off the handle at every little thing; they are very needy and sometimes deflect dealing with their own feelings by focusing on other people's needs, telling everyone else what's wrong with the other person instead of focusing on their own problems; they play 'the martyr' and fall into patterns of 'love addiction' whereby their entire happiness is defined by being with another person.

Counterdependency is the flipside of codependency. Instead of needing people too much, counterdependents push people away; act as if they don't need anyone; have trouble feeling emotions, including compassion for other people; learn to put up walls around their real feelings; and rely on themselves too much. Sometimes counterdependents can seem like very happy, upbeat, positive people, impervious to sadness, but this is because they are spending a huge amount of energy trying not to feel the pain that is underneath. This is why sometimes friends of people who have taken their own lives cannot understand it and say the person who committed suicide seemed to be one of the happiest and most carefree people they knew.

There is much disagreement about how this process develops, but it seems to me that counterdependency is a reaction to codependency. I believe counterdependents can't cope with their oversensitive feelings and so shut them down, convincing themselves that they are hard, tough and untouchable.

Pia Mellody, author of *Facing Codependence*, believes that not all codependents are addicts, but that, in her experience, most addicts are codependents. At the base of all this are unprocessed feelings of shame and childhood trauma.

The tip of the iceberg

The iceberg theory of addiction seems to have been developed from the experience of people in Anorexics and Bulimics Anonymous, as noted in their manual.

It asserts that addictions are symptoms of an unseen problem with self-hatred and fear at its core, surrounded by all manner of problematic compulsive behaviours and attitudes. (Again, this can be a way that anyone who has suffered severe childhood trauma can react, not just some gay people.) In order to survive, the traumatized and shamed child becomes desperate to be better than everyone else (**perfectionism**), fearing it's the only way he or she will be accepted. This leads to him or her becoming **self-obsessed** and to a feeling of superiority (**grandiosity**), which needs to be bolstered by constantly looking down on other people (**judgementalism**), which relies on having a very narrow and set worldview (**rigid, black-and-white thinking**). But because in reality no one is better than anyone else, the feelings of **low self-worth** continually come flooding back and he or she develops anger at other people (**resentments**) and starts feeling hard done by (**self-pity**), believing that everything is pointless

THE ICEBERG THEORY OF ADDICTION

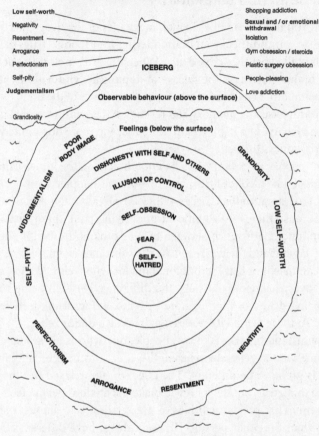

Low self-worth
Negativity
Resentment
Arrogance
Perfectionism
Self-pity
Judgementalism

Grandiosity

Shopping addiction
Sexual and / or emotional withdrawal
Isolation
Gym obsession / steroids
Plastic surgery obsession
People-pleasing
Love addiction

ICEBERG

Observable behaviour (above the surface)

Feelings (below the surface)

POOR BODY IMAGE
DISHONESTY WITH SELF AND OTHERS
ILLUSION OF CONTROL
SELF-OBSESSION
FEAR
SELF-HATRED

JUDGEMENTALISM
SELF-PITY
PERFECTIONISM
ARROGANCE
RESENTMENT
NEGATIVITY
LOW SELF-WORTH
GRANDIOSITY

and everyone against him or her (**negative thinking**). This is why one of the most classic and commonest symptoms of people with addictions is **irrationally swinging from feeling better than everyone else to feeling worse than everyone else**. The phrase 'feeling like the biggest piece of shit that the whole world spins round' is an expression of feeling better than everyone else yet totally worthless at the same time. It's a horribly confusing place to be.

How addiction takes hold

When you use a drug like alcohol, molecules of the drug enter your bloodstream and affect your brain, altering your mood. Drugs that do this are called **psychoactive** drugs. When the drug molecules get into your brain, they cause the release of **dopamine, endorphins, serotonin** and other chemicals that stimulate the parts of the brain linked to reward, pleasure, memory and relaxation. Dopamine is what gives you the feeling of a high, so it follows that the more dopamine your brain produces the better you feel.

For people who don't feel bad for much of the time, using a substance like alcohol just makes them a bit happier than normal. It's not a dramatic effect. Because they are already calm and content, and because there's no significant underlying pain, there isn't such a pronounced difference between being drunk and sober. It doesn't feel *that* great and the desire to take the substance again is not as big; they can take it or leave it. But for someone who feels bad a lot, or is often overwhelmed by anxiety, the difference between being sober and being drunk or high is more extreme. Being drunk feels *really* good. To these people **it's not just a drink, it's major relief**.

For instance, if you take two people, one who is always anxious and one who is generally relaxed, the effect on them of smoking a joint is going to be different. The effect on the relaxed person will not be that great. But the joint will make the anxious person feel very different. That person will have a greater desire to smoke a spliff again than the other person. Different drugs have different effects so will feel different for different people. A person who is warm and loving will feel less of a dramatic effect on ecstasy, which produces feelings of love and togetherness, than someone who is uptight and doesn't usually feel love and warmth for other people.

Control

When we are plagued by feelings of low self-worth and anxiety we feel out of control. Changing those feelings with a drug gives us a sense of being in control. This is ironic, because in fact drug use easily leads to loss of control.

Use any drug regularly enough to medicate bad feelings and your brain will learn to expect that drug when you have those bad feelings. You develop a habit. There's evidence that the neuro-pathways of your brain actually start changing and soon, without even thinking about it, you will start to crave whatever it is you use. This is when a person becomes 'dependent' on the drug to feel OK and get through the day.

An important feature of most addictions are 'rituals': the things we always do as part of the experience of using the drug. It might be the excitement of leaving work knowing you are going to go to the pub or bar, or calling your dealer or preparing equipment you use. Some people say the excitement of the ritual is more satisfying than the actual using.

All this can easily become a vicious circle. When a drug leaves your brain you feel worse than you did in the first place. This is called **withdrawal**. To feel good again you have to use the drug again. This has its own complications. If you drink regularly you can find yourself going from drunk to hungover to drunk without ever really breaking free of the effect on your mood. The same goes with any drug: using it can put you into a constant state of binge and withdrawal – one moment down, then up, then down again.

This is known as the **cycle of addiction** and it shows how people are unwittingly stuck in a pattern: see the diagram overleaf.

Tolerance

Older readers will know that when you are young you get drunk more quickly than you do twenty years later. This is because if you use a mood-changing drug regularly, your brain gets used to it: it regards unnaturally large amounts of dopamine as normal and tells you that you need even more to get that old high. This is called developing **tolerance**.

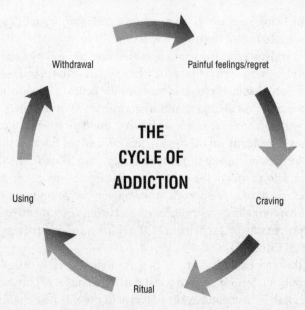

THE
CYCLE OF
ADDICTION

Withdrawal

Painful feelings/regret

Craving

Ritual

Using

On top of this, some drugs cause a physical tolerance as well as a psychological one, so your body can only function when you are using the drug. This is why severe alcoholics can shake and tremble if they haven't had a drink. In advanced stages of alcoholism people have to drink in the morning just to feel normal. In these cases stopping can be extremely dangerous and usually doesn't feel like an option.

When does something become an addiction?

At one time or another, most people will have overused alcohol, got drunk and done something they regret. Some people learn from the experience: they recognize their limits and in future stop before things get messy. They have a glass of wine after work and then go home. Others find this difficult. They might tell themselves they are going to have one drink but find themselves out till the early hours, or at a sauna, or taking drugs or doing dangerous things they might not do when they are sober, or they may black out. They might get into work late or not at all, make serious mistakes in their job, miss meeting up with friends or family events. A key point is that an addiction, in this case alcohol, is not about whether you drink in the morning or in the gutter: **it is about whether once you start drinking you are in control of when you stop.** There's a saying in recovery: 'One drink: one drunk'. This describes the key experience of alcoholics: they tell themselves they will only have one (or two, etc.) drinks but one drink always leads to 'one drunk'. It is the same with every other addiction, be it drugs, sex, shopping or food.

The fuck-it button

Addiction doesn't make sense. Why does someone always end up out late drinking or drugging and damaging their performance at work, for instance, when they don't want to? It isn't that they are struggling with an invisible hand forcing a bottle or other drug to their lips. It's very hard to understand, but addiction and compulsion make a person, in the moment, truly *want* that drink or drug even if they know that it's not the logical thing to do.

We've all had that voice in our heads that says 'I really should go home now, I have work tomorrow'; or 'I really shouldn't take that drug, it's dangerous'; or 'I really shouldn't download Grindr again because I have a boyfriend'. Lots of people learn from previous mistakes, listen to that voice, act on it and do the responsible thing. 'Compulsion' overrides the part of the brain that knows the right thing to do. Even though we may have made this mistake a thousand times before, it makes the urge to use seem like the best idea in the world. It makes us think, 'Fuck it! To hell with the consequences – I'm going to do this.'

In recovery language this is called '**pressing the fuck-it button**'. It's the psychological override moment where you decide to ignore your common sense or your own personal moral code and do it anyway:

'Fuck it, I'll have another drink and worry about the fact I've got to be up for work tomorrow.'

'Fuck it, I'm trying to lose weight but I really want that piece of cake.'

'Fuck it, I'm having a great time, I'll take that line.'

'Fuck it, this is so hot, I won't use a condom this one time . . .'

Pressing the fuck-it button feels as though it's dissolving the potential consequences of our actions. But it is an illusion. It dissolves the consequences *in that moment* – but those consequences are still there, suspended, waiting to crash back in as soon as the drugs wear off. The next day we wake up full of regret. We feel frustrated that we did something that makes us feel bad yet again. This feeling itself feeds into the cycle of addiction and makes us want to escape our feelings again. If this has become a pattern, then the regret and shame can seriously affect our self-esteem, confirming the original feelings we had as kids: 'Everyone was right. I *am* a flawed, unlovable human being.'

This is called 'false evidence' and it is part of a subconscious self-destructive pattern of making ourselves feel worse. When we feel bad we can use every mistake or slip-up – even the tiny ones that every human being makes – as further evidence that we are flawed people.

Because compulsive, dependent or addictive using is about blocking out feelings, we often can't see the reality of what is happening. We make excuses – it's not that bad, everybody does it – and the thought of stopping or seeking help seems like the craziest and scariest thing in the world.

It's not just drugs and alcohol!

When we talk of addiction we tend first to think of illicit drugs or alcohol (of course, alcohol is a drug) – to which I'll return in Chapters 11 and 12 – but because, at least in part, it's the release of dopamine and endorphins into our brains that gives us the feeling of pleasure, it stands to reason that anything that causes dopamine to be released – *anything that affects our feelings* – can become addictive.

Food This is often the first thing we use compulsively. When we are feeling down we don't stuff ourselves with salad. We turn to ice

Common Addictions

People can suffer from **substance** and/or **process addictions**:

Substances
alcohol, caffeine, food (especially sugar, white flour, carbs, fat), recreational drugs, prescription drugs (such as tranquillizers, pain-killers), solvents

Processes
eating, vomiting, losing weight, exercise/the gym, bodybuilding, gambling, shopping, sex, watching pornography and masturbation, internet surfing (including Twitter and Facebook), obsessing, losing yourself in fantasy (including music, films, theatre), creating drama, falling in love, relationships, having someone take care of you, taking care of other people, putting yourself in dangerous situations, self-harming, hurting other people, doing well at work, criticizing yourself, criticizing other people, never earning enough money, being pitied, feeling bad, self-sabotage

Anything that can change our feelings and give us the illusion that we are in control can become addictive.

cream, chocolate, cake, starchy foods like pasta and potatoes, and things with heavy sugar, fat or carb content because they give us a form of high – not as much as a drug that makes us dance all night, obviously, but enough to affect our feelings. You might scoff at this (pun intended), but the term is familiar: comfort eating. We will look at eating as an addiction in Chapter 10.

Disordered eating Eating too much or too little, bulimia, obsession with carbs, etc. (eating or avoiding) seems to go hand in hand with emotional problems. Without doubt the emails I most regularly receive at *Attitude* are from men describing how they were chubby, overweight kids, only to come out, go gym crazy and pump their bodies up. Exercising releases dopamine and endorphins but this too can become obsessive and addictive, just as the thrill of people ticking our shirtless selfies can.

Fantasy Escapism is another way in which traumatized people, as children, disassociate from their feelings. Anything from simple day-dreaming to reading to watching TV or films, music and all types of entertainment can fall into this category. I'll address this specifically in Chapter 8.

Self-harming If you hate yourself it's not hard to understand why you might want to hurt yourself. Study after study shows higher rates of self-harming in LGBT than in straight people. The Metro Youth Chance study found that over half of LGBTQ young people had self-harmed compared to 35 per cent of straight, cisgendered young people. The PACE RaRE study found that young LGB people were almost twice as likely to make a suicide attempt than their straight counterparts. A study by Tracy Alderman in 1997 found frequent reasons for self-harming were 'escaping intolerable emotions, pro-ducing pleasant feelings, communicating with others, nurturing one's self, establishing control and self-punishment'. The common theme was one of hurting oneself in a misguided effort to 'cope'.

Sex Of course sex absolutely affects our mood. The whole process of preparing for it, finding it, doing it is exciting and mood-altering – I will look at it in detail in Chapter 13. The same is true of **being in love and in a relationship**. Researcher Helen Fisher showed through brain imagery that the same parts of the brain light up when someone is in love as when a person is using cocaine.

Gambling An addiction to gambling can be hard to understand if you don't do it, but it is accepted as a real problem that affects many people. The possibility of winning is exciting and produces a thrill, then a crash, which keeps the cycle of addiction turning. As they develop tolerance, addicts have to gamble more money to get the same thrill. This can escalate to the point, in extreme cases, where people end up losing their homes. The makers of scratch cards know they can be addictive and the cards carry a helpline number 'in case you are playing too much'.

Shopping This is something for which two of the world's most famous addicts, Elton John and Michael Jackson, are/were both known. Something about the process of purchasing things makes us happy. Again, there's a familiar term for it: retail therapy. Feel bad? Then go shopping. Lots of advertising is designed to make us feel not good enough – for which the solution is 'go out and buy things'.

Affirmation/validation

This is a major one. People who have low self-esteem will get some relief if other people show that they like them or give them positive attention. Some forms of validation might be:

- being praised
- someone finding you attractive
- someone 'liking' a shirtless selfie of you on Facebook or Instagram
- getting messages and interest on apps like Grindr
- being the centre of attention (or, conversely, melting into the background and feeling invisible)
- feeling you are important
- feeling special and different from others
- putting other people down to make you feel better about yourself
- having material possessions

- dominating conversations

- being the best at whatever you do

- wearing fashionable clothes

- perfectionism (proving your worth by doing everything absolutely perfectly and having the best things – clothes, parties, possessions, job, home, body, partner)

As strange as it sounds, we can even become addicted to feeling bad. This is what you might commonly call 'being a victim' or 'a martyr'. It's usually used as a term of condemnation, but that's unfair. It's perfectly logical that when a person (again, of all types, any sexuality) is extremely traumatized the only thing they know and are comfortable with is feeling bad. It is very common to become addicted to **self-sabotage**, sometimes subconsciously enjoying the feeling of 'being special' when we are left out in the corner, or feel unattractive and spend another night in on our own.

Most of the things on the list above do make us feel better. It's great when someone finds you attractive, for example, and there's nothing wrong with that. Everyone enjoys the ego-boost it brings. But as with alcohol, it's a problem when we come to rely on it to feel OK about ourselves. Everyone likes to be valued and praised. It's when these things are a means of medicating painful feelings that they become a problem, because they take on extra significance.

Again, like someone using a hard drug, if a person who is generally happy with themselves gets a compliment it's quite nice but not earth-shaking. But for a person who feels terrible about themselves a compliment is really powerful and can become something they obsessively need. I have handsome friends who think they are ugly and constantly obsess about their looks, posing and pouting for selfies, but are never satisfied. This is what you can see happening all across Facebook with people gay and straight – posting shirtless pictures or uploading photos of themselves in the 'Gold Circle' at a concert or with celebrities: all things that validate or affirm them.

Where it changes from just being fun into being a problem I don't know, but it does for many people.

Bringing other people down can also be powerful if you don't feel good about yourself. There's such a strong tradition of sarcasm and bitchy put-downs – or 'throwing shade', as younger people might call it – from gay people that we've come to celebrate it as part of our culture. Kenneth Williams did it so much that there's a book of the bitchy things he said called *Acid Drops*.

Being the centre of attention generally makes us feel good, which is why so many people with low self-esteem, both gay and straight, go into show business. That's all show business is: affirmation and escaping feelings.

Self-obsession and perfectionism

Self-obsession and narcissism are always viewed as terrible personality faults. Self-obsessed people talk about themselves, don't ask about you and find any excuse to turn a conversation back to themselves. But it isn't as simple as them being horrible, unpleasant people. Self-obsession is simply a natural next step from hyper-vigilance and insecurity. An example is a friend of mine who called me and moaned on about how devastated he was after the end of a three-month relationship, and how tragic and scary it was that he was single and washed up at twenty-seven, not stopping to realize that he was talking to someone who was forty and single. He is not a bad person, just traumatized. In fact, I've done the exact same thing and moaned about being forty and single to a single friend of mine in his early fifties.

Often hand in hand with self-obsession comes perfectionism. It is the most common characteristic I have noticed in gay people. In her book *The Drama of the Gifted Child*, Alice Miller, as quoted by John Bradshaw, writes that many 'super achieving and successful people are driven by a deep seated chronic depression, resulting from their true and authentic selves being shamed'. This is what Alan Downs refers to in *The Velvet Rage* when he talks of gay people having to have the best bodies, the best parties, the best boyfriends.

We believe that if it looks as if we're having successful, happy lives on the outside then we will feel that way on the inside. But sadly, these things don't give us **true esteem** – that is, self-esteem, an innate feeling of being OK with ourselves that comes from within. Being validated by other things or people means we receive **outside esteem**, the direct opposite of self-esteem. Building our bodies in the gym doesn't give us true esteem because it can't last – we all get older and our bodies will eventually sag. Sleeping with someone hot doesn't give us true esteem because as soon as it's over we're alone again. Relying on being in a relationship in order to feel better about ourselves does not give us true esteem because that person may not stay with us. Take all of these things away and, until we deal with them, we're left with the original feelings of low self-esteem and shame.

Self-esteem comes from within ourselves. It needs no control because it is stable and continues without our influence. It isn't dramatically affected by the way we look or who is praising us or whether we are being sent lots of Grindr messages or get into an exclusive party or what other people think about you. Ups and downs still happen, but our self-esteem is always available as a resource and it gives us a sense of calm and inner peace.

Outside esteem comes from other people, places and things. It is at the whim of external forces that we can't control, although sometimes we may literally die trying. It is temporary, transient and needs to be constantly sought – which is exhausting.

In fact, relying on affirmation and validation from outside ourselves actually makes us feel worse. It may work for a while, but the feelings we are trying to escape always seep through. Though we may not consciously understand it, we know we aren't doing the right thing. Even if we spend a lot of time slagging people off, deep down we know it's wrong – and unattractive to other people. We know that wearing cool clothes or chasing guest lists and VIP status – something that's common within the gay scenes of big cities – is meaningless and hollow. As editor of *Attitude* I would walk the red carpet to film screenings and get whisked into VIP entrances, jumping queues; and it does feel great – for that moment – but then even as I took my seat I'd return to feeling just as awful as I did before. Sometimes, instead of enjoying it for what it is, a fleetingly fun but meaningless perk of my job, I just felt I wasn't good enough, I was an imposter. If we don't feel good about ourselves, these things often come with a message that we don't deserve them. In David Furnish's documentary about Elton, *Tantrums and Tiaras*, Elton's therapist said that Elton had only just started to believe that his sell-out audiences genuinely wanted to be there. Despite outside esteem on the biggest scale possible, for a time his success made him feel worse than ever before.

Russian dolls

A good analogy of what we're left with when we rely on outside esteem and other ways of coping is a Russian doll: the round-hipped wooden dolls that contain five or six additional dolls inside, each one slightly smaller than the one before, until you reach the tiny baby doll in the middle. This little one represents the original **wounded child**. Each of the outside shells represents a defence mechanism, be it a behaviour or addiction – thick layers piled on top of the inner child. The outside shell, the person we present to the world, is not our authentic self: this is the **adapted adult child**. It's a child who has adapted to deal with the wound but not been able to develop into an emotionally authentic adult.

In *Attitude*, with our monthly 'Truly, Madly, Deeply' page, I made it my business to show that there are countless people in successful same-sex relationships. But it is also true that significant numbers of us – myself included – find it hard to form and sustain healthy relationships (as Alan Downs acknowledges in *The Velvet Rage* when he notes that therapist offices all over the Western world are jammed with gay men trying to work out why they can't keep a boyfriend). Can you see why relying on outside esteem might make it hard to have an authentic relationship? The up-and-down rollercoaster of being drunk, high, on a come-down or experiencing the intense energy that sleeping with lots of people brings makes it really hard to know who you are, let alone share it with someone else. (Don't panic as you read this. These things can absolutely be worked through, as we'll see in the last part of the book, and some couples do seem to evolve together with, or sometimes without, help.)

If we're understandably emotionally fragile, then even when we're not drinking or drugging, etc., relationships can be difficult: being too needy or jealous, or feeling we aren't worthy of the other person, can make things hard. Often people who are too emotionally sensitive will subconsciously pick someone who is emotionally shut down to partner with. It can feel exciting and we can convince ourselves that we can be the one to change them – usually we can't. Even though we blame the other person, subconsciously we've made it happen as much as they have.

An extremely common thing I have heard over the years is something that *Attitude*'s former dating columnist Pip McCormac described in one of his columns. He met a guy; they felt a powerful attraction, enjoyed the night together and saw each other over a few more, similarly charged, drunken nights. The guy said he was excited at the prospect of dating Pip, but when Pip returned the sentiment the guy went cold and ran away. It is common for people (gay or straight) to chase someone passionately, but as soon as the other person responds they freak out and run off. These people are often desperate for a relationship – but when they get close they can't handle it. That's because for a real relationship we actually have to let that person connect with our authentic self. We might desperately want it, thinking it will fix us, but if we are self-shamed, letting someone else get close to the inner Russian doll, the part of us with all the pain that we have been subconsciously doing everything we can to avoid, is unbearable – and we bolt. This is an incredibly painful place in which to be: desperate to open up to another person and find true, substantial love but terrified of it at the same time.

It's no wonder it traps people in the cycle of addiction. Next we'll look at how all this actually manifests in the real world.

8

'I know a place where you can get away': Fantasy and Entertainment

'I am a gay black man from Houston, Texas. Beyoncé is my Lord and gyrator. She is the beginning, end and body roll to me. I should have known better than to ever bother with such haters.'

Michael Arceneaux, 'I would never
date a man who hates Beyoncé',
Guardian.co.uk, August 2015

'I think what you guys like is a strong woman that's having a breakdown constantly. And that certainly is me. Judy Garland's got nothing on me.'

Cher, at the Attitude Awards, 2012

DOROTHY BEGAN IT FOR me. It's a cliché but it is true. At six or seven, to the bemusement of my parents, I would perform *Wizard of Oz* songs that I had memorized. A child who didn't know what was real or safe, I was obsessed with Dorothy, obsessed with the witch, obsessed with the film to the point where I couldn't think of much else.

It seems I wasn't alone. The 'Friend of Dorothy' connection has been documented to the point where it feels like parody. In a 1967 *Time* magazine review of a Judy Garland concert, the writer noted that 'a disproportionate part of her nightly claque seems to be homosexuals', men who would 'roll their eyes, tear at their hair and practically levitate from their seats'. Gay US news magazine the *Advocate* has called Garland 'the Elvis of Homosexuals'; in 2006 singer Rufus Wainwright paid homage by recreating her most iconic live appearance in *Rufus Does Judy at Carnegie Hall*. The musical *Wicked* (music by Stephen Schwartz, original story by Gregory Maguire, both gay) entrances heavily gay audiences from New York to London to this day, and Garland's offspring Liza Minnelli, a 'gay icon' in her own right, officiated over cinema's first and most OTT gay wedding in *Sex and the City 2*. ('Anytime there's this much gay energy in the room,' declared Miranda, 'Liza manifests!')

In an interview to promote the 2009 London Palladium production of *The Wizard of Oz*, actor Lee MacDougall (playing the cowardly Lion) succinctly commented, 'Well, my friends and I quote the movie all the time, it's the language we speak . . . for some reason gays have always attached ourselves to Judy. I met my husband in a production of *The Wizard of Oz* in 1989. I was the Scarecrow and he was one of my back-up dancer crows. So we really are the friends of Dorothy.'

Why is this? Apparently we love the tragedy of Judy Garland's life – the failed relationships, the drunken carnage. Certainly we may glibly enjoy the dark tragi-comedy of her life story, but I didn't know anything of this when I was a child. Yet the powerful connection was there. Why?

What is it with entertainment, the arts and gay people? Why is it that when you go to a Madonna, Lady Gaga, Beyoncé or Kylie concert anywhere in the world there is such a huge proportion of gay people, gay men in particular, who are obsessively devoted to the artist? And why certain performers and not others? Why Lady Gaga and not Nine Inch Nails? Why Barbra Streisand and not the Rolling Stones? Why Beyoncé and not Jay Z? In an article for Attitude.co.uk in summer 2015 called 'Why do gay men love divas so much?', Brian O'Flynn, in his twenties, wrote, 'The phenomenon has always fascinated me, simply because I find myself helplessly subject to it. Despite my best efforts . . .'

Yes it's a generalization, but one you'll see reflected all over the world, from gay-bar playlists to gay men with tattoos of their idols – quite an extreme thing to do – such as actor Guillermo Díaz, who has Madonna on his arm. For some this idolization becomes obsessive. 'Superfan' Adam Guerra, who appeared in the TV series *My Strange Addiction*, spent $116,000 on plastic surgery to look like Madonna and a further $100,000 on dressing like her. Guerra works as a Madonna impersonator, but his boyfriend believes his obsession is 'psychotic', saying 'I want to date a boy not a fifty-six-year-old woman' and is worried that his partner will die during one of his many surgeries.

Written down it sounds ridiculous, but industries related to perform-ance, theatre, glamour and artifice are heavily populated with gay men. Look at theatre, fashion, personal grooming, TV, even celebrity magazines and websites; or at TV gossip-show couches across the world; or at online pop-music message boards: they are edited, run, dominated by gay men. Why is this so common that we take it for granted? If being gay were no more than just a sexual preference then it wouldn't be so. I didn't have a passion for theatre and film because I knew these were apparently 'safe' industries in which to be gay. I didn't even know I was gay, but I was absolutely decided on a career in show business before I was ten.

The simple answer, as may well be obvious by now, is because at a time when we are overwhelmed by the danger of our existence, clutching for a rope to pull us out of the pit of fear, this shiny, unreal, neon world of artifice, of glamour, of making something beautiful out of the dullness offers us a way to escape – to disconnect from reality. Fantasy is often the first way we disassociate from the world around us, alongside food to which I'll come later. It may start as daydreaming, then move on to reading books, watching TV, then music and film, and it progresses to become the most powerful escape route we will ever have – and one of which some of us refuse to let go even in adulthood.

Entertainment offers us a way of having some control over our feelings. If we feel bad, then a musical offers gleeful hope and romanticism. If our way of coping is slowly to grow comfortable in the position of unlovable victim, then listening to a sad song or watching our favourite weepy can affirm our sense of tragedy and unlovability. Feeling in need of empowerment? Then there's nothing better, for different generations, than a Diana Ross, Madonna, Beyoncé strong-woman anthem. Want to indulge in obsessive, simplified, happy-ever-after love? Then watch *Pretty Woman* or our favourite Disney film for the umpteenth time. Calm, balanced people are not interesting to those of us who have emotional problems, but people expressing intense, overblown emotions – those that are too painful or too dangerous for us young LGBT people to explore in our real lives – are attractive. It is not just a 'gay thing': it's the story of all show business. A line from the musical *Chicago*, written by (gay) duo John Kander and Fred Ebb, expresses it clearly:

> **Roxy Hart:** I'm a star! And the audience loves me! And I
> love them and they love me for loving them and I love
> them for loving me and we just love each other!
> **Dancing Boy:** And that's 'cos none of us got enough love in
> our childhoods . . .
> **Roxy Hart:** And that's showbiz, kid!

Lady Gaga wrote a whole song about it in which she sings that she 'lives for the applause'.

You might want to stop and think about your favourite pop stars, films and theatre (if you went) when you were growing up. Not just things you liked, but the films, music and shows you *really* loved and could watch over and over (and probably did, if you were anything like me). They often tell a story about our emotional state at the time. My brother's favourite films were *Herbie Goes to Monte Carlo*, *That Darn Cat*, *The Cannonball Run*. For music, he had a period of loving Guns N' Roses. My favourite music was from musical theatre, then as

I got older Pet Shop Boys, Madonna, Kylie, Stock Aitken Waterman, and then Tori Amos. Along with *The Wizard of Oz*, my favourite films and shows were:

Annie The story of a mistreated, unloved orphan, desperate for affirmation, who suddenly finds herself with all the love and riches she could possibly want.

The Sound of Music A person who has removed herself from the possibility of love, sex or family life faces hostility from a family whom she wins over, becoming mother to all of them.

Superman A man from another place, different from his family, who grows up with a secret and, though he is haunted by the fact he can never be one of them, wins the universal devotion of society, but is never able to reveal his true self.

Halloween and **A Nightmare on Elm Street** Outcasts taking revenge on the family.

Starlight Express A loser whom nobody loves, who wallows in self-pity but finally triumphs and wins the day, with everybody realizing they underestimated him.

The Phantom of the Opera A deformed freak, so disgusting he has to live outside society in the sewers.

It's no coincidence that science fiction is disproportionately popular with those, regardless of sexuality, who have been traumatized growing up. If this world doesn't accept us and isn't safe for us, then actually getting off it and finding other worlds where we are accepted is highly attractive. Some sci-fi holds more gay appeal than others. The specific queer appeal of Marvel's *X-Men* series has been well documented: genetic mutations lead to a minority of 'mutants' living secret lives hidden amongst the general population.

If sexuality were simply a matter of sexual preference and there was no commonality of experience, there shouldn't be large gay fandoms for programmes or genres that aren't specifically about homosexuality – and yet the LGBT appeal of sci-fi reaches across many different programmes. The appeal doesn't arise from sexuality but from the fact that LGBT children are so traumatized that they subconsciously latch on to anything in which they can sense otherness.

Russell T. Davies told me about the celebrated relationship *Doctor Who* has with gay fans. 'There's famously a high number of LGBT viewers tuning into *Doctor Who*,' he wrote in an email, 'and it's a well-known fact that the fandom is predominantly gay. In fact, when I took over *Doctor Who*, I saw it as my job to turn the programme away from niche viewing – which includes the gay audience – and to open it up to women and straight men. I took a lot of my writers from fandom, and many of them are gay – Mark Gatiss, Gareth Roberts, Keith Temple. If you include my episodes, that's about 70% of episodes of post-2005 *Doctor Who* written by gay men . . . So, yes, there's something about escapism there, especially when you're closeted. And *Doctor Who* notoriously, among other fandoms, is still famous for having a high gay ratio, more than *Game of Thrones* or *Supernatural* or *Star Trek* or *Buffy* or any other franchise, which is kind of interesting if you consider that *Doctor Who* is more escapist than any of those other shows. Literally, it's in a different time and place every week, a feature which no other show shares. It's even in a different genre, week on week. So its capacity to [provide] escape is greater.'

Russell believes the escapism narrative put forward to explain science fiction's appeal to gay people is negative because it implies terror. He believes instead that it is attractive because gay people are freer, happier, more able to accept colour and campness – but I don't agree. In our teenage years we are desperate for connection but we know that it is too dangerous. I think we are drawn to Doctor Who precisely because he is a stoic loner, emotionally detached and literally leaves before anyone gets close enough for him to have to face his emotions.

As I was writing this I noticed a man on one of my social media networks with the surname 'Gallifrey', the fictional planet from which Doctor Who comes. I spoke to him and he told me he'd changed his name by deed poll. 'I suffered a lot with depression when I was younger and am still on the meds to this day,' he wrote. 'I use *Doctor Who* to get away from the pain sometimes of my head and a lot of the time it was down to my sexual orientation or really, to be honest, the normal fact of me being who I am, a gay man. It's my escape to a world of fantasy.'

Russell says when he was researching his TV series *Queer As Folk* in the nineties, he found out that, though *Doctor Who* wasn't then being made, gay people were latching on to another popular sci-fi series. 'In order to research the character of fifteen-year-old Nathan, I went and spoke to a gay youth group, only to discover that they loved *Star Trek: the Next Generation* just as much as I'd loved *Doctor Who* when I was a teenager.'

Star Trek is set in a world where all the things that separate us – race, skin colour, gender – are irrelevant. In *Star Trek* you may be green with tentacles but you are still worthy of respect.

Horror also holds a disproportionate appeal to many LGBT people. Harry Benshoff, author of *Monsters in the Closet: Homosexuality and the Horror Film*, told me, 'I think queer audiences tend to like the horror film because they can and do easily identify with the monster who is out to topple white heteronormative culture. In classical horror films the monster must be destroyed at the end, unlike in more recent horror (and of course in fantasy or science fiction one can be different in a million ways without necessarily being monstrous). All of these genres create spaces more or less welcoming to queer spectators in ways that more realistic genres do not'.

Any medium that allows us to fantasize that we are someone else, to express the inexpressible, to triumph over 'normality', or, simply, that offers us an experience powerful enough to soothe our feelings, is likely to be popular with those of us who are traumatized – sometimes overwhelmingly so. In January 2014, trans writer Laura Kate Dale, the founder of the aptly named indiehaven.com, wrote a piece in the *Guardian* about how she lost herself in online gaming as she struggled for acceptance from herself and others:

> Almost five years before I came out to my family and friends as transgender, I started playing the online fantasy game, *World of Warcraft* . . . I was fourteen and in deep denial about my own feelings regarding my gender expression and identity . . . Right from square one I was hooked; I didn't want to leave. At the time I assumed this was mostly to do with the compelling game mechanics, but looking back I'm sure it was a lot to do with how I had presented myself in the world. I found a place where I had friends that treated me as female, for better or for worse. I had found a world where I got complimented on my appearance in game, where people were not scared away by my gender presentation. A world where I felt happy with who I was. I didn't want to leave. I didn't want to go back to the real world where I felt I needed to be masculine to remain safe.

*

Addiction therapist Sarah Graham says for many LGBTQI people there is an addiction to 'surface': 'It can manifest in different ways – in gym addiction, in cosmetic surgery addiction, in having sex with younger people addiction, and all of that.'

The Velvet Rage author Alan Downs says that gay men hide their true selves through manufactured beauty: 'Something about growing up gay forced us to learn how to hide ugly realities behind a finely crafted façade . . . We hid because we learned that hiding is a means to survival. The naked truth about who we are wasn't acceptable so we learned to hide behind a beautiful image.'

Whilst it is not true that all gay people care about design and style, it is true that the global fashion industry is absolutely dominated by gay men. Think for a moment: Lagerfeld, Dior, Yves Saint Laurent, McQueen, Calvin Klein, Marc Jacobs, Valentino, Oscar de la Renta, Gaultier, Armani, Versace, Pierre Cardin, Tom Ford, Galliano,

Louboutin, Christopher Bailey, Jeremy Scott, Dries van Noten . . . The domination of fashion by gay men is something we take for granted, but it is shocking and illogical; again, it should not be the case. Escape from unacceptability is what drives it.

But it is music that offers many of us a safe space for the expression of things which as children we weren't allowed to express and as adults we're often too scared to explore.

Andy Butler of group Hercules & Love Affair said in an interview with the *Guardian* in 2014, 'I still look in the mirror and see an awkward, ginger, unattractive, feminine queer. My music is really about being able to express that sensitivity and vulnerability but it's a constant struggle to truly accept that aspect of who I am, y'know? It's strange because it can transport you back to twelve or thirteen years old, and that's when music was the only thing keeping me alive.'

For so many of us, keeping us alive is truly what music does. We should be grateful to those passions we developed as teenagers, whether they be art and design, the Eurovision Song Contest, or gaming or film and theatre. As I became an adult, for me it was Madonna. Just months after I'd come out to the local gay youth group, in summer 1990, I saw this defiant, hyper-sexual woman telling a packed Wembley Stadium, full of the kind of suburban people I lived my life surrounded by, to fuck off. For the first time I realized the possibility of fighting back, of not feeling ashamed, and I went Madonna bonkers. I bought a CD player, all her back catalogue and plastered my bedroom walls with her pictures. I learned dance moves, obsessed over interviews, wrote an A-level paper comparing her to Shakespeare's Cleopatra and forced bemused relatives to watch videos of simulated masturbation over Sunday lunch. She was all I thought or spoke about. Over the two years of sixth form, I used Madonna's persona as armour, strutting around 'striking a pose' at anyone who got too close. Sometimes the other boys ignored me, sometimes they threw chairs. Occasionally they'd celebrate the oddness. When two friends and I performed 'Express Yourself' and 'Vogue' in front of the whole school in full Madonna and back-up-singer drag during a lunchtime mini-concert, the room erupted with five hundred hormonal teenage boys cheering on every bra flash and high kick.

Out on the gay scene of the early nineties I was shocked to discover that my personal connection to the Material Girl wasn't so personal after all. From the clubber with the *Erotica* artwork tattooed on his arm, to the lip-syncher at G-A-Y every – and I mean *every* – Saturday night in full Madonna drag, to the friend whose anxious reaction to 9/11 was to ask if it meant Madonna's new album might be postponed, it was apparent I wasn't the only one obsessed.

It has become clear as I've got older that many of my friends had similar artists on to whom they latched. Ryan is a thirty-nine-year-old friend of mine. He's successful, funny, clever and the Pet Shop Boys are never far from his thoughts. He goes to exhibitions and films that have been mentioned in their work, nags friends into coming to concerts and will always find a way of turning any topic of conversation round to them. He also had a really hard time growing up. He told me that a straight friend he was in love with introduced him to their music.

'I was known as the Walkman Boy as I just walked around listening to them on my Walkman every day,' he told me. 'It was a safety net, it was losing myself in another world. I'd spend hours and hours in my room listening to them, barely breaking for food.'

Today his best friends are fellow fans and he still spends a lot of time thinking about the group. Clearly, as addictions go, drink or drugs are more damaging, but I asked Ryan if he thinks he spends too much time focusing on them. 'Maybe. That's a fair comment,' he acknowledged. 'It has become a problem, possibly, sometimes. When you're that much of a fan you take it personally. I once got into a row with a guy in a pub who was slagging them off. Another time I was searching for mentions of them on Twitter and someone was criticizing them and I drunkenly started attacking them, saying "You work in IT, you're so boring, fuck you." A big part of it is about emotional trauma. The friends I share that love them have that in common. I think it's because they create this other world.'

The artists that inspire obsessions are the ones who create the immersive world that Ryan talks about – Madonna, Beyoncé, Kylie, Taylor Swift, Rihanna, Ariana Grande, Tori Amos, David Bowie, Britney Spears, Kate Bush and many more.

The kind of pop music that has become so popular with us isn't accidental. Super-producer Nile Rodgers said in the Channel 4 documentary *Queer Pop* that disco music evolved specifically to cater for the tastes of black and gay marginalized audiences. Much of the output of pop music of the 1970s or 1980s was designed to appeal to gay audiences without it ever being stated. Some songs were almost explicit in their appeal, such as 'I'm Coming Out' by Diana Ross (the meaning of which Diana Ross was not told at the time) and other anthems of defiance, like Gloria Gaynor's biggest hit, 1978's 'I Will Survive'.

There was also a huge amount of music of the time that wasn't officially aimed at gay people but none the less ticked the boxes of the emotionally traumatized audience's needs. Much of Stock Aitken Waterman's needy-schoolgirl emotional output became massively popular with gay men. As homophobia accompanied the rise of HIV and AIDS and the Conservative government implemented Section 28, songs that reflected the time, such as Bananarama's 'Love In the First Degree', Erasure's 'Ship of Fools' and 'It's a Sin' by the Pet Shop Boys were iconic hits with gay audiences, with the Pet Shop Boys' tantalizing synth soundtrack of the closet going as far as many of its listeners could in their own lives.

Over the last thirty years you can see a trend in the kind of pop music that is popular with gay audiences because of the way it expresses our emotional needs. It's commonly accepted that the kind of women that appeal to gay men are strong women, when in fact it's a streak of vulnerability and even victimhood that these women often show that is actually closer to the truth. Remember, we are an audience who were told we were wrong, immoral, not allowed to have relationships. It's no wonder overblown and childish emotional themes of rejection, loneliness and empowerment were so appealing.

The songs that seem to hit an emotional button for us fit broadly into four categories. Here are a few examples of each.

An assertion of aggressive sexuality, typified by songs such as:
'Dirrty' – Christina Aguilera
'You Think You're a Man' – Divine
'Hot Stuff', 'Bad Girl', 'She Works Hard for the Money', 'Love to Love' – Donna Summer
'It's Raining Men' – Weather Girls
'Outside' – George Michael

Escape through music, typified by songs such as:
'Vogue', 'Into the Groove' – Madonna
'Lost in Music' – Sister Sledge
'Your Disco Needs You' – Kylie
'Just Dance' – Lady Gaga

Empowerment/I'm too good for you, typified by songs such as:
'I Will Survive', 'I Am What I Am' – Gloria Gaynor
'Respectable' – Mel & Kim
'Believe', 'Strong Enough' – Cher
'Survivor', 'Independent Woman' – Destiny's Child
'Single Ladies' ('Put a ring on it'), 'Run the World (Girls)' – Beyoncé
'Express Yourself', 'Human Nature', 'Sorry' – Madonna
'Get Outta My Way' – Kylie

I'm not good enough for you/victim, typified by songs such as:
'I Don't Wanna Get Hurt' – Donna Summer
'Dancing On My Own' – Robyn
'Counting Every Single Minute', 'You'll Never Stop Me from Loving You' – Sonia
'To Deserve You' – Bette Midler

Kylie's appeal to gay audiences is legendary and, again, taken for granted. But why? Why is it that so many young gay boys respond with devotion to her and not to other artists? She's pretty and vulnerable, but I think a significant part of it is that the majority of Kylie's early output fits into the 'I'm not good enough' category. 'I Should Be So Lucky' is one of the ultimate victim anthems. Think of the lyrics if you are sceptical. It describes exactly how I and much of her audience would have felt: not worthy, not good enough, never able actually to get the man. She continued the theme later in her career: 'Je Ne Sais Pas Pourquoi', 'Wouldn't Change a Thing', 'Never Too Late', 'Tears On My Pillow', 'Hand On My Heart', 'What Do I Have to Do', 'Can't Get You Out of My Head'. Think of the lyrics of her greatest hit, 'Better the Devil You Know' – a brilliant song, but one none the less that is explicitly about accepting second best, begging a lover to take her back. This will upset fans – proving the point I'm making – but if you're in any doubt, google the lyrics. It's a song I love, but it is truly an anthem of disempowerment.

The gay appeal of certain artists isn't because we know they had difficult lives. It's because we sense in them the vulnerability and strength that we have too, the dysfunction that often pans out into difficult personal lives the way it does for some of us. Like is drawn to like. Healthy people attract healthy people. Codependents are drawn to codependents. I was attracted to Madonna because subconsciously I could sense a mixture of emotions – her anger, her defiance, her need to be loved and also to reject as a reaction to her own childhood trauma – and the same is true of most performers who attract large gay audiences. Madonna's ambition, she said, was driven by feeling unloved after the death of her mother; Streisand has said she felt unloved and ugly; Gaga has broken down in tears on stage, expressing how she felt not good enough growing up.

The connection with Dorothy and *The Wizard of Oz* is not simply because of the campiness and colour, but because the film is a tale of codependency portrayed by one of the most famous codependents of all time. Those of us wounded children, gay or straight, who connect to it do so at a very powerful subconscious level. Like us, Dorothy is a girl who has been through deep emotional trauma (she's lost her parents). Through no fault of her own, she indulges her feelings of not being loved: even though she is being raised by her aunt and uncle she doesn't feel their love is enough. So she runs away from home and ends up in a colourful fantasy world where she meets other misfits, all of whom have self-esteem issues too: a problem-solving man who thinks he's stupid, an overly emotional man who doesn't think he has a heart, and a lion who is afraid of everything and everyone. The film is about their journey to self-acceptance and self-esteem.

This is the nature of the appeal of *The Wizard of Oz*, of Judy Garland, of Dorothy. A codependent played by a codependent living out the progression and recovery of codependency. We didn't know it, weren't aware of it as we watched it, but that is what it is.

Fortunately for us, as for Dorothy, there is a way out of the mess we're in and, as for her, it comes from within ourselves. But like her, most of us go through a lot of pain before we can get there.

9

'Either fuck me – or fuck off!':
Small Town Boys on Old Competition Street

'It's quite brutal. If you're beautiful and you have the right genes, then the gay scene is a place where you can be worshipped. But if you don't, it's a different ball of wax. I sort of have a lot of anger around that because coming out was tough enough, dealing with the people that hated you because you were gay . . . to then go into the gay scene and realise that it's even worse there, that was, well, fucked.'

Singer John Grant, *Guardian* interview, 2014

ON 8 MAY 2015, the day after the UK general election, a young man from a small British seaside town without a large gay scene emailed *Attitude* unprompted to tell us how isolated he felt. 'If there has been some massive change or revolution in the last few years,' he wrote, 'it's passed me by.'

He wrote that he had a severe problem with depression, anxiety and debilitating panic attacks, which he blamed, in part, on not being able to afford to live in a place that had more gay people. 'Today I'm twenty-eight years old. I have no job or life, really, but the thing that gets me the most is that basically I have no friends, no one to turn to and, literally, no one who cares about me apart from close family members . . . this is no life for a young person.' He went on to explain how badly affected his life had been by his anxiety and ended on a sad and frustrated note: 'I think that because everyone seems to think that it's OK now, no one talks about those who still have issues and need a little guidance or encouragement. I feel worse about being gay today than I ever have . . . things may have changed for others but those changes don't include the likes of me . . .' He signed his email off 'A very unhappy and excluded young person'.

Isolation and poverty are the elephants in the room for LGBT people in the UK in 2016. Despite all the talk of the pink pound – the assertion that gay people have more disposable income, which dominated 1990s consumerist thinking – and the explosion of acceptance and positivity, things can be bleak for those who don't have the significant financial resources to live nearer to other gay people.

I put a request out in January 2015 to hear about *Attitude* readers' experience of living outside big towns and cities. Scores of people replied. Happily, many reported positive experiences. Indeed, some had moved away from cities like London to be in the country and one, having expected a bad reception, was so surprised to find the opposite that he had started a blog about his positive experience. Some in tiny villages were outgoing and gregarious with a good circle of friends and said they had great, enriching lives. Others had a positive experience – until an issue arose that meant they didn't. One man told me he and his partner enjoyed where they lived but 'were attacked in an unprovoked homophobic attack in the area over four years ago and we encountered homophobia from our local police force and discovered absolutely no support was available for victims of hate crime in our area.'

It seems easier if you are a gay couple not looking to socialize or meet new gay people, otherwise the small pool of the same people in the local pubs, if there are any, or on Grindr can be restrictive. A young man from a town about fifty minutes outside London told me 'the people on the scene itself are as dire as the [one gay] pub. All the gay guys with ambition upped and left, so all that's left are mostly unemployed twentysomethings and old men.' He said his local village had 'all the phobias. It's a very white, very middle-aged, very Tory area. These are the people likely to vote UKIP. They've probably never seen a gay person in their life . . . I think a large number of the residents don't really believe [homosexuality] happens, because there just aren't that many of us. We're a bit of a myth/novelty.'

When you are a novelty you stand out more, something that was backed up by a 2015 study by Dr Stevie-Jade Hardy at the University of Leicester. She found that many LGBT people living in rural areas were 'lonely and isolated with nowhere to turn'; often they would be homophobically bullied in their homes but wouldn't report incidents to the police because they believed it would make it worse. People who looked noticeably different were more likely to suffer harassment. Dr Hardy told the *Telegraph*:

> Within rural locations those differences are maybe magnified, and so young people will often target someone who they see as being different in that context. The impact can be devastating. Some LGBT people are scared to leave the house, feeling anxious, fearful and vulnerable. I heard from some people who had taken practical steps to feel safer such as installing CCTV. In a rural location hate crime can be especially damaging, particularly for older LGBT people. There often isn't that sense of community or a social group where you can access support.

Being visible can be dangerous. One young man from a small place in Yorkshire who was labelled 'the only gay in the village' told me that he spent a lot of his life trying to act as 'manly' as possible. 'I'm not overly camp but neither am I macho,' he wrote. 'School was quite difficult. I was known as the "gay one" but I would quickly shoot down these comments and reiterate that I wasn't. I even had girlfriends to try and dismiss claims.'

Another told me, 'In my past relationships I have often had to censor myself and avoid holding hands or showing any kind of affection in public through fear of [homophobia]. I think this stems from the fact that I have been jumped and physically assaulted due to my sexuality in the past and also had verbal altercations with customers at my workplace due to ignorance.'

A man in his mid-thirties from Swindon told me that homophobia on the streets is far worse there than in London: 'It's just not comfortable to express yourself on the streets. I get looks and have seen other expressive guys get full-on looks, comments or verbal abuse. Lesbians don't get bothered and many will hold hands or express themselves completely maturely, but will always be noted by others . . . It is because of all these things I very rarely go out in Swindon on a night out compared to London. I don't feel safe and if anything I feel quite vulnerable unless I am with a large group of friends.'

One man from Scotland told me, 'When you think of a small, Highland town you don't automatically think "gay-friendly", which, to a certain extent, is true. I find myself being overly cautious when I'm being introduced to new people or starting a new job because you just have no idea how they will perceive you. I can actually feel myself trying to be more "manly" so that I don't rock the boat too much. This isn't just a negative for the place that I live, but for me as well. I am a proud gay man, but I personally feel that I have to be a bit more guarded about it because of where I live.'

Some people cannot avoid homophobia no matter what they do. A nineteen-year-old from near Manchester told me he had been bullied throughout school and was still enduring abuse every day. 'I was beaten up and punched, kicked and spat at in school and college, and verbally [abused]: fag, gay, queer, fairy, puff, bender, batty boy (just to name a few of the daily ones),' he told me. He said he has continued to be abused since leaving school. 'It is literally daily. Some people on the bus call me a dirty queer every morning, I'm called fag/puff by some people that pass me on bikes and people in my village stopped using my name and called me "that queer".'

A man who lives in Dover, which he described as 'a very odd place filled with odd people [with] no gay bars, no scene', said that using apps like Grindr becomes the de facto way to meet other men. 'I have an entire folder of them on my phone,' another young man told me. 'Grindr, Tinder, Gaydar, Hornet – you name it, I've got it. Why? I have no idea, given it's the same people on every single one.' Another said, 'There's lots of sleeping around. Everybody seems to have had everybody else and on the rare occasion you do meet someone new, you discover you have a minimum of five mutual friends with them on Facebook.' Another wrote, 'I tried Grindr but didn't find much luck there as most people liked to keep secret about what they did. I even had sexual relations with some straight people but again they would fiercely deny they were gay/bi which has impacted me in ways of trust and commitment. So after rejections like that I started to not bother about meeting anyone.'

This was echoed by lots of people who mailed me. One said, 'There are lots of partnered guys using [Grindr] and also lots of married straight guys using it, which I find interesting.'

Other complications of socializing in small circles were raised. 'Being an HIV-positive man, I also experience further prejudice,' one man told me, 'not only by the straight community but also by my own LGBT community, which makes meeting people even harder on such sites where everybody knows or professes to know your business'. As I was writing this, another young man I know who lives in Northern Ireland and is open about his HIV-positive status posted about the anonymous harassment he receives on Grindr, this time when someone sent a message calling him 'an AIDS Fucktard'.

Poverty is a key factor in the oppression of so many LGBT people. A twenty-four-year-old man living in the centre of the UK told me that he has no option but to stay with his homophobic mother and stepfather. His mother is white, his stepfather from a different culture and ethnic background. He wrote that when he came out his mother was 'crying in shame' for a long time, while his stepfather calls him disgusting, does not include him in family meals, suggests he is going to turn his younger brother gay, blocks his car in the drive and tells him 'In my country they kill people like you.' He wrote to me, 'It's like living in a prison. I am a human being . . . It's like domestic abuse . . . Mentally, I am drained. It's made me so low in confidence. I feel scared to gain a new partner or even try and look. Catch-22 situation . . . It takes two to move out and pay bills these days (especially on my wages). I am really so badly trying. I am at college gaining some extra qualifications to make a better living for myself . . . I am also applying for jobs and I've had so many interviews . . . It hurts when they say your low confidence came across and we need someone who has a lot of confidence . . . I just want a normal, understanding family.'

And so it's clear why, whether it be London, Leeds, Manchester, Brighton, Glasgow, Dublin or some other city, so many young gay men gravitate to places where there are bigger gay populations. Who can blame them? I did. But this is where another problem can occur.

A twenty-three-year-old man who escaped from a small town to the outskirts of London to be nearer more gay people said that he 'was mesmerized, astounded' by being so close to such a large gay scene, but also found it intimidating. 'I loved the fact that there were so many different LGBT people, but again I felt that I was being judged and since haven't plucked up the courage to go [out on the scene] again.'

One afternoon in 2014 when I was arranging to meet a friend on Soho's Old Compton Street, I sent a text message that the predictive text autocorrected to 'Let's meet on Old Competition Street'. When we met we both laughed and winced, recognizing what felt like a Freudian slip. The gay scene can be a transformative, life-saving place where we find solace and acceptance. It absolutely was for me. David Stuart of 56 Dean Street told me he commonly watches from his office window as couples link hands when they enter the relative safety of Old Compton Street, then disconnect as they leave it. I spent a huge amount of my time on the gay scene in my twenties and thirties and lots of it was great.

This is something that many people expressed. One man I interviewed told me how rich the diversity of the scene in London is – somewhere for people to come from places in the world where being gay is far harder.

'If you come out in Jamaica, for instance, there's nowhere to go,' he told me. 'That's why you get so many gay guys come to England, to get away from that. When I first went to Heaven I was fifteen and I thought I was the only gay person in the world. I went to the RnB room and I was surrounded by all these gay black men – it took my breath away. It wasn't just one or two, it was a whole clubful; some of them I recognized from my area. It was like, woah! There's a huge West Indian community on the gay scene in London who have come here to find solace. Gay guys get killed there, they get found murdered, so they come here. The gay scene was quite seedy, but the black part of it was more about the music where you were able to be yourself and dance in a way you coudn't with your straight friends. The stigma in those communities is really bad, but it's not just the black community. It's all round the world, even in London.'

But there is another side to the experience and many people have expressed to me their dissatisfaction with 'the gay scene' and its values. I asked what *Attitude*'s Twitter followers thought and these are some of their replies:

'Depends on location. Hideously depressing in the sticks, I avoid it. More fun in London. I prefer "straight" bars.'

'Like meat markets. Not into the whole drug/popper scene.'

'It feels threatening at times, and overwhelming. It feeds on your weaknesses. It is *not* healthy.'

'Cliquey, in your face, stereotypical, sad. Gives a bad impression of the gay life I would say.'

'Hate it, wish it didn't exist, a giant school yard of playground bullying, bitchiness and spreads a lot of hate from within!'

'Been on it for 600 years. Bitchy, fast, shallow, extreme, dull, vicious, a family, damaging, healing, static, sporadic #LoveIt'

'It's like anything else in life, it's what you make of it. You can choose to be mired in the drama or simply rise above it:)'

'I wouldn't advise going until you know who you are and
how to ignore the old men standing by the radiators.'

'Gay people destroy each other. Knock each other down then
ask for society to stop doing the same to them. NEXT!'

I was surprised at how condemnatory the majority of the
comments were and at how we seemed to have moved so seamlessly
from the experience of those young men we saw at the beginning of
this chapter, desperate for a place to be themselves, to others who
experienced so much negativity when they found it.

The problem seems to boil down to the fact that often we don't
treat each other very nicely or with much respect – something that
I feel also happens on Grindr, where racism and HIV shaming are
commonplace. Again, I want to re-emphasize that lots of people love
the gay scene and that, like most things in life, to some extent you get
out of it what you put in. Clearly lots of gay clubs and pubs are still
packed; but, on the other hand, something we don't acknowledge when
bars such as the Black Cap in Camden shut and people are up in arms
about it is that lots of us love *not* having to go to those bars any more.

Our complicated relationship with the scene comes from how we
feel about ourselves and other gay people, and from the context of
how we arrive on the scene and what we expect from it. If you accept
that to some degree, as Dr Joe Kort says, many, if not most, of us
are abuse survivors, then the gay scene is unique in that it is a place
where we are mixing with lots of other abuse survivors. Traumatized
people socializing with lots of other traumatized people. Sometimes
this can mean we bring specific behaviours to our relationships with
each other – what I call negative mirroring, invalidation potential
and extreme objectification.

Negative mirroring

Human beings don't like others who display the things that they don't
like in themselves. A formerly very overweight friend of mine thinks
fat people are disgusting, worthless and have no self-respect – because

that's what he thought about himself. If – and again, it's not everyone – we don't like ourselves, then other gay people are a mirror of the thing that we aren't comfortable with in ourselves, and that dislike will come out directed at them. This is why time and again so many rabidly homophobic politicians and religious people are revealed as having had illicit gay sex. It's an aspect of themselves that they cannot accept and that they have tried so badly to submerge that it makes them attack others passionately; sometimes they make whole careers out of it. We all enjoy seeing an anti-gay bigot caught in a public toilet, or with an escort, but the reality is that these are just very damaged, shamed men. We also encounter it on dating apps when men express an aversion to campness and an obsession with being 'masc'. It's OK to find masculinity attractive, but not OK to shame other people, which is what happens to every single person who sees those messages, regardless of how masculine they are, as more than likely all of us will have doubted our masculinity as we came to terms with our sexuality.

If we aren't comfortable with ourselves, then a gay bar is like being in a house of mirrors. It would be like my formerly overweight friend socializing exclusively with people who are obese, having his self-loathing triggered over and over again. This is problematic, because when we don't like people we're usually not very nice to them.

Invalidation potential

Gay or straight, if you have low self-esteem sleeping with someone is a great boost – there's little more powerfully validating than someone finding you attractive. That's why when people split up others advise them to 'get over someone by getting under someone'. But for people who are validation junkies – gay or straight, male or female – desire for sex is often more about a compulsive need for a hit of validation.

Seeking this validation is a dangerous thing because it risks invalidation – rejection – and a connection to our ever-present, just-below-the-surface feeling that we are not good enough. This is something we'd do anything to avoid. It's not only being rejected that is painful;

just not being validated can leave you feeling crushed. I've heard men say they were devastated if they didn't pull on a night out and their whole week was ruined. One friend told me if he didn't meet someone every single time he went out he would feel suicidal and drive home in tears. It's why, in response to my question about the gay scene, we got Twitter comments like 'I always feel the judgement gaze from all the "regulars" there'. For someone with good self-esteem a moment of rudeness isn't a big deal. If a shop assistant is rude, for instance, a person with good self-esteem can shake it off – they understand it has no relation to who they are; maybe that person was having a bad day – it's about them. But if we start from a place of feeling worthless, a rejection or rude remark devastates us because it *confirms what we subconsciously believe about ourselves.*

Because feeling invalidated is so painful, we often employ the defence mechanism of rejecting before we are rejected. This is why sometimes we are sneery and nasty to each other and why, as I was told by some men, sometimes in Old Compton Street men look down at their feet or avoid the street altogether: they are scared of being rejected and (in their minds) having their feelings of low self-worth confirmed. Of course we don't understand this on a conscious level, so we walk away from such experiences with the belief that 'those gays made me feel bad – gays are mean' rather than the more realistic 'I have a problem with my self-esteem which I have to work on and if anyone was unpleasant to me it's because they probably have a problem with anger management or with their self-esteem too.'

Extreme objectification

Both negative mirroring and invalidation feed another problem, which again affects straight people too, of course, but which dominates aspects of gay men's experience: objectification. My sexual behaviour got really out of control in my late twenties after the end of a serious relationship. I made a semi-conscious decision not to engage emotionally with anyone as I just couldn't cope with feeling hurt like that again. I shut down that part of me because the risk of pain was too scary. My sexual behaviour became intense. I didn't understand that I was constantly seeking validation. I felt terrible, and the hotter the person I could attract, the better I felt about myself. But it only lasted while they were there and it walked out the door with them as they left.

This is common amongst people who have been shamed. One handsome young man in his mid-twenties told me his experiences of gay men were so bad he was giving up dating. He wrote, 'I don't give a damn about them (men) anymore and that's why I don't have relationships . . . I don't even cuddle'. When I used to go to get my hair cut as a teenager I'd hear one of the hairdressers talking about her 'gay mate who doesn't do relationships'. Taken to an extreme, when people withdraw from relationships it is called **emotional anorexia**, while withdrawing from sexual intimacy is called **sexual anorexia**; this is the flipside of sex addiction. Often people switch from one to the other: all then nothing then all again.

A problem of using sex as a way of fixing our feelings is that we always need a hotter guy to make us feel good about ourselves, meaning no one is ever good enough. An extraordinarily handsome older friend of mine has recently found himself single and on the scene again. He said, 'Guys fall over themselves to speak to me and when I do it's almost like they achieved what they set out to do and so now they are on to better and bigger things. They can't look me in the eye because they are busy looking elsewhere.' Again, of course this happens with straight people, but because for us there is not much alternative to either going on the scene or using apps where the dominant culture is of hooking up, then being sexually attractive assumes more and more importance, to the point where it can feel it's all that matters.

Looking for a boyfriend, there are various meaningful things on a checklist: personality, interests, character, kindness, sense of humour, for instance. But if we're just looking for a hook-up, then physical appearance becomes the main requirement. Such a huge focus on casual sex isn't problematic for reasons of morality, but because it demands higher and higher standards of physical perfection – better bodies, bigger penises, bigger chests, more attractive smile, perfect skin and so on. The most desirable man receives the greatest validation and is himself most prized because he can give the most validation to other people.

Standards can spiral ever upwards until even stunningly attractive people feel they're not good enough. Gym and diets become, for many of us, obsessions absolutely crucial to our sense of self-esteem, with 'likes' of shirtless selfies becoming the way we get our hits. Being sexually objectified sounds great! What's not to like? But objects don't have feelings; people can't truly connect with them or have deep relationships with them. Combined with our sexual self-objectification as just 'tops' or 'bottoms' – at its extreme, as seen in app culture – a herd mentality arises of no boundaries, no respect for ourselves or others, no line that cannot be stepped over no matter how it hurts us or others.

Taken to its limit, when this 'extreme objectification' dominates, only men who validate us are even worth talking to. The old drag trope becomes the motto by which we relate to one another: 'Either fuck me or fuck off!' Everyone else is dead to us. At its worst we become Primark people: no longer brothers, or even friends, just holes and human dildoes; throwaway people having throwaway relationships.

This is when you hear things like this, from the young man I mentioned above who had withdrawn from relationships after being cheated on. I told him he seemed nice and had lots to look forward to. He replied, 'I'm far from nice. You can't survive the gay world being nice . . . I used to [be nice] but it only made me suffer . . . You have to adapt'. He told me his partner cheated on him, called him a piece of shit and told him that 'all he could see when he looked at me was my belly'.

In 2013 on BuzzFeed, Louis Peitzman, referencing activist Dan Savage's 'It Gets Better' youth campaign, wrote an article entitled 'It Gets Better, Unless You're Fat'. He said that although he no longer experiences homophobia from the wider world, he is ostracized by gay men because of his weight. 'I deleted Grindr after one night when a stranger messaged me to let me know that if I shed a few pounds I "might actually be cute",' he wrote. Fat gay men are ignored or ridiculed, he said: 'We just don't matter. It doesn't get better for us'.

The more cynical will say, 'Tough – that's life: hotter people get more attention,' and that's true. But when sexual desirability becomes the overridingly dominant currency, then we're all on borrowed time, even those who might feel secure in their hotness. None of us is twenty-five for ever. Even my extraordinarily attractive older friend told me, 'I am marvelling at the speed at which I am slowly becoming invisible . . . as I hit my mid-forties I am disappearing before my very eyes'.

In 2015 *FS* magazine published the results of a survey about men's experiences of racism on the gay scene. It is extremely painful to read. Between 64 and 80 per cent of people from BAME (black, Asian and minority ethnic) backgrounds said they had encountered it. Commonly they'd been blocked on apps or called racist names. Of black and South-east Asian men interviewed, 63 per cent said that racism on the gay scene was a bigger issue for them than homophobia. Men talked of being asked if they were drug dealers or terrorists. Some respondents pointed out that racism was also a problem in the mainstream bars and clubs, but there seemed to be a painful expectation that the gay scene is meant to be a place where prejudice has been left behind. One man said, 'I'd rather be somewhere that's homophobic than somewhere that is racist, because I can't pretend to be a different skin colour or race.'

Another disturbing theme in *FS*'s report was how race played such a dominant part in sexual objectification: black men were trophies and fetishized; South-east Asian men were considered gold-diggers who were only attracted to white men; Asian men were either ignored or just treated as someone to have sex with but not to date. (Obviously there are lots of gay men who aren't racists and lots of people in happy, healthy mixed-race relationships, but racism is clearly a significant problem.)

Having their value as sexual partners put before anything else – before any consideration of their merits as human beings – is inevitably a factor in the greater than average levels of low self-esteem, suicide, HIV infection and other related problems in gay men from ethnic minority backgrounds. A 2011 study by Louis F. Graham at the University of Michigan in Ann Arbor showed a disproportionate amount of depression and low self-esteem amongst black gay men, with 'homo-negativity' being a significant part of the problem.

Again, I want to emphasize that being 'on the gay scene' is not all like this. Lots of us just go out, have a drink, have fun. But all these people have told me there is a problem that seems to be getting worse. So many of us come from a place where we've felt not good enough and have had to change to fit in, and then we've found ourselves in another place where we still feel not good enough and have to change to fit in.

If our physical appearance is what we actually see of ourselves, then it is this that is, so often, the focus of our low self-esteem – and our desire to change.

10

Compare and Despair:
Food, Perfection, Body Image and Control

'I have body issues, absolutely, slight body dysmorphia . . . it's about self-esteem and confidence . . . on a bad day . . . I will look in the mirror and what I see will not be how I am . . . I know it's crazy'.

Dr Christian Jessen, presenter of *Embarrassing Bodies*,
interviewed in *Attitude*, 2010

'When I got my diagnosis, I was thrilled. I said "Oh, AIDS! Doctor, thank GOD! I thought you said I had aged!"'

Robert Patrick, *Pouf Positive*

SOMETIMES ON A FRIDAY night Tim would load so much food on to the conveyor belt he would talk into the phone to himself.

'I would say, "Yeah, babe, how many people are coming round?"' he told me. '"Ten? I'll get enough for ten people then."'

Back at home he'd eat the lot; it was usually all gone in around fifteen minutes. Then he'd roll over, pass out and spend the next day bingeing, watching films, smuggling food in, keeping up a pretence to his flatmates that nothing was wrong.

Tim was seriously obese even by the time he was at secondary school. At thirteen he weighed thirteen stone. Strangers regularly abused him. Women sneered at him in clothes shops, kids threw eggs and adults made faces and shouted at him from cars. But all this did was make him eat more. It also drove him to perform. 'I would do anything to take the focus away from being called gay or fat, so I was attention-seeking, performing on buses, chatting girls up, pinching their bottoms, getting slapped, making people laugh.'

When he came out on to the gay scene something switched and he exercised like crazy, shed pounds and found that inside was an attractive young man. He had several years of making the most of his new slim body, but then after he got cheated on he started overeating again and regained the weight. He found himself in a continuous cycle of piling on weight, losing it, then putting it back on again. 'I was swinging from bingeing on food to bingeing on exercise,' he explained. 'It was the same with all my behaviour. I could not do anything in moderation.'

In his early thirties, at nineteen stone, things reached a climax. Guys in bars regularly laughed at him. A tramp in the street told him to 'lose some fucking weight'. He found himself drinking in the darker gay venues (in both senses of the word) because the people in them 'were even unhappier than I was' and a grope in a dark corner was the only physical contact he could get.

'The worst thing about being in those bars is that people wouldn't even look at me,' he said. 'It was like I represented their worst fears. I could handle being rejected, but people just stare through you. I couldn't even pull in darkrooms, because though people can't see you, they can touch you. That was probably the loneliest time.'

Tim started making himself sick to create room for more food and the cycle swung from the shame of bingeing to the exhilaration of knowing that he could empty his stomach. Sometimes he would find himself repeating this cycle up to ten times a day, with bags of sick all over his room.

'It was horrendous,' he said. 'I know it doesn't make sense, but I couldn't stop. I would throw up in the street, terrified people would see, or vomit in the shower at work, having diarrhoea at the same time. I'm sure colleagues were aware of it. You cannot have a normal life when you are doing this.'

Dieting is a global sport. In 2013 the diet industry in the UK alone, according to the *Independent*, was worth £2 billion. But despite this there is little conversation about what really causes severe obesity, or about the fact that overeating can be an eating disorder just as anorexia is. We all see regular newspaper stories of people literally eating themselves to death, such as Brenda Flanagan-Davies from Tyne and Wear, who died from a heart attack in 2013 aged forty-four weighing forty stone. Often these people claim they want to lose weight, whilst doctors and media commentators scratch their heads, saying it's a metabolism or lifestyle problem, as I saw on television recently. They talk in desperation of cases where people have burst their gastric bands after continuing to binge on food, yet people rarely mention the word 'addiction' or talk of mental health or, crucially, recovery.

But scratch beneath the surface and you will find seeds of understanding that eating disorders, for gay and straight people, are fundamentally symptoms of emotional problems.

Eatingdisorderssupport.co.uk states that those suffering with anorexia 'have a low self-esteem and often a tremendous need to control their surroundings and emotions. [Anorexia] is a reaction to a variety of external and internal conflicts, such as stress, anxiety, unhappiness and a way of dealing with the feelings of the rest of the person's life being out of control.'

The website for the charity B-eat.co.uk includes comments from people suffering with bulimia: 'I used to eat as much as I could, as quickly as possible, to try to make myself feel happier and fill the hole I felt inside.' And: 'I thought that people wouldn't like me if they knew what I was really like . . . the deeper my hunger became, the greater the sense of control I felt being restored'.

The charity Men Get Eating Disorders Too quotes the National Institute of Health and Clinical Excellence (NICE), which suggests that 1.6 million people in the UK were affected by eating disorders in 2004 and 180,000 (11 per cent) of them were men. Other studies suggest similar figures. In 2007 the NHS Information Centre carried out a snapshot survey of people in England over the age of sixteen and found that 6.4 per cent of adults had a problem with food, a quarter of them men. They also state that gay/bisexual men are at particular risk and note that the Eating Disorder Association found that 20 per cent of male sufferers were gay, several times the estimated 4 per cent of gay/bi men in the population.

In *The Invisible Man: A Self-help Guide for Men with Eating Disorders, Compulsive Exercise and Bigorexia*, the author John F. Morgan, writing for his majority straight male readership, explains that for many of the men he has encountered with body-image and eating disorders, trauma is often the basis for their condition:

> If someone mugs you at the bus stop, you will probably feel very anxious for a few weeks then put it behind you and get on with your life. But if you get mugged every month or beaten up by your dad every Saturday night it begins to get under your skin and changes you as a person, altering the way you see yourself and the way you see the world around you. It even changes the wiring in your brain, and the brain adapts to constant fear.

Sound familiar?

As we saw in Chapter 7, if people feel constantly bad or anxious, they often reach for the thing closest to hand to medicate their feelings, and the first thing available to them is food.

It's no surprise. Studies have shown that, like drugs, ingesting sugar and other complex carbohydrates which convert to sugar (such as white-flour products) causes a dopamine release that gives us a high.

In recent years the world seems to have begun to realize how addictive sugar is. In 2013 the *Daily Telegraph* reported that the head of Amsterdam's health service, Paul van der Velpen, had declared that sugar should be restricted and regulated. 'This may seem exaggerated and far-fetched,' he said, 'but sugar is the most dangerous drug of the times.' He went on, 'Whoever uses sugar wants more and more, even when they are no longer hungry . . . Sugar is actually a form of addiction . . . Thereby diets only work temporarily. Addiction therapy is better.'

As with the iceberg theory of addiction (see page 113), body-image disorder is just one of the behaviours that arise from child-hood trauma. Our bodies are the physical manifestation of who we are, so it makes sense that if we don't like ourselves then the first thing we don't like is our bodies. Of course everyone experiences not liking how they look sometimes, but when you *really* don't like your-self then it will manifest as *really* not liking the way you look.

Body dysmorphic disorder is when a person cannot see the reality of what they look like. Often they believe they are ugly or become obsessed with a perceived flaw.

There are plenty of examples of people in the public eye who seem obsessed with changing their looks. One is Alicia Douvall – real name Sarah Howes – a former model who appeared on *Big Brother* in 2015. She has had more than 150 procedures at a cost of more than £1.5 million, including having her toes shortened because she didn't like the way her feet looked in sandals. She believes her need for surgery is an addiction. 'It's like being an alcoholic,' she is quoted as saying. For her it seems to have stemmed from childhood trauma. In an interview with the *Sun* in 2009 she said she had been abused. 'I had a very, very unhappy childhood. From the moment I woke up I lived in fear . . . I killed off Sarah Howes a long time ago and for years I wouldn't allow myself to think about her or to remember anything because it was too painful. I never told a soul about the abuse. All I ever wanted to do was reinvent myself as Alicia Douvall because I hated myself so much. I thought I was the ugliest person in the world.'

Alicia's words are mirrored in a study by J. D. Feusner *et al.* published in the journal *Psychiatric Annals* in 2010, which found a strong link between body dysmorphia and childhood abuse and neglect; other studies suggest a link with anxiety disorders and obsessive compulsive disorder.

When men appear in the media with similar body-image or surgery obsessions they always seem to be gay. Jordan James Parke is a twenty-three-year-old make-up artist who hit the headlines at Christmas 2014 after he spent £100,000 trying to make himself look like Kim Kardashian, blowing his lips up until they looked like pillows. A twenty-two-year-old orange-coloured man called Ryan Ruckledge appeared in the media in February 2015, addicted to potentially dangerous illegal tanning injections despite the fact that they were giving him heart palpitations. A month later a twenty-year-old called Nathan Thursfield, who has spent £40,000 in a bid to look like Katie Price, appeared on *This Morning*. Several men have had thousands worth of surgery to look like a 'Ken doll', including American Justin Jelica and British resident Rodrigo Alves. In August 2015 thirty-five-year-old Tobias Stebel, who had appeared in the TV shows *Botched* and *My Strange Addiction* after spending $100,000 to make himself look like Justin Bieber, was found dead in his hotel room. He had recently broken up with his boyfriend and police found drugs in the room.

In March 2014 I noticed an article in the press headlined 'The teenager addicted to selfies'. Nineteen-year-old Danny Bowman took hundreds of selfies every day, pawing over perceived flaws and blemishes in his appearance until the point where he tried to kill himself. I had no idea if he was gay or not, but I met him for a coffee and he brought his charming boyfriend. He is very handsome, but in 2012 he was so convinced he was hideous that he didn't leave the house for six months. I asked him about growing up.

'I went to a school where you had to aim high,' he told me. 'There was pressure on you for success and lots of good-looking boys and girls. I couldn't control what exam results I got, I couldn't control how well I did at sports . . . the only thing I could personally control was my image.'

As I said in Chapter 7, the issues of **control** and **perfection** are central to addiction. Feeling constantly under threat makes us feel out of control and anything that affects our mood even temporarily gives us the illusion of regained control.

Danny said he was bullied at school because he liked fashion and things that pinpointed him as gay. 'They called me homo, gay, made jokes about "up the arse" and things like that . . . That was kind of what started the ball rolling of trying to seek perfection.'

Did he feel that there was a link between the bullying and the body dysmorphia? 'Yeah, there's definitely some connection,' he agreed. '[I thought if I controlled the way I looked it] would enable me to become more popular and get more friends. [I channelled all my insecurity] to the way I look. People said my nose was hooky. I thought my bone structure wasn't right, that I had splotchy skin. I thought I had extreme acne at one point and I would cover my face with spot cream. It escalated to the point where everything was a problem. I'd go to the hairdressers six or seven times even after I had my hair cut. I thought I was fat and would throw up to make myself skinnier. It became my life. [Feeling bad] wasn't a one-day thing, it was every single day.'

Although there is little research on how sexual orientation affects body-image and eating disorders, the few studies that there are do bear this out. In 2014 statistics in the *International Journal of Eating Disorders* found that 42 per cent of men in their study who had an eating disorder were gay or bisexual, and that gay or bisexual men were three times more likely than straight men to have body-image issues. It suggested that 4 per cent of gay men suffer from bulimia and a staggering 20 per cent appeared to be anorexic. (In a salon.com article about the study entitled 'A hidden epidemic: eating disorders in the gay community', writer Troy Roness said his own eating disorder was a way of controlling anxiety.) In the UK, the PACE RaRE study 2015 found that gay and bisexual men had higher levels of dissatisfaction with their weight, body shape, musculature and eating habits.* Meanwhile a 2013 study by Brigham and Women's Hospital in Boston, Massachusetts,

---

* Amongst respondents to the survey, 59.6 per cent of gay/bi men were dissatisfied with their weight compared to 45.5 per cent of heterosexual men; 59.2 per cent of gay/bi men were dissatisfied with their body shape compared to 40 per cent of straight men; 58.2 per cent of gay/bi men were unhappy with how muscular they were compared to 40.6 per cent of straight men.

stated it 'is now well established that women of minority sexual orientation are disproportionately affected by the obesity epidemic'.

Over the years I have worked at *Attitude* I have been amazed at the number of people who have written to me asking to have their weight story in the magazine – it's usually how they were overweight as kids and how happy they are to have lost it, usually compulsively, and that they now fit into the gay world. Emails like this one from a PR agent which arrived while I was writing this chapter:

Dear Matthew,

X, aged 21, recently came out as gay.

As a teenager he was depressed and overweight. Since coming to terms with his sexuality, in the last year he has shed 5 stone (started off at 20 stone) and has another 1 stone to lose. He goes to the gym 3 or 4 times a week. He's now confident and looking for love! Before and after pictures are attached. He is happy getting his shirt off for a photo shoot etc. Would you like to feature him?

If we did a study – and I hope someone does – I am absolutely confident that it would reveal a common pattern in gay/bi men of weight gain (due to compulsive comfort eating) as children followed by obsessive weight loss as adults and bulking up, in part, to 'fit in' to the pressured 'gay world'. But there are also other, unique complications for gay people. We have complex relationships with our bodies and those of people we find attractive.

Michael, typical of many gay men I know, a regular, handsome guy in his late twenties, goes to the gym often, doing a mixture of weight training, swimming and yoga from seven to ten times a week, as well as street running at least twice a week. He told me he'll never be happy with the way he looks. 'Depending on what day of the week you ask me, I'll tell you that I'm too fat or I'm too thin. I have an unhealthy obsession with trying to get a six-pack, as though getting one will somehow make people like me.'

Michael's compulsive exercising began after he had a nervous breakdown and his doctor encouraged him to go to the gym as part of his recovery, something on which he became hooked.

He said he has a complicated relationship with images of hot men. 'I find it difficult watching porn or looking at photo shoots of people I find attractive because I end up feeling more sad than turned on,' he explained. 'This has resulted in a constant battle of following and unfollowing hotties on Twitter and Instagram.'

He touches on an inherent complication for gay people. Heterosexual attraction is a state of being attracted to 'the other', whilst homo attraction is a state of attraction to 'the same'. That's not to say straight people don't feel insecure about their looks, but in homosexual attraction there is, on some level, an act of direct comparison. There is a saying in recovery, '**compare and despair**', which means you'll always feel bad if you judge yourself against other people; but for us, every feeling of attraction to another person – a man, like us – is also a direct comparison to what we perceive as attractive, and it can be continually painful.

Google-Image the word 'gay' – try it – and mostly what you'll see (and probably what you're after) are shots of perfect bodies in pants. A world that does not tend to show the full expanse of our lives and relationships represents us, instead, as uniformly hot and available.

Michael said that when he was coming out the gay press was very important to him but that now magazines such as *Attitude* and *Gay Times* seem to be all about buff white guys, which he finds depressing. He says he's aware of 'how ridiculous it is to feel bad because of what you see in a magazine . . . but still I look at their glowing skin, toned muscles, then directly compare it to myself and all I see is the bags under my eyes, fat around my waist and my chin slowly sinking into my neck.'

As you can imagine, this is a sensitive issue for me. *Attitude* has been very sexual; over the years both the readers and staff, including me, have been enthusiastic about sex and sexual content. As amongst straight people, sex sells. *Attitude* has always had lots of non-shirtless covers, but they aren't the ones people remember. But when I took over as editor we ditched the annual 'Porn' issue and the adult chat-line ads. We did a 'Stonewall Youth' issue, and on the covers we had celebrities like Take That, James Franco, Beth Ditto (the first lesbian on an *Attitude* cover) and Kele Okereke (the first black gay man on the cover). But they didn't sell well. Someone angrily challenged me at an event: 'You'd never put Stephen Fry on the cover, would you?!' So we did – and it was the lowest-selling issue I'd produced at that time. This was not a reflection of Stephen Fry's popularity, but of the reality that our readers wanted flesh from us. My boss, who naturally wants to sell magazines, shouted at me. Who can blame him? No business aims to sell less product.

But, despite commercial pressures, I intentionally continued to mix up the popular shirtless covers, which do sell well, with non-shirtless covers, which sometimes do, mostly don't. Inside, I've made sure we are as diverse as possible – we do real people, an interview with a man over fifty every month, real couples, a monthly body feature that shows a regular man with a normal body, and more. Lots of people don't notice – there is a general perception that all we do is 'Naked' issues, presumably because those are the ones most readers buy – but some do. When gay health magazine *FS* ran a survey on body image in 2015 and asked which magazine does the best job representing the diversity of gay men, *Attitude* scored highest with 51 per cent, *Gay Times* next at 32 per cent, *QX* at 5 per cent and *Boyz* at 4 per cent.

The situation is frustrating though. Whilst writing this book someone complained to me that they loved *Attitude* but wished we would put a guy with a regular body with his shirt on on the cover. The issue on shelf at that moment was *Sherlock*, *Spectre* and *Pride* star Andrew Scott, clothed. In June 2015, when we launched the Attitude Pride Awards, celebrating twelve 'real' people who embodied the spirit of gay pride – including a ninety-year-old man, a Ugandan refugee and more – I made the decision to put them all on the cover, against the wishes of many of the staff. That cover is the one that I am most proud of. But, as expected, the sales dipped from the shirtless cover the month before. When it comes to gay magazines, people say they want something that in reality they don't buy.

A gay interest in buff bodies is not a new thing and there was never a golden age when gay magazines didn't use sexy images to sell copies. Back in 1982, in the same issue in which *Gay News* first warned its readers about AIDS, it featured an article about the growing popularity of bodybuilding. 'Regulars on the male gay scene,' it reported, 'if they are not too busy snapping the tops off beer bottles with their own biceps, will have noticed some of their acquaintances undergoing dramatic changes in the last two or three years.' Asking why gay men were working out, one man said, 'I'm certainly not the man of my dreams', while another revealed, 'Five years ago I was a drag queen. I've gone from one extreme to the other . . . It got hold of me. I wanted to do more and more.'

In short, we all drive the body obsession that we complain about. It comes from us. It's rife on apps. On Facebook a noticeably bigger proportion of gay friends' images are shirtless and hyper-self-conscious, often looking like they've been desperate to find an excuse to post a selfie. Davey Wavey is a gay internet personality who posts lots of sexy selfies to his 140,000 Twitter followers. On his website – daveywaveyfitness.co.uk – he made an entry about the phrase 'Straight skinny, gay fat', meaning that what is skinny to straight people is fat to gay men. 'A few extra pounds on a straight guy isn't a big deal,' he wrote. 'But in the gay world, it's a different story altogether . . . Maybe the idea of "gay fat" wouldn't bother me so much if it wasn't killing people.'

As I described in Chapter 9 on the gay scene, when sex becomes the main thing we want from each other then we throw fuel on the fire of body fascism and standards get higher and higher. Combined with our childhood-trauma-driven need for perfection, our insecurities about our masculinity and the fact that in the 1980s skinniness was a marker for unhealthiness and disease, this means many of us become obsessed with bulking up.

'Bigorexia' is a term coined in 1997 to describe a form of body dysmorphia where men obsess about having bigger muscles and cannot see how muscly they are – it is the flip side of anorexia, the condition in which people starve themselves – and it is a significant problem amongst some gay men, for whom steroids become part of their lives.

Sam is a friend of mine in his early forties, six foot something and built. He is one of the biggest, most attractive men I know. Elements of his story are predictable, but the way his need to feel good enough has developed is not.

Growing up, Sam felt incredibly anxious and unsafe. He soothed himself by beginning to masturbate over characters like Superman and The Hulk. 'It was a way to cope,' he told me. 'It was about feeling powerless and having some power – which is what *The Incredible Hulk* is about. In my mind I was really big and strong and standing up to people – being powerful, basically. The hulk thing is like sexualized trauma for me. It's basically an expression of sexualized rage.'

As he grew up, Sam felt more and more strongly that he was 'not enough', saying he felt 'all wrong'. 'I have this core shame focused on my body, so I became obsessed with it. The feeling was: I know I'm shit in every other way, but if my body was OK it wouldn't matter.'

During his teenage years Sam was convinced there was something wrong with him and demanded doctors test him for growth problems. There was nothing wrong. He began obsessing about protein powders and buying bodybuilding magazines. After recovering from a suicide attempt at university when a relationship ended, he found himself being complimented about his body for the first time when, high on ecstasy, he took his shirt off in a club. 'This drag queen said, "Oh, nice body," and honestly it was like, "What? You're being serious?? Wow!" It was really powerful. I had no interest in him; it was just someone giving me validation for my body. After all that time, that was quite a life event.'

At the age of twenty-two Sam came to London and started going to the Love Muscle night at The Fridge and then to the all-nighter Trade. 'It just ticked all the boxes for me. I could go and stare at all these bodies. I felt completely inadequate but really drawn to it. If someone gave me some attention with my top off I would be through the roof and if nobody did I would be through the floor.'

He says he wasn't successful at meeting men because he looked so paranoid. 'I made some friends, but a lot of my time in clubs I was feeling incredibly lonely. People used to ask if I was a drug dealer because I looked so tense.'

Sam told me he believes most of the men in those clubs who look amazing – gym bunnies, as he calls them – take steroids. Steroids were used in the 1980s to treat gay men with AIDS who were suffering loss of body muscle; used incorrectly they can cause liver failure, acne, aggression (known as 'roid rage'), shrunken testicles, infertility, high cholesterol, high blood pressure and neurological issues. Back in 2004 the BBC news online website ran a story called 'Body of deceit' about the growing number of gay men injecting steroids. Pete, a twenty-nine-year-old accountant, is quoted as saying, 'All my gay friends work out and about half use steroids . . . When I look in the mirror I think I want to get bigger . . . I have an image in my head of what I want to look like and who I want to attract.'

In 2007 Sam did two cycles of steroids, injecting into his buttocks, but found the results disappointing. He looked awful, he said, with a permanently flushed face.

He eventually moved on to using bodybuilding websites where he could spend hours speaking to men, masturbating, even though they don't actually talk about sex. Officially, the forums he goes on are mainstream sites for straight men and women to swap workout tips. But according to Sam, many of the people on them, even those who say they are women, are actually like him – gay or bi men getting off by talking about being massively muscly and how awful it is not to be like that.

'It is the most weird, self-hating place,' he told me. 'It's about rejecting and being rejected. There are people going, "Oh there are gay people in here and they are the worst." Really sexualized gay-bashing. They're obviously gay themselves. It's bonkers.'

Sam is one of the nicest guys I know and he cringed as he told me that the thrill comes from talking about humiliating men who are not muscly. In one scenario he pretends he is a woman discussing with bigger men how wimpy her boyfriend is; in another he is a stacked schoolteacher who gloats over the bullying of averagely built students. 'We'll discuss how all youngsters today want to be muscly because that's all that's acceptable and that being thin is absolutely unacceptable and they deserve to be bullied.'

Some of you reading this may think, 'Who cares? It's not hurting anyone.' But Sam says he's like an alcoholic who cannot stop once he starts. A session can be for just two hours or it can last through the day and sometimes on until the early hours of the morning. Several times he has sat masturbating for over twenty-four hours solid without sleep.

'It's horrific,' he said. 'It's so self-shaming and destructive and nihilistic. I can't sustain an erection for that whole time and I've hurt myself doing it, but once I start I just can't stop. How do I feel afterwards? It makes me think I really do need to take steroids, that maybe that'll be the answer. Basically I feel sort of suicidal, not that I'd ever act on it, but I feel real despair and pain.'

Sam is now in recovery and has reached the point where this is happening less and less. He knows that building his body is not the thing that will alleviate the pain that is the basis of all this.

'I could take all the steroids in the world, but it would never be enough. It's the same with sex and romantic obsession. I say I love sex, but actually I think I'm terrified of sex and I don't really like it. For me, it's all about control, because for some reason my child-hood left me feeling out of control and that was terrifying because I thought I was going to be killed.'

Our bodies are how we present to the world and they are the key to one of life's greatest pleasures, the ultimate affirmation, the thing that everyone desires: love, sex, a relationship. If we have difficulty with how attractive we feel, it's no surprise that most of us can't actually attempt to find relationships, love or even friends without some liquid courage.

11

'You only tell me you love me when you're drunk': Alcohol

'I suppose it was inevitable that I'd turn to other ways of managing my feelings and I found alcohol. The more I tried it the more it suppressed my feelings. And a few years later when the black periods grew more frequent, I found that the more I drank, the better I felt – or rather, the less bad I felt, although that only lasted till the next morning when I woke up.'

Australian Olympic swimmer Ian Thorpe,
This Is Me: the Autobiography, 2012

'At the age of 30, I have found it quite difficult to remain socially active within the gay community while reducing my alcohol intake. And when I say difficult, I mean impossible'.

Tyler Curry, senior editor of *HIV Equal*,
writing on advocate.com, 'The Fine Line Between
Gay Pride and Alcoholism', 11 July 2014

DESPERATE TO GET TO a lock-in in a pub, driving drunk at seventy miles per hour down a narrow village road with two friends in the back of his Ford Fiesta and his wife next to him, David hit a humpback bridge with such force that his car flew over the roof of an oncoming vehicle, almost killing everyone in both vehicles. Happily still alive thirty years later, he now says that it didn't seem such a big deal at the time: at the height of his drinking when he was in his twenties and thirties, drunk-driving was just a normal part of his life.

David grew up in a working-class family in Lancashire in the 1950s and was a massively oversensitive child. At fifteen, awkward, with no friends, he began an apprenticeship at a local factory alongside four thousand boisterous Coventry City fans, an experience he described as 'terrifying'. One evening a representative of the local Conservative club knocked on his door trying to recruit new members. At the first meeting he realized that alcohol enabled him to relax and to be funny – and his dysfunctional relationship with drinking began.

During his time at the factory he had a fumble with a workmate, who promptly told their colleagues. In that moment, David decided that whatever those feelings were they could not be acted upon in the future. 'I decided, "No one's ever going to put me in that situation again, it's too dangerous."'

And so he drowned his feelings. Under pressure to find a girl-friend, he would stand around dance halls with colleagues watching the women and when he was drunk would move in and kiss a girl because that was what you were supposed to do.

David met a recently widowed woman and began what he calls 'the perfect codependent relationship'. On the day of their wedding his father hugged him for the first time – 'with a sigh of relief that he'd got this pansy to get married' – and a daughter soon came along, whom David adores. 'I was convinced there was going to be something wrong with her as I felt so bad about myself,' he said, 'and of course there wasn't. [But] the pain of being responsible for another human being was untenable. I couldn't cope with it. I was drinking like a fish.'

During the worst days of his drinking David was damaging himself in multiple ways. He developed gastritis – an inflammation of the stomach that is common in people who consume too much alcohol – and nearly killed himself several times falling out of trees and from the flagpole in the town centre. Sober, he was terrified of heights. Drunk, he would climb anything.

Eventually, in his mid-thirties, David finally found his way to Alcoholics Anonymous where he got sober. Then after about seven years of sobriety, one day driving down a village road with his wife and daughter in the car, he noticed a man, a cyclist, in shorts.

'I looked at him and it was like being kicked in the stomach. It was so visceral I had to look at Jane [my wife] to see if she'd noticed what had happened. The desire was so great. I thought Christ almighty, what's that about! I couldn't get over it.'

His attraction to men, which he'd suppressed for so long, was rising to the surface and didn't go away. He turned it over in his mind and discussed it with friends at AA meetings, then one day, when he was certain, he came home and told his wife he was gay. She said she'd known for three years and they agreed to split up there and then. He still finds the memory distressing.

'It was incredibly painful for everybody and I still can feel guilty. As far as I'm concerned I should have known at eighteen, fifteen, ten. But I couldn't. Didn't. When I should have been openly gay it was against the law.'

Although gay people no longer have the added pressure of il-legality, blocking out our feelings with alcohol remains a problem for some of us.

In the UK we are all, gay and straight, in denial about how dangerous alcohol really is. For 2013 the government estimated that costs to the NHS directly from alcohol misuse were more than £3.5 billion – more than £120 per taxpayer. I'd suggest this was an underestimation. Many deaths caused or contributed to by drinking are officially attributed to other causes. In 2012 Transport for London did some research into recorded pedestrian deaths on the city's roads. It found that of the 198 people aged between thirty and forty-nine who were killed, nearly half were impaired by alcohol. In the deaths of pedestrians aged between sixteen and fifty-nine, alcohol was a contributory factor in 38 per cent of cases. It reminds me of an accident I witnessed one evening in 2002. Standing on the corner of Old Compton Street and Wardour Street, I watched a young, effeminate guy and two young women fall into a seemingly drunken, giggling heap in the middle of the road. The women got up; he didn't, but sat there laughing instead. The minicab that drove into him simply did not see him.

A man I'll call Fiez, who works in A&E in a London hospital, agrees that often deaths caused by alcohol are not registered as such because the person has actually died of secondary injuries. He tells me they see many incidents with all sorts of people who, after a night out, or at home, have been so out of it they have fallen and banged their head, causing internal bleeding, the pressure of which bruises the brain and kills them. It is that fall and blow to the head that will be registered, not the alcohol that caused the fall.

This may have been what happened to Simon Hobart, one of the most influential and culture-defining gay club promoters of our time, the man behind Popstarz, Trash Palace and Ghetto. I knew Simon to say hello to, as I was always in his clubs. It was clear to anyone there that he drank too much – especially to those like me who were as paralytic as he was – but it was still devastating when, in late October 2005, the news came that he had died. Rumour spread that he had fallen down the stairs.

Tommy Turntables, a DJ who ran Popstarz with Simon, was his flatmate and best friend. He's never spoken about it publicly before but over email he told me, 'Simon was very drunk and it seems he fell over outside the door to our flat. He banged his head and passed out. It was a particularly cold night. No one knows for sure whether the head wound or the cold or the alcohol caused his death. At the inquest it was suggested that it was a combination. It's widely believed he fell downstairs, [but] this is not true.'

I asked him about Simon's drinking.

'Simon didn't really warm up till he was drunk. I think because he never drank in the daytime we, and he, believed it wasn't much of a problem. It wasn't like he needed a drink to get out of bed. But he did worry about it from time to time. Just a few weeks before his death . . . I sat him down and told him how worried I was. I also wrote him a long letter telling him my concerns.'

There's no doubt that Simon was one of the most important people in contemporary British gay life. He changed gay culture and gave a significant amount of his profits to charity. Who knows what he would be doing if he were still with us today. His death remains a deep loss to us all.

Of course, alcohol misuse is not just a problem for LGBT people. Tommy rightly pointed out to me that in the clubs he works in he sees straight people behaving messily just as often as gay people. Look on any British street at closing time at the weekend and you will see a lot of alcohol-based street violence and disarray. Glance at the internet and you'll see alcohol also contributes to a great amount of serious violence and domestic abuse in heterosexual relationships.

Again, most gay people do not have drink problems, and as with all aspects of our (gay) lives not a huge amount of research into alcohol abuse amongst LGBT people has been done, so it's hard to be sure of what's going on. Because sexual orientation is not recorded by the NHS, if there were, for instance, higher rates of liver cirrhosis amongst LGBT people, we simply wouldn't know. There are, however, a few studies that suggest alcohol use is more common amongst our community. A study by King *et al.*, published in *BMC Psychiatry*, found that LGBT people were at least one and a half times more likely to use alcohol and drugs than straight people, while the American Centers for Disease Control and Prevention acknowledges that, compared to the general population, gay and bisexual men, lesbians and transgender individuals are more likely to use alcohol and drugs and have higher rates of misuse.

Clearly, a significant part of the problem is that for generations we have had to go to bars and clubs in order to socialize and meet partners. In TV programmes such as *Absolutely Fabulous* we celebrate our overuse of alcohol, as writer Tyler Curry – who has admitted having to seriously address his own drinking – said in the *Advocate*: 'It is a part of the gay culture to laugh off alcohol abuse as part of our charm, a silly joke or a harmless offence. And for a while, it is funny! But every joke only lasts for so long, yet I was still part of the worn-out punch line'.

Liam is a friend of mine whom I've known for more than fifteen years. I used to think of him as a socialite: one of the faces I'd see in bars and clubs who was always out and knew everyone. I had no idea what was going on in his private life – probably because I didn't have much more of an idea what was going on in mine.

He told me he never felt safe at school, understood gay feelings were not acceptable and said the only gay person he knew was a boy who joined his school after being locked in his room at his previous school; the room had then been set on fire. Liam would share cigarettes with this boy but didn't want classmates to see them together. At university he found himself surrounded by students, many of them from Eton, casually throwing homophobic insults around.

'I was terrified about what I said and did and I think that's where a lot of my drinking problems started,' he said. 'I had a crippling fear of what other people thought about me, or what I thought they would think about me if they knew.'

Liam's drinking got worse when he ventured into the local gay club for the first time, where he used alcohol just to enable him to go in, and it stepped up again when he moved to work in London. There he became a classic example of 'Catholic School-girl Syndrome', which refers to people who are in a repressive and restrictive environment for so long that they go berserk when they get any freedom, like kids who've been denied sweets suddenly given the keys to the chocolate factory.

'I went from being ashamed of being gay in this smaller place to thinking I'm so fucking lucky to be gay in this amazing, dazzling world. There was a sense of there being no limits and no script – like no-holds-barred hedonism, which appealed to me massively.'

Liam never drank in the morning or sat in parks with a four-pack. What made him a problem drinker was the fact that once he started he couldn't stop – something we looked at in Chapter 7.

'After a while, every time I drank it would be a fast track to oblivion,' he said. 'Total chaos would always ensue from a night out. In many ways that was [what was] so exciting about it: I never knew where the night was going to take me. I would always lose my jacket, my keys, my wallet, my phone. That first drink was the start of a hellish inevitability that would always end the same way.'

He first had inklings that his behaviour was problematic when he saw the reaction of straight friends at birthdays and weddings. On one occasion he vomited in front of guests, went back for more and vomited again, and on another was escorted out of someone's home after smashing a bottle of vodka into a glass door.

Remember the cycle of addiction that I wrote about in Chapter 7? You can see how it worked in Liam's case below.

Despite loving his first serious boyfriend, at least once a week Liam would end the night in a sauna, sandwiched amidst a group of men. 'I was constantly paranoid,' he told me. 'If I had any feeling in my groin I was absolutely terrified that I'd caught crabs. I knew after a while that once alcohol touched my lips all bets were off. I would do things in blackout – or not – that you don't do when you're in a relationship.'

A 'blackout' is when you have no idea what you did for a period of time, usually after drinking too much alcohol. To have one means you are not in control of what you are doing. It is a sure sign of a

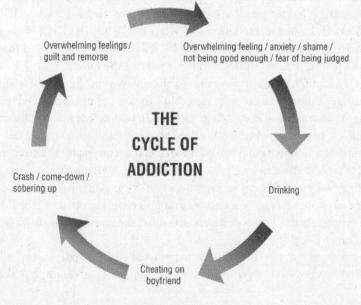

Overwhelming feelings / guilt and remorse

Overwhelming feeling / anxiety / shame / not being good enough / fear of being judged

THE CYCLE OF ADDICTION

Crash / come-down / sobering up

Drinking

Cheating on boyfriend

problem. In blackout people drink-drive, take sexual risks, argue with cab drivers, pass out in the streets or cheat on their partners.

'I felt terrible,' Liam said. 'The feelings of shame and regret became very intense and got worse and worse. Every time I drank, the feelings of not wanting to do it were overridden by this overwhelming feeling of wanting to do it. It's hard to explain.'

Liam pressed the 'fuck-it button' I described in Chapter 7 a lot. On the last night of a holiday to Berlin he had unsafe sex with a man whom he later found out was HIV positive. The next day he went to his local sexual-health centre from the airport and asked for PEP treatment – a month's course of HIV medication which, if you begin within seventy-two hours of exposure, can prevent you from becoming HIV positive. But to give the drugs the best chance of stopping the virus from getting hold, you cannot drink whilst taking them.

'I met up with a friend and I had all the pills laid out in front of me,' Liam said. 'I remember saying to him, really wrestling with it, "Fuck, I might have HIV and if I take this course of treatment it could eradicate it but it will mean I won't be able to drink for a month. What do you think I should do?" My friend, who has HIV himself, looked at me and said, "What the fuck? That's not even a debate. Take the pills."' It was only his friend telling him to do it that made him struggle through with the pills for the month.

In Liam's case, as his tolerance to alcohol went up, he started using drugs. 'I didn't like coke,' he said, 'but I took it because it allowed me to drink more and keep going. You couldn't drink that much without falling over otherwise.' By this time he was in his second major relationship, but his sexual behaviour was also becoming more extreme. He took home a homeless guy whom he came across slumped next to a cashpoint and, on another occasion, took a disabled guy home, he says out of pity. The next morning, feeling ashamed of treating someone badly, he hurried him out so fast the man was nearly hit by a car.

'I started to get really frightened of what would happen because I had no control of it. When I was with men, I'd take Viagra to make sure I could get a hard on, which isn't good – a mix of alcohol, Viagra and cocaine is enough to kill you. I'd often get chronic chest pain. I had trench mouth [acute ulcerating gingivitis] as I'd never brush my teeth at night. I had pleurisy. My body was begging for help. But the main damage was being done to my brain and my self-esteem. What had enabled me to get over my nerves of going to a gay bar when I was eighteen was completely controlling me. I was dependent on alcohol to be at all social, but then it became the reason I would fuck up at social occasions. It was a downwards spiral.'

Jack is twenty-nine and in recovery for his drinking problem. We heard from him back in Chapter 5: he was the child whom an adult called 'a poof' when he was about six years old and who said the bullying at school was so relentless that he stopped telling his mother about it and at eighteen was wishing that he could just have one day off. He told me that the first time he walked into London's biggest gay club, G-A-Y at the Astoria, and saw hundreds and hundreds of people with the same sexuality he thought he'd found freedom.

'I was so filled with excitement,' he remembered. 'It felt like I'd arrived; it was all going to be great now . . . '

Because he was slim, older men found him attractive and he went with them, sometimes because he wanted to, sometimes because he felt he should, sometimes because he didn't know how to say no. He said he felt intimidated at times, that some older men seemed to enjoy treating younger men badly, through a kind of homophobic assumption that being young and slim – a 'chicken' or 'twink' – meant they were lesser men, not deserving of respect. He began a relationship with an older man, in part, he says now, because it gave him some power, but regularly found himself in dangerous situations because of his drinking. On one occasion he was refused re-entry to G-A-Y at Heaven, after going out for a cigarette, because he was so drunk. Then he remembers coming out of blackout lying on the other side of the Thames, on London's South Bank, in just his T-shirt and pants, no shoes, socks or trousers, with a group of girls asking him if he was OK.

'I was hammered, crying, I looked like I'd been beaten up. I was so drunk they were asking me where I lived but I couldn't remember.' The girls took him to their flat in North London and in the morning he travelled home in a pair of their tracksuit bottoms to his angry boyfriend.

Another time, he visited friends outside London and instead of leaving the club with them to get his last train he stayed on for one last drink. He came out of blackout the next morning in a stranger's house. 'I felt I had to do something [sexual] with him to get out. So I said do whatever you want to do. I got to Paddington and I remember bursting into tears and crying all the way home on the tube – I could not stop sobbing. There were so many times like that. That's when I first started realizing that the only way was down and that I was really losing it.'

I began this chapter with David's story from the 1960s, where he got married in an attempt to make his sexuality go away. You might find that situation unusual, but fast-forward fifty years and it's remarkable how similar David's story is to that of twenty-seven-year-old Rugby League player Keegan Hirst, who came out in August 2015. In his late teens Hirst started dating a woman, whom he eventually married. He said, 'At first I couldn't even say "I'm gay" in my head, let alone out loud . . . Now I feel like I'm letting out a long breath that I've held in for a long time.' He also drank too much to bury his feelings. He told the *Sunday Mirror*, 'I was playing matches on a Sunday and then I'd go out and get in some ridiculous states . . . I was drinking 20 pints plus every time. I'd roll in at 5.30 on a Monday and have to be up for work at six . . . It wasn't that I wasn't happy with [my wife], it was that I wasn't happy with myself.'

For some people it is food that dulls their painful feelings, for some it is alcohol, for others it is drugs. Often alcohol is a gateway drug to harder substances. In the past, drugs popular with gay men have been substances such as ecstasy and cocaine, but today there is a new group of drugs that are far better at numbing internalized homophobia and shame – and far more dangerous.

12

Horny and High: Let's Talk About Gay Sex and Drugs

'Gay or bisexual adults were more likely to have taken any illicit drug in the last year than heterosexual adults. In particular, gay or bisexual men were the group most likely to have taken any illicit drug in the last year (33.0% had taken drugs in the last year), with higher levels of illicit drug use than gay or bisexual women (22.9%) and heterosexual men (11.1%).'

UK Crime Report, 2013/2014

It was 3 a.m. on a Friday morning in South London when Sean overheard one of the two men whose flat he was in saying that they should kill him. Sean challenged them: 'What? What did you just say?' They answered, 'Nothing, we didn't say anything,' but when he turned away he heard one of them whisper it again.

Panicking, he looked around the flat, his mind racing. He realized that he hadn't told anyone where he was, so if anything happened to him no one would know how to find him or who he was with. He looked up to see where the door was and saw that one of the men was whispering about him again, staring at him suspiciously. He knew he had one chance: he jumped up and bolted out of the door before they could stop him.

'My heart was beating out of my chest,' he told me over a beer in a London gay bar. 'I'm amazed I didn't die. I ran out of the place barefoot, headed on to a bus. I jumped on it . . . and then jumped off as it was moving, ran down the Clapham Road, completely high, running into shops asking for them to call the police.

'I was running down the High Street convinced that every single car going past was part of a South London drug gang that was trying to kill me. I turned into my road and thought thank fuck I'd made it home. There was a guy at the end of my street who I was convinced had a gun. I was like, "Come on then, let's have ya!" Looking back, I think he was a tramp. I was having conversations with people: "I know you're fucking going to do it, fuck you, just do it now then!" People were like, "Eh?" I got home, called an ambulance – but I thought the phone was hacked, still thinking somebody was after me. I had to ride that out for about a month. I should have gone to A&E, been knocked out, slept it off.'

Hallucinations are a common side-effect of crystal meth use, especially after you've been up for three days solid with no sleep. Once they start, they are likely to come back whenever you use. Sean's story is similar to that of a friend of mine, intelligent, early thirties, job in the media, HIV positive, who ended up using the same website Sean used to meet other positive guys – with whom he started injecting crystal meth, something he'd never done before. Similar to Sean, my friend found himself running through the streets of Stockwell banging on strangers' doors demanding to be let in, screaming that the government was after him.

Sean is a thirty-one-year-old, confident, brassy, gay man from the north-east of England who sometimes works as a DJ and who came to London eleven years ago to go to university. He was diagnosed with HIV in 2011 after 'getting twatted' on booze and cocaine, then going to a sex party. He says he dealt with his diagnosis and the feelings of being 'made to feel like a disease by my community' by meeting men on barebackrealtime.com, a website for men who want to have condomless sex.

Sean said his friends are worried about him, but he's not quite yet at the point where he's ready to commit to giving up drugs. He is worried about the hallucinations, though.

'It's happened several other times,' he told me. 'Once it's been trig-gered, I don't think you can go back. It keeps happening. The last time it happened was about a month ago.'

When I was growing up and out on the gay scene, the main popular drugs were alcohol, obviously, and poppers, speed, ecstasy and cocaine. Cocaine can do serious damage. I know a formerly successful man now living in a hostel after having lost his job, home and partner due to a severe cocaine and alcohol addiction. It's not news, as many have said, that gay men like using drugs to have sex. What is different is these new-generation drugs and just how powerful and dangerous they are.

A tall Australian ex-pat named David Stuart has virtually single-handedly brought the misuse of these new drugs to the attention of the public and the agencies charged with dealing with the health of gay and bisexual men, none of which seemed to have much of a clue what was going on. When I first met David, he was a manager at Antidote, London's only dedicated LGBT drug and alcohol service, which is part of London Friend, the LGBT health and wellbeing centre, working alongside a heroic gay woman called Toni Hogg. He now works at 56 Dean Street sexual-health centre in Soho as their first Substance Use Lead.

David explained why these drugs have become so prevalent. 'On the whole, we use drugs differently from straight people. Heroin was very popular amongst straight drug users in the eighties, and is used by people with a specific type of childhood trauma or abuse. Its effect is like having a warm blanket put over you and it makes you collapse for days on end on a sofa. Cocaine is popular in the gay commu-nity but it is almost used like alcohol, as part of an evening out. Yes, people become addicted to it and it does cause serious problems, but many people use it casually without too much harm. But internalized homophobia is ninety-nine per cent of the reason why people are coming to Antidote and that needs different drugs to fix it.'

David said that, beyond the drug use, men will talk of shame about being gay and having sex. 'It's all still there – things like the shame, feeling physically inadequate, a core belief that sex is dirty, that it's a sin and is associated with disease, and it's just a shameful, shameful thing. Internalized homophobia is made better by social activity and heroin doesn't enable that. What does help it are drugs that will keep you dancing for days, that will enable you to feel confidence, for your inhibitions to go – and will also facilitate sex.'

Let's have a look at these drugs.

Ketamine Also called K or ket, this is an anaesthetic used, infamously, to tranquillize horses. It creates feelings of disassociation from reality. Prolonged use damages the bladder, kidneys and the urinary system, and is responsible for a large number of people having to have their bladders and sometimes kidneys removed – yet the public are unaware of how dangerous it is.

Mephedrone Also known as MCat, meph and miaow miaow, mephedrone is in the amphetamine class of drugs. It is a stimulant and produces euphoria, sexual enhancement and feelings of love and joy – but also often paranoia, hallucinations, erratic behaviour and dehydration. It puts pressure on the heart and circulatory system. By 2016 it seems to have become the drug of choice for young men on the gay scene.

GHB (G) The full name of this drug is gamma-hydroxybutyric acid and it's sometimes known as 'liquid ecstasy', or G for short. A 'date-rape' drug, it is colourless, tasteless and easily mixed with drinks. It is a depressant, suppressing the central nervous system, and when taken with alcohol is even more dangerous. Overdoses lead to unconsciousness, which can induce coma and sometimes death. G makes people highly sexually aroused and can be extremely addictive. Withdrawal can be very dangerous. Often taken in the form of GBL, a wheel-cleaning solvent and paint-stripper sold online, which, ingested, metabolizes into GHB.

Crystal meth Methamphetamine, also known as Tina, T or ice, is expensive to produce and exceptionally powerful, addictive and dangerous. It gives an intense rush of euphoria, makes people incredibly confident, increases sexual desire and sexual confidence. The come-down is considered so bad there have been reports in America of people shooting others to get money to buy more crystal to alleviate it. Users can become paranoid, obsessive and sometimes violent – a specific part of the come-down known as 'tweaking'. It can permanently damage dopamine receptors in the brain, affecting the user's ability to feel pleasure for the rest of their lives.

For years G was sold in Soho sex shops as 'liquid ecstasy'. Mephedrone too was sold online and only banned in 2010. This 'legal high' status contributed to the mistaken belief amongst some that they could take these drugs without serious harm.

The 2013 EMIS Study [European Men who have Sex with Men Internet Survey] of over 15,000 men found that drug use is higher in London than in the rest of the country. In the capital, in the last four weeks of the survey: 11 per cent had used cocaine, 7.1 per cent ecstasy, 5.9 per cent ketamine, 5.5 per cent GHB/GBL, 5.2 per cent mephedrone, 2.9 per cent crystal meth and 0.2 per cent heroin.

When it came to men living in areas of South London – Lambeth, Southwark and Lewisham – figures were higher: 18 per cent had used cocaine in the last four weeks, 11.7 per cent ecstasy, 10.5 per cent GHB/GBL, 10.2 per cent mephedrone, 9.6 per cent ketamine, 4.9 per cent crystal meth and 0.1 per cent heroin.

A development amongst a small but not insignificant minority of men at sex parties in recent years has been 'slamming' – slang for shooting up (injecting) drugs, usually crystal meth or mephedrone. Getting the drug straight into the bloodstream heightens its effect and avoids damage to your throat and lungs, but it damages your veins and puts extra strain on your heart because of the intensity of the high. It can cause pulmonary embolism, where a clot goes to the lungs; it can make veins tighten and collapse; and it increases the risk of HIV and hepatitis.

Gay men have traditionally not injected drugs, but in the last ten years this has changed, because – people have suggested – many positive men are desensitized to needles after having bloods taken so often, and also because steroid use has become common. This tallies with what I have heard anecdotally. One friend I've known since we were teenagers told me he started injecting because he was at a sex party where men were smoking crystal and he had a packet of needles with him from his steroid use, so he showed them a quicker way to get a hit.

Since 2014 there has been more and more media coverage of the use of these new drugs by gay men. *Attitude*, *QX*, *Dazed & Confused*, the *Independent*, the *Guardian* and BBC radio have all covered the subject of 'chill-outs' – parties in people's homes that were originally simply a way of continuing after the clubs shut but have slowly come to be understood as sex parties, often held in their own right, usually fuelled by drugs and a never-ending supply of men from apps like Grindr and Scruff, and often lasting for days.

Some have accused the media of hysteria. Some online voices have been especially critical, one writing in January 2014 in response to an *Independent* article that talk of 'slamming' was rubbish, and saying of Antidote that they have exaggerated the problem in order to gain more funding. When the vice film *Chemsex* was released in autumn 2015 there were more suggestions that the problem was being exaggerated, based on homophobia and that David Stuart had a vested interest in talking this up.

Attention increased as the media covered the release of *Chemsex*. Then, at the end of October that year, forty-year-old Stephen Port was charged with the murder of four men in their twenties, allegedly killed with overdoses of GHB. Weeks later the *British Medical Journal* wrote that 'chemsex' was leading to increased risks of HIV and other STIs and should be treated as a public-health priority. The accusations of hysteria continued.

There's been more balanced criticism too. In August 2015 Jack Cullen wrote in *QX* magazine that he welcomed discussion of the issue but wanted to assert the social aspect of chill-outs and that people don't always take drugs. 'I for one have made some brilliant friends at chill-outs and after-parties,' he wrote. 'Often you end up just having a chat . . . It's a welcome respite from the stressful lives we ALL live . . . it's certainly not because we hate ourselves. If anything it's because we LOVE ourselves'. Former *Attitude* deputy editor Jamie Hakim, in the *Independent*, also focused on the pleasures and the 'bonding' that occurs, and questioned the link between drug use and unsafe sex, writing that 'the recent rise in HIV infection is, in fact, more likely to do with the poor quality of gay sex education available in Britain'.

I wanted to speak to someone with direct knowledge of the gay scene, so I went to meet Anthony Gilet, a twenty-four-year-old working-class man from Sydenham, South London, who worked as a promoter for many of the city's biggest gay clubs and runs a popular blog called Cocktails & Cocktalk. He told me what he believes is the experience of many young men arriving in London: the cheap drinks of the Ku Bar and G-A-Y are usually the first port of call and often the drugs come soon after. Anthony says that one morning, after Heaven shut, he and his friends discovered they could go on partying at an early-morning club in Vauxhall, where they began casually dabbling with mephedrone.

'We got there and we were like, this is the greatest place in the world, everyone's fucked! We went on like that for a couple of years. We'd go out at nine or ten p.m. [and] finish at about nine or ten in the morning. Sometimes we'd go to a sauna. Mephedrone had just come on the scene. It wasn't illegal then, it was a legal high. You'd order it in bulk off the internet, ten grams for £70. I was taking about twelve grams a weekend. We'd come home [from the club] and sit in our bedrooms and sniff meph while our parents did their Saturday stuff.'

Anthony and his friends then moved on to G and started going to sex parties. GBL is taken as a liquid, measured by pipette in 'doses' of millilitres that have to be timed and dropped into a drink such as cola. Getting the dose and timing correct is crucial: if you overdose you can go into a coma, commonly known as 'going under'. Under, sometimes people swallow their tongues or choke on their vomit. G suppresses your respiratory system and heart, so get the dose even more wrong and you might not wake up again. It doesn't take Einstein to realize that, high, it's easy to make mistakes. One man told me people sometimes keep a spreadsheet open to monitor timing. But going under happens all the time; it is a normal occurrence when a group of people take G. David Stuart estimates that although 95 per cent of people who go under wake up again, 5 per cent do not.

'G is *so* dangerous,' David says. 'It's more dangerous than heroin. People do die from overdosing. More than ten a year officially, which doesn't sound too high, but it's definitely more because it's really hard to establish that this is what killed them as it doesn't always show up in the bloodstream after death. Three new people a week were coming to [Antidote], every week for five years, because they were addicted to G and using it every hour. Once you are addicted you are really addicted. If they don't get their G on time their withdrawals are really dangerous and people can die from that alone, whether it's a physical thing like their heart stops or a seizure. They go into this confused state where they don't know where or who they are, and they walk out in front of traffic, for instance. And those deaths wouldn't be attributed to G. It's very, very dangerous and people are not educated about it.'

Accidents easily happen. One morning Anthony Gilet woke up, hungover, and drank from a bottle of water which he'd forgotten was in fact a half-litre of unmixed G that friends had given him because they believed their own use was taking over their lives. He tried to spit it out but had taken a gulp. He called his brother and then passed out, waking up in intensive care twenty-four hours later. His heart had stopped beating for a minute in the ambulance. Anthony has said that these days he avoids both G and mephedrone.

As long ago as 2007, *Time Out*'s then gay section editor Paul Burston wrote a powerful piece entitled 'London's Gay Scene in Crisis'. The article quoted Dr Sean Cummings of private gay GP practice Freedom Health as saying:

> GHB is a nasty, poisonous drug which is killing gay men on
> a regular basis. We've had a number of deaths of our patients

resulting from use of the drug, either together with other drugs or alone. Death often occurs during or immediately post-sex and so the victims are found in humiliating circumstances. The scenarios are usually awfully upsetting for all concerned, especially partners and family members. Coroners will frequently be coy to spare the feelings of loved ones [by recording accidental death], but this has the inadvertent effect of concealing the likely real numbers. There is nothing glamorous about finding a young man dead in a harness, having fallen, struck his head, inhaled his own vomit and suffocated.

In the same article, Burston also quoted Duckie club promoter Simon Casson, who asserted that he'd had countless invitations of unsafe sex since revealing he was HIV positive, and that he believed there was a strong connection between substance misuse and HIV risk. 'I think there is a significant constituency of gay men . . . who use a lot of drugs and who are into unsafe sex,' he said. 'It's actually not that socially taboo. It's quite accepted.'

I went to see Dr Cummings (a gay man) to ask how things are now. 'Dreadful,' he said blankly, adding that he is seeing 'lots of new positives' and people requiring urgent psychiatric treatment. 'To be honest, I find it depressing – the amount of drug taking and the psychological unhappiness that results from this mishmash of things that occur to us when we are younger seems often to lead to an almost never-ending cycle.'

He said that while drug use is common in the general population, as are depressive disorders, in his gay patients they often manifest as 'particularly destructive behaviour', adding that he frequently has a sense that the people who come to him are 'running away from who they are'.

'It surprises me. People commonly experiment and rebel at an early age, find a drug of choice, stick to it and eventually give it up. But I see a significant number of gay people who go completely off the rails in their forties and fifties. That's commonplace. It's not unusual for me to get a brand-new psychotic, whom I've never met before, who comes in with a friend and is off his head on something, and is, at a comparatively late age, still looking for who he is. They'll be agitated, physically unwell, not sleeping, paranoid, jumping up at the window thinking that the police or someone else is following them. They may ask me to take my phone out of the room and think they are being spied at through the windows. They may be fairly successfully navigating their lives until their late forties, then they develop an enthusiasm for crystal or other drugs and very often those will send people completely insane. I've got several of those on the go at any one time. There will be lots more in the pipeline.'

In 2010, consultants at Chelsea & Westminster Hospital's HIV and AIDS Kobler Clinic were concerned about a trend they had noticed in some of their patients who were not taking their HIV medication on time. Even occasionally skipping doses can facilitate drug resistance. If you stop taking tablets as directed, then the medication – which prevents HIV from progressing to AIDS, which will kill you – can stop working properly. A small research project had found that the vast majority of these men had begun using crystal meth and G. They reported their findings to the leaders of the hospital's drug treatment centre, Professor Owen Bowden-Jones, chair of the Addictions Faculty of the Royal College of Psychiatrists, and Darren Kingaby of the Central & North West London Mental Health Foundation Trust.

Darren and Professor Boden-Jones got an innovation grant to set up a new clinic that would focus on people who had issues with the new so-called 'club drugs'.

'When we opened the Club Drug Clinic in 2011,' says Darren, 'we expected it to be about eighty per cent heterosexual students taking legal highs and maybe fifteen per cent gay men. But in fact it was the opposite: it was eighty per cent gay men.'

I asked Stacey Hemmings, an assistant psychologist at the Central & North West London Foundation, what they were seeing in the people who come to the clinic.

'Lots of HIV, lots of problematic crystal use, lots of injecting G, coke, mephedrone – combinations of everything,' she said. 'Lots of fetishized use around injecting. Over half this clinic is injecting. Injecting one another, sharing needles, having lots of sex. It's a little recipe for a public-health disaster.'

David Stuart adds, '[Amongst the drug users] there is often an obsession with sex beyond eating, beyond breathing, beyond showering, beyond their own health and care . . . [Sometimes they are up for three days in a row.] They are devastated when they wake up. They are like, fuck, I missed a day's work and I've got to do PEP again and they have the paranoia that is always associated with the third day. They say, "It's like people are watching me, or hating me or judging me." It's really sad to watch. They are in tears, they are exhausted and they are dishevelled. They don't sleep; they've just been fucking everything that moves for the best part of three days. They don't know why they are doing that every week. They tell us they know they will be doing it again the next week but they don't know why.'

In December 2011, after the drug-related deaths of five men in Vauxhall over the space of one week, Alex Hopkins, a writer for now defunct *Beige* magazine, wrote a piece for *Time Out* called 'Clubbed to Death' in which he stated, 'The police are sick of it, the hospitals are despairing and, most alarmingly of all, people are still not adequately addressing the problem'.

Two and a half months after Hopkins' piece ran, in February 2012, a forty-one-year-old man died in the Pleasuredrome sauna in Waterloo; four months later, another in the Central London sauna SweatBox; and a month after that another in Chariots sauna, Liverpool Street. All three died from cardiac arrest with GHB and mephedrone in their blood. Then, on 27 October 2012, three men collapsed in the Pleasuredrome sauna. A forty-one-year-old died at the scene. Another man, forty-six, was taken to hospital, where he died two days later. The third man recovered in hospital. All three had taken GHB and one had also taken cocaine.

In summer 2014 I went to see Fiez, the gay man we met in Chapter 11 who works in A&E in a large London hospital. I had heard he was worried about the increasing numbers of guys coming in needing emergency help after drug overdoses. He too was stressed that because the NHS doesn't monitor sexual orientation no one could be sure of the exact numbers, but he was concerned that most of the people coming in with regular drug overdoses were gay/bi men.

'We have this chunk of people who will come in through the night, two or three at a time, and have all been at the same place,' Fiez said. 'You can see the stamp on their hands, the flyers. We know because their crowd come in and take them back to the club as soon as they have been "resuscitated". [The patient will] get up and say, "Is that place shut yet?" and they take off. We look at the blood results and say, how is that possible? Sometimes people pile out of a taxi and come in asking if their friend has been admitted. "Yeah, he's in Resuscitation Room 1." They ask "How is he?" "Well, he died twice but we've brought him back." "Oh great!" They'll get on the phones and ask where are we going next?'

Did he think the situation was getting worse? 'Oh my God, yes. In the last three or four years it's gone bananas . . . The amount of trauma in clubs, it's not just 10 per cent up – we're talking quadrupling from 2009, 2010, maybe ten times up. It's a steep graph – almost a vertical lift-off.'

I asked him about the saunas, which if you believe the hype are liberating pleasure palaces of love, respect and safe sex. Saunas are surprisingly popular. In a study in 2007 (before Grindr's explosion in popularity) by Sigma Research, 37.8 per cent of men interviewed who said they had met new sexual partners in the last year had met them in a sauna. I'm sure many men use them relatively safely but there's no doubt there's a lot of dangerous drug taking. In the *Chemsex* film, the owner of Soho's SweatBox describes an incident where one man collapsed into a G coma and was rushed to hospital without his partner, who continued cruising. The next day his partner delivered G to him in hospital, and they both went into comas.

At the inquest of Stephen Green, a forty-six-year-old man who was found dead on 17 March 2013 in the H20 sauna in Manchester, the coroner criticized the sauna, saying there was blood on the walls, urine and faeces in the sauna room, and used needles thrown in general rubbish bins. Staff had cleaned faeces off Green's body, not realizing he was dead, and then made sandwiches. The coroner said, 'This is not a judgement of morals but merely a matter of health and safety.' In Alex Hopkins' article for *Beige* magazine in 2012, 'Gay Sauna Deaths: How Many More Will Die?', he wrote that he had had good times in saunas but also witnessed more troubling things: 'I've seen men in their twenties lying partially unconscious as predatory older men crawl all over them. I've witnessed guys pushed into wheelchairs when they've collapsed in the shower, their bodies spasming violently. I've crawled across a cold stone floor crying out for water and an ambulance after taking too much K and then been thrown into a cubicle and told to "recover" by panicked, untrained staff.'

Fiez told me that at the hospital they receive lots of 'blue lights' – life or death emergencies – from saunas. In his words, they are being 'wheelbarrowed' in.

'One thing that really infuriates me,' he said, 'is that saunas are particularly bad places for people to die because the victims are just so badly neglected. Someone thinks the guy has fainted from the heat but that might not be the case at all. How these places aren't shut down I don't know. There are so many people coming from saunas, it's unbelievable.'

Mark is a highly successful, thirty-one-year-old, upper-middle-class young man who looks like an Abercrombie & Fitch model. He told me his drug use became problematic when he got into a relationship with a wealthy married man who, he said, had deep shame because he had a wife and child. Mark told me he himself had very low self-esteem and went from using G, passing out on it, to becoming dependent on crystal meth, which he scored off apps and used at chill-outs.

'I used to call [gay app] Manhunt "Tinahunt", because if I was abroad it was the quickest way I could find drugs. I know Manhunt have made an attempt to edit profiles but they can't possibly catch all of it. People write "parTy" with a capital T for Tina or "P&P" which means "party and play". [They also write 'H&H' meaning 'high and horny'.] It's not so much out in clubs. The people involved in the sex-party scene are doing it in a private space for a reason. They don't feel comfortable [for instance, about] the way they look; [they have all the] insecurities which most of us have. The sex-on-drugs scene appeals to so many gay men because of the issues we have. The Los Angeles Lesbian and Gay Centre describes [crystal meth] as the perfect gay men's drug, because it's the glove that fits the hand, that's what's so terrifying.'

In the United States, crystal is popular with gay and straight people alike, but it has had a particularly devastating effect on the gay community for a number of years. A 2003 article in the *San Francisco Gate* talked of an epidemic fuelling a lack of safe sex, while a *New York Times* article the following year referred to crystal as 'the beast in the bath house', with gay commentators calling it 'the second epidemic' (after HIV and AIDS). In Frank Sanello's 2005 book *Tweakers: How Crystal Meth Is Ravaging Gay America*, West Hollywood psychologist Michael J. Majeski bleakly describes the two fashionable 'places to be' for gay men on a Saturday night in Los Angeles: 'One is West Hollywood's most popular gay dance club, and the other is the emergency room at Cedars-Sinai Medical Center'. Studies have shown that positive men have been using crystal at twice the rate of negative men.

Some, though not all, believe that drug use in America is now receding, but the jury still seems to be out. In the UK, clubbers have spoken out about the growing use of crystal meth, which many assert has been leading to unsafe sex and HIV transmission. A man (whose name I have left out at his request) was dismissed as a lunatic for years for continually lobbying the British gay health organizations, demanding they take the coming threat of drug use seriously. I don't believe they listened.

A research project by the London School of Tropical Medicine and Hygiene in 2013/14 spoke to thirty men using drugs for sex and found that one third said that when under the influence they could not control their behaviour and engaged in 'HIV/STI transmission risk behaviour, which they subsequently regretted'. It also found that more than a quarter of the men, who were all HIV positive, made pre-determined decisions to have unprotected anal sex with men they believed were also HIV positive.

Anthony Gilet told me he was particularly worried about two friends of his. 'I've been at sex parties and I've seen my mate not use condoms. That makes me worried. It's dangerous, the amount of drugs that you're taking . . . My mate was out a couple of weeks ago for five days non-stop.'

'Condoms?' says Mark. 'They're out the window. No matter how important safe sex is to me, if I put crystal in my body it's like that part of my brain shuts down. I relapsed during my early recovery and, even though I knew about recovery and safe sex and how lucky I was to be HIV negative as a recovering crystal-meth addict, in relapse that just left my mind.'

Mark disagrees that coverage of the drugs problem and of injecting has been sensationalized. He set up London's first gay Crystal Meth Addicts Anonymous Twelve Step meeting groups and has no money or grants to apply for, as Twelve Step groups fund themselves. The groups are well attended and growing as every month goes by.

Richard is a forty-four-year-old professional man with a very impressive job – a big, beefy, muscly guy. He said he was always anti-drugs after seeing friends experiment at university. On the scene, though, he felt there were 'a whole set of rules you have to adhere to' and he had his first E in a gay sauna. 'I became a scene guy, tried to fit in, did a couple of courses of steroids, buffed up the body. By the time I was in my early thirties I was in a relationship that was abusive.'

He first used crystal meth to help him finish his MA dissertation. Initially, he says, it was 'in a very controlled way, a couple of puffs on a pipe while I was working in the evening. But it doesn't stay like that. The relationship's crumbling, you get your kicks elsewhere because it's an open relationship and the boyfriend's a pathological liar who occasionally hits you, and you're doing more and more drugs to escape that. And someone suggests, rather than smoking crystal, 'cos it ruins your teeth and probably your vocal chords, there's a much, much more efficient way of doing it – and that's slamming.'

It took Richard eighteen months to progress from smoking crystal meth to injecting it. 'The first time I did it, it did nothing for me. So I did it again. And I had it done to me. The guy I was doing it with couldn't find his own vein. I thought I need to know what I'm doing, so the next three guys I had sex with were a doctor, a nurse and a paramedic who taught me how to slam'.

In January 2014 Leigh Chislett, the manager of 56 Dean Street in the heart of Soho, inundated, took on David Stuart as a full-time drugs worker. In the first three months three hundred men who said they used drugs were questioned, resulting in the following statistics:

- 65% reported four or more partners per 'bender' (highest being thirty partners)

- 70% could not remember the last time they had had sex sober from drugs or alcohol

- 46% were HIV positive

- 34% of those on HIV medication said they missed doses when high (typically every weekend)

- 10% were currently on hepatitis C treatment (in five cases it was the second time they had been infected) and another 15% had had hepatitis C in the past

- 45% of these 300 men had injected drugs in the last three months

- 54% of these had only ever been injected by other people (sexual partners)

- 45% reported sharing needles

No one wants to overplay this problem. It's clearly a minority of men doing this, but not a tiny minority and nor does that make it something that should be ignored. Log on to Grindr and you will see people selling drugs or looking for people to take them with. And it is not limited to London. In January 2014, I went to meet David Viney, the Health and Wellbeing Manager at the Birmingham LGBT. I asked him if this kind of drug use is common on the not insubstantial gay scene in Birmingham. He said, 'It happens here. It's probably similar to Manchester here – we're the same size – and it's very similar in Leeds. It's mephedrone, ketamine, people do crystal but it's not as big up here. G is popular here. There's polydrug use [using a variety of drugs]. Different drugs come in and out of fashion. House parties, all being organized online, BBRT . . .

'That subculture's developed over ten years,' he tells me wearily, 'but no one's responded to it.'

This was no surprise to me. I was fifteen minutes early to meet him and I switched Grindr on as I walked from Birmingham New Street station. Literally the fourth profile nearest to me stated that the user, a guy in his twenties, is 'looking to ParTy'.

Back in London I asked Sean, whom we met at the start of the chapter, how he would respond to those saying this issue was being sensationalized.

'It's very hard to get away from,' he said. 'My friends say "Promise you'll never do it again," but I can't promise that. It's setting yourself up for failure. You know what it's like. You go on Grindr and probably in the first six to eight squares you can easily get drugs and far too freely. Some of the gay men who are dealers are vulnerable gay men and nice guys who get roped into doing these things and use it as a source of income. You befriend them and it can become a friend-ship circle and it can become toxic. It is hard to escape. I do think it's rife. To think young guys these days, their introduction to the scene is by online hook-ups and chill-out parties – it is quite scary. It's not a community any more. We've turned into a community of individuals.'

13

Looking for Warmth in Cold Places: the Sex Issue

'I am a total bottom who is always horny. To make sure I am satisfied on a daily basis I make it a rule to LET ANYONE WHO WANTS TO FUCK ME! I really mean this. Think of me as a whore who does it for free. I am a slut – I hope this is OK for u'

Gaydar profile, 2014

'There's always some new bloke, some better bloke just waiting round the corner'

Vince, in Russell T. Davies's *Queer As Folk*, 1999

JAKE CANNOT STOP CHECKING Grindr. It's the first thing he looks at when he wakes up, then when he's making a cup of tea, while he's waiting for the train, as he starts work, in his lunch break, and on it goes throughout the day. He has deleted the app from his phone many times, but always goes back. It's not just Grindr; he has all the gay social media apps: Scruff, Hornet, Recon, Gaydar. He checks them all, then goes back to the beginning.

I heard him speak at a 'Let's Talk About Gay Sex and Drugs' event in Soho and we shared a pot of tea in Patisserie Valerie in Old Compton Street on a sunny summer's day. He is lovely – handsome, young, funny. He told me the only reason he uses the apps is because he thinks he might find a boyfriend on them. 'Once in a blue moon you meet someone interesting,' he said. 'There is the potential for meeting someone really amazing and falling in love, because it's happened to other people. [But] most of the time I'm just getting contacted by guys who want a cock pic or a fuck or whatever.'

Jake said he has a problem with compulsive behaviour. He got into the habit of going to sex parties via Grindr after he left Vauxhall clubs high, something he did about twice a month. For some this might be an ideal way to spend a weekend, but Jake never felt very good about himself afterwards.

'Oh God, I always feel ashamed afterwards,' he said. 'Guilty and ashamed, always, always.' On one occasion he spent three days without sleep, at five different parties, where he had sex with fifteen men. He's been on PEP treatment four times.

At one regular sex party he used to go to Jake met a handsome young man, also in his twenties with a good job, with whom he felt he connected on a deeper level. They swapped numbers and talked about going on a date. Jake texted him and waited to hear back but no reply came. He felt a bit down about it, wondered what he was doing wrong if the first guy he had really liked in a while wasn't interested in taking it any further. But then a few weeks later he went to another party and learned he hadn't been rejected at all – in fact, a few days after they'd met the other man had overdosed on G and died. Jake was shaken. 'It felt like that could be me . . . Very upsetting for his family. What if that was my family? That was when I really decided to stop taking drugs. And it's been a struggle. I don't feel like you can go to a sex party without having drugs.'

Clearly, most people don't have addictive problems with sex. And of those that may do, most are not as extreme as Jake's. Take Chris, an attractive, popular guy with a great job who is another of those annoying, seemingly perfect gay men who is like a walking fragrance ad. Like many of us, he uses Grindr a lot. I often used to see him on Gaydar, but now it's the famous orange-and-black app where I find him online. Sometimes he advertises that he has a very large penis, sometimes he doesn't. Again, what's the problem, you might reasonably think. But on social media I regularly saw him moaning about his love life. He knew I was writing this book, so we arranged to have a chat online.

'I know that in the past my desire to be desired has been compulsive,' he wrote, 'and that often it was the sole reason to go out. Friends would comment on it. I could find myself stuck for two or three hours messaging guys, swapping pics, inviting people over. I'd try to quit the computer, and a few times deleted my profile, but I could be sat there for hours at a time, chatting away pointlessly.'

He told me he'd felt unsafe with strangers in his flat and he did a course of PEP treatment after having unprotected sex with a guy who found out he was HIV positive the next day. I asked if he'd had sex with men he didn't find attractive. 'Absolutely,' he answered, 'all the time. You have no idea what you are going to get when you invite people over. Sometimes I do feel ashamed afterwards. I regret it immediately if I don't actually find them attractive.'

I asked why he would have sex with someone he didn't find attractive. 'Loneliness,' he replied. 'I've only had two or three boyfriends and not for very long times. I know that I pull away from guys very quickly, and am very quick to step back.'

'Loneliness' is another of those key, controversial words that is problematic for the guardians of modern gay culture. I understand why. It's been used as a weapon against us: the phrase 'a sad and lonely lifestyle' has been employed so much it's become a cliché. Just one look on Facebook or Twitter shows that huge numbers of gay people today aren't lonely in the slightest. That's great. We've shifted very quickly from being represented by shadowy, haunted figures to being shown as wedded couples happily clutching toasters. And yet, researching this book, the word 'loneliness' came up again and again.

I met Robert Palmer, a man who runs Burrell Street sexual-health centre in London. He is a sex-positive man, meaning he is someone who will never criticize people's sexual behaviour. He is keen to point out there are lots of gay men enjoying sex on drugs whom he doesn't see at his clinic; but he too is seeing more and more men who are having a difficult time negotiating sex lives dominated by drugs.

I ask him what his gay male clients in therapy tell him when they say they are having problematic sex. He smiles before he answers, as he knows he is telling me something that is politically incorrect and doesn't fit into the modern gay narrative. It's as if he's saying something he doesn't want to.

'They're lonely,' he says and pauses. 'There is a real sense of sadness about it, to be honest. In a sense these chill-outs, they kind of become community centres where guys meet and use drugs at the same time.'

You'll remember Sean, the man from the previous chapter who had a psychotic episode in Clapham High Street. He told me that using drugs had worked for him, 'someone who never felt attractive, still hasn't had a boyfriend, never very good at approaching people'. I don't believe that having a boyfriend is the be all and end all but I meet a surprisingly large number of adult gay men who have never had one. Ever. I asked Sean if he wanted a boyfriend? 'More than anything. I think maybe it's because I'm too needy at first, too aggressive. I think I have a lot of shit to work out. Rejection is a huge thing for me. Drugs and sex make that go away instantly. I was talking to a guy last night and he said, "I would never, ever have thought you were like that. I thought you were a hard-faced cow." But ultimately those kind of people have the biggest insecurities.'

He says it's something he believes is common. 'It's easier to drop your pants than to emotionally connect with someone. We can do that easily, whereas it's hard to say "I like you, let's do something with this."'

Psychologist Patrick Carnes first made the world aware of sex addiction with his 1983 book *Out of the Shadows*. He suggested it was similar to alcoholism and other addictions except that, instead of alcohol or drugs, the person was using sex, fantasy and masturbation as a way of managing difficult feelings. Critics assert that sex can't be addictive because it doesn't involve ingesting a chemical. But in the introduction to Robert Weiss's *Sex Addiction 101*, Dr David Sack pointed out, 'Imaging studies show that the brain on cocaine and the brain when sexually aroused are virtually indistinguishable. In other words the human brain reacts to sex the same way it reacts to cocaine – one of the most highly addictive substances known to man.' Others have argued that the concept of sex addiction is a religious or puritanical way to stop people having sex, or at least anything other than monogamous, heterosexual, 'vanilla' sex. It's logical that we might be suspicious that the concept of sex addiction is another part of the homophobic arsenal. In reality, however, there are millions of men and women, straight and gay, in recovery for sex addiction – not with the intention of giving up sex, but to help them have the sex, straight or gay, that they want to have. These are people whose extreme sexual behaviour has sometimes cost them their jobs, their health, their relationships and even landed them in prison.

Carnes describes the process that takes place in sexual addicts (regardless of sexuality or gender):

1. **Flawed belief system** Low self-esteem; convinced people would reject them if they knew about their sexual behaviour; belief sex is the most important thing in their lives, etc.

2. **Impaired thinking** Straight men might tell themselves women expect men to cheat, or men are just hardwired to want sex constantly. Gay men might tell themselves gay men can't be monogamous, everyone barebacks, people who object to seeing men cruising in parks are uptight/conservative, etc.

3. **Addiction cycle** The ritual may be as exciting as the actual sex: sitting at the computer, getting changed at the sauna, or driving to a location, etc. Carnes describes sexual addicts going into a kind of 'trance', from which nothing can liberate them until they have orgasmed. Some describe it as being in a bubble that they can only escape when it bursts.

4. **Unmanageability** As with alcohol and drugs, the more your brain becomes used to the dopamine release, the more

sex – or the more intense sex – you'll need in order to get the same thrill. Unmanageability is when out-of-control sexual behaviour causes the person harm, which may include:

- catching sexually transmitted infections

- finding yourself in dangerous situations

- wasting excessive amounts of time

- spending money you cannot afford on porn, prostitutes, sex clubs, etc.

- anti-social or illegal behaviour, such as masturbation or sex in public places, voyeurism, etc.

- detrimental effects on relationships – cheating, passing on to a partner a sexually transmitted infection, including HIV

- emotional stress: shame and anxiety about being found out, or breaking your own moral boundaries

- sexually harassing people

- work suffering through an inability to focus, being disciplined for sexual behaviour on premises, viewing porn at work, etc.

- using dangerous drugs as part of the sexual behaviour, with all the risks that entails, including physical danger and arrest

Straight people have got nothing to be smug about. There are more straight people dealing with sexual addiction – or compulsivity as it is sometimes called – than gay and, as the Ashley Madison website data leak in 2015 showed, the fallout can be worse, especially as children are more likely to be affected. As I have mentioned before, the thousands of same-sex couples in happy, monogamous (or non-monogamous) relationships are largely invisible. As far as I can see, only *Attitude* features them with any regularity. Most gay men are clearly not sex addicts and lots of straight people are also sexually shamed growing up. But, I believe, there are reasons why sex addiction can so easily become an issue for us.

Our first sexual experiences are usually enmeshed in shame – if not our own, then that of others. Part of the unspoken deal with the straight friends with whom I first had sexual interaction, often instigated by them, was that they had to assert how disgusting they found it. For me, that disgust and rejection became tied up with the excitement, and sexual shame became painful and addictively thrilling in itself.

In an interview with me in *Attitude* in 2015, singer John Grant said, 'I believe that gay men were forced to have their relationships in certain places and seek each other out in certain places . . . I joke whenever I go through an alleyway that smells of piss and shit, I'm just like "Ah, the smells of my childhood, I feel so comfortable." Role play and the forbidden, because it was always forbidden to be with another man, that's what gets me off now; it's got to be forbidden and fucked up and wrong, as it's as if this [alternate] thing that's OK and accepted is not very much fun . . .'

The key points of difference for gay men, I think, are:

1. Our teenage sexual awakening is usually in shame – either ours, our partner's, or both.

2. These negative feelings are relieved when we do the very thing that causes them, meaning shame and sex can become subconsciously fused.

3. We learn that if sex happens in secret it has no consequences. We can develop a murky relationship between sex and honesty. Many of us therefore 'split' our experience (see page 109).

4. We receive constant messages that gay relationships are always wrong and are solely about sex, never romantic or emotional.

5. We come out into a gay scene and culture that is overwhelmingly focused on sex and so seems to reinforce point 4.

If you have heterosexual brothers or sisters you might want to compare their experience to yours, as I do here with mine:

- My brother grew up with an awareness that his feelings were natural and normal. *My feelings were so horrifying to society they weren't even explained or expressed other than being presented as an abomination, against nature.*

- My brother grew up talking about girls with his friends. *I grew up doing everything I could to hide the fact I liked boys.*

- He had my parents and other adults reinforcing what felt right for him – 'When you marry . . . When you have kids . . . When you have a wife . . .' *I was told the same thing: that I had to marry a woman – any possibility of what was natural for me was portrayed as illegal, immoral and impossible.*

- He experienced adolescent experimentation with the nurturing help of his friends, who would never have shamed him about the basic fact of his attraction to women. *Everyone shamed me for my feelings – media, friends, teachers, even my gay friends and I homophobically abused each other.*

- As a teen, it was socially acceptable for him to meet women in public or in any bar or club he walked into. *I knew I risked physical violence if I showed attraction to any man in public. If I wanted to meet a partner I had to seek out a shadowy niche bar or club. The messages I received were that parks and toilets were where people like me went.*

- My brother could hold hands with his girlfriend in public and sit kissing on a park bench or at a bus stop. *I was afraid my first boyfriend would be imprisoned. To this day, outside of gay areas I am self-conscious about kissing friends, let alone a partner, in public.*

- He conducted his relationships at our or her family home and she was allowed to spend the night with him; sexual intimacy was implicitly approved. *My early sexual relationships were literally illegal and conducted in absolute secrecy, like a military operation. I believed if my parents knew I was having sex my life would be over.*

- When my brother had sex he and his girlfriend had to be careful they did not create a new life. *When I first had sex, the overriding fear was that I could contract a virus that could end my life.*

Catherine Bewley, a sexual-abuse caseworker at Galop, the UK's leading anti-LGBT hate-crimes charity, agrees that young LGBT people are often driven towards sexual subcultures because there are no places where they can have the kind of innocuous 'kissing behind the bike shed' moments that straight people take for granted and that help them gently explore their sexualities and identities.

'If you're a young gay person you might be lucky, in a fantastic school with fantastic friends,' she says, 'but you might not. Where is the safe space? If school isn't really safe [and] home is not safe, where do you go? You go online or on to apps. I think young people of all sexualities are pushed in this way currently, but it's particularly true for LGBT young people. If you go online it is highly sexualized. It's about what you look like physically, what you do, what you're prepared to do. One click and you're going to get barebacking, drugs. If you're fourteen, how do you assess what is normal? As a young person, naturally, you want to explore sex; you want to explore all of this. There's a certain attractiveness to this being underground, clandestine, that's my world – that's quite exciting, until it does your head in or something bad happens and there's no protection.'

Jason is a twenty-eight-year-old whom I arranged to meet in a pub in Manchester after I heard him talking about some of his experiences at discussions about addiction – which he says he doesn't have but is very interested in learning about. He tells me how he was sixteen years old and on a school trip to France when he first had sex in a toilet with a 'not very attractive man who said he was thirty but was more likely forty' who was masturbating at the urinal on the ferry. Back at home, he found a website listing public places where men have sex and spent most days for the next two years in a toilet near his school. He had sex with 'a mixture of everyone on the dirty-old-men scale', aged from late twenties up to sixties. 'Not everyone was really disgusting,' he adds, 'but a lot of them were.'

Jason is a highly intelligent man. He talks about sex in toilets with the enthusiasm of someone who runs a vintage car club. He has a strong assumption that 'this is what we all do'. At one point he rummages in his bag for a diagram he drew of the toilet in a library, which he describes as the ultimate cruising experience; or at least it was until 'a bunch of meth heads' gave the game away and a man was arrested. His current favourite is at another public venue where there's so much sex happening, he says, that it's inconceivable the general public haven't cottoned on. The management is scared to clamp down, he believes, because of the venue's liberal gay friendliness and, he thinks, because he's seen some of the staff having sex there too.

When I ask him why he doesn't just go on Grindr or to saunas, he explains, 'One of the things I really like is the control. I'm really good at this. I know what I'm doing. That is an enormous part of the thrill for me. None of it is about the risk of getting caught. This is a space where we are operating in a completely different way and I know how it works.'

He is not always in control, though. On one occasion when he was seventeen he found himself in a cubicle in a station toilet with a man who, when he lifted his shirt, had a skin infection over a large part of his torso and some kind of sore on his penis. Before he could get out there was an angry knock on the door and a voice threatening to call the police. It was security. 'We open the door; I try and make up some story that he's my disabled brother and I'm helping him use the bathroom. I lift up his shirt and say "He's sick!" I'm shitting myself. If I had been cautioned they would have had to tell my parents, who I wasn't out to at the time. The guy just said, "Fuck off – just go and don't come back!" I went home thinking I cannot believe I put myself in that situation.'

On another occasion, in a secluded toilet, a man in his sixties sexually assaulted him after offering his hand to shake and then grabbing his crotch, something Jason shrugs off. 'He didn't get much power over me. He just tricked me into letting him do something kinda gross. I think he made me feel his stuff through his pants. I mean, big news. Old man's bits . . . I've touched them loads. I think if that happened to me before I had cruised anyone it might have freaked me out, but by that point I was fairly jaded.' At the time he was seventeen.

'Minimization' is a psychological term to describe how people play down the impact on them of something that has happened. It feels like something the British do a lot: 'Don't make a fuss, I've been through worse.' I've heard lots of gay people do it with regard to their experience at school. It is also common when people have been sexually assaulted under the influence of drugs. David Stuart wrote in *FS* magazine in 2015, 'We rarely hear the word rape, or assault . . . but that's what it is. What's worse is the sentence we hear in most of these cases: "It's my own fault, I took too much G."'

Minimization happens because to connect with the reality of what really happened – and what you really felt – is too painful.

Jason has spent a lot of time intellectualizing what he does and was keen to tell me how happy and emotionally well rounded he is. He says he would like to be in a relationship, which seems to embarrass him. He believes his behaviour was addictive in the first couple of years, but doesn't accept the 'hawkish narrative that it's dangerous and disgusting' and maintains that he is currently in control of it. When I say lots of gay men believe that in this day and age it's only closeted men that cruise in toilets and public places, he says that's not true: 'A lot of people do it. A lot of people who are not English. A lot of Spanish, Greek, Portuguese, a lot of Filipino guys, Asian guys, a lot of black guys who have covered their faces with hoods and caps, clearly quite furtive. It's current. More so than ever for some people.'

Today, meeting for casual sex, something that once might have involved a lot of time hanging around, can be arranged in minutes.

Clearly a vast number of people love Grindr and similar apps. They are so popular that in the Apple App Store Grindr is, extraordinarily, used as the symbol for all social-networking apps; it seems always to be disproportionately high up in the top-ten charts. One friend in his thirties is a happy customer. He told me, 'I hate meeting people in bars, yet I feel entirely comfortable talking to people online. What would feel like a crushing rejection in person has absolutely zero impact to me on Grindr. I think I use it in the absence of anything more intimate, and sometimes for less-than-positive reasons (horniness and the need for validation isn't a great combination), but I'm definitely not avoiding intimacy (as far as I know!) and I don't think anything I'm doing is getting in the way of that.'

His is a minority view amongst the men I have talked to. At the 'Change of Scene' discussion events I help run, frustration with Grindr is something that comes up over and over again, with many men saying they continually delete then re-download it.

Gay social-media apps promise so much. But tentative research suggests social-media networking apps in general don't actually deliver the feeling of community that they promise.

Jeff van Reenen is a South African gay man who lives in London and works as an addiction therapist. For his Masters degree he looked into the effect that Grindr had on gay men who were in recovery from drug abuse. He found the men in his study were getting a potential constant stream of affirmation and rejection – as he put it, 'reward, reward, reward, mixed with rejection, rejection, rejection'.

'It started off under control,' he said, 'but gradually became obsessive to the point where it was addictive and compulsive and being used almost every waking moment.' He found they were using Grindr to relieve loneliness and boredom in a way that you might assume was useful for gay men. 'But what I found is that ultimately it does the opposite,' he explained. 'Eventually the sex became unimportant. It was only about being affirmed, reaching out, getting that communication back, then losing interest and moving on to the next one.'

What Grindr facilitates so well, Reenen discovered, is the illusion of authentic relationships. In other words, you feel like you are making a connection with someone but you are not. Jeff's findings were similar to a major study of Facebook published by the University of Michigan in 2013. People logged on because they were lonely and wanted to connect, but ended up feeling even more disconnected. Co-author John Jonides suspected it was because Facebook facilitated a never-ending comparison to other people. 'You get lots of posts about what people are doing,' he said. 'That sets up social comparison – you maybe feel your life is not as full and rich as those you see on Facebook.'

On Grindr the comparison is of how hot you are. Users are being judged against scores of others: too fat, too thin, too small, too black, too brown, too pale, too foreign, too camp. Aside from the racism that is so common, the worst possible thing, it seems, is being anything less than hyper-masculine. If overcoming low self-esteem is about finding a safe space with people who respect and value you, then seeing hot guys listing off the reasons why you're not good enough for them *before you've even spoken to them* is the last possible thing any of us needs, especially as we'll likely all have felt insecure about our masculinity. Again, like in childhood, the message we receive is: 'You are not man enough and therefore not good enough.'

Grindr might not be so problematic were it not for the fact that, as gay bars shut, it is becoming the dominant way many of us experience and interact with each other. I can't help but think about those people who fought so hard for LGBT rights over the last fifty years – outside the Stonewall Bar in 1969, the House of Commons in 1994 and on Pride marches across the years – and wonder whether they were all 'masc' and looked like porn stars . . .

The American website Douchebags of Grindr was set up to showcase some of the more unpleasant profiles. Here are a few examples of real American profiles:

'Hate everything. No fats, fems, olds, uglies or ethnics.'

'Sorry, I'm not into people who are beautiful on the inside.'

'Recent ex cop and new to the area. If ur only personality is gay, move on. No pics/stats no chat. Not into fem or older.'

'Gym hot ONLY! No pic no chat.'

'Hey, hi, yo, sup = not interested. Yes, I know I have a great
    body, say something more interesting. Thin isn't fit. Stop.'

'Neg clean guy here and love to BB. Neg guys only. No
    Asians, old, black, or fat hairy guys.'

'Be fit, handsome and smart. No fatties, femmes or uglies.
    Have a face pic. It's 2006.'

'I find 99.9% of you disgusting, don't message me about it.'

'Old? Weigh twice what I do? Ugly? (Be real, you've seen a
    mirror.) If you answered "yes" assume I hate you.'

'A different kind of SF boy. Can someone ask the Asian
    swarms to stop asking me to top? Also please be
    interesting and maybe want to explore SF.'

I asked Luke, a friend of mine in his early thirties, how he feels
when he uses Grindr. He replied, 'Erm . . . makes me feel crap – when
even those who put they are looking for friends don't reply. Would I
make an ugly friend?'

Luke is not ugly. He should have been snapped up by now.

'I'm stable, with a house and a good job, financially sound, caring,
make people laugh, can cook . . .' he wrote, 'but cos I don't fit into a
guy's unreachable physical looks . . . I'm left on the shelf.' He added,
'And of course, this is before all the top, vers and bottom talk, which
just makes things even harder.'

In the seventeen years since I had my first AOL gay chat-room
discussions, the dialogue has mutated from 'What are you into?' to
'I'm active/passive', to 'I like to top' or 'I like to bottom', to 'I *am* a top'
or 'a bottom', to 'Looking for tops', 'Looking to bottom for hung tops',
and on and on and on.

Being able to hook up with men so easily, sober, drunk or high, at
any time or place, means we can often take risks we might not in the
cold light of day.

Wayne, a black guy in his mid-twenties, had just begun his fifth round of PEP treatment the day before we met. He told me he was on his way home from a club the previous Sunday at five in the morning, talking to a guy on Grindr who had been at a chill-out for two days and who asked to come round. When Wayne's doorbell rang there were four of them on the doorstep. Upstairs, they took mephedrone and G.

'I got with one boy and that was cool,' he said. 'I went to top another one and change the condom but there was no more. In a moment of madness I went to have sex with him without a condom. It was less than a minute and I thought, "What are you doing?" The boy said, "It's fine, I'm negative."

'Then one of the other guys took me to one side and said, "Mate, I was trying to get your attention – he made a comment to me earlier, which was 'You can only catch HIV once.' He really doesn't care about catching HIV. I thought I'd let you know." The reality dawned on me and I kicked them all out. Then I went to the clinic to get PEP again.'

Grindr poses other risks. Going to a stranger's house or letting them into your home is inherently dangerous. I'm not pointing fingers; I've done it myself. There are many cases of men being attacked, robbed or murdered by people they have met off Grindr, here and in the US. I haven't listed them here as it is too much, but they happen. I've known one myself. Clearly this is rare, but I have had a handful of men tell me they have either seen intentional overdosing or had it done to themselves, some have been raped or assaulted and have been too embarrassed to go to the police.

I believe the reason the episode of Russell T. Davies's *Cucumber* where Lance is murdered by the 'straight' man is so powerful is because we have been shown the value of his life. We see him at his birth, as a child, a teenager, we see his family, his relationships, the man he loves, the people who love him – not just as a profile pic – and then he is murdered by a confused, mentally ill 'straight' man he was trying to seduce. When the ghost of Hazel says earlier to Lance, 'Sometimes it's better to just go home', we know that is a painful truth: we are all worth far more than a risky shag.

*

A lot of this happens because being gay has traditionally been an act of breaking a societally imposed boundary. There's an unarticulated feeling that all boundaries must be wrong. It's as if we've thrown the baby out with the bathwater and anything goes. With no sex or social education, and with my generation robbed of many elders by AIDS, we have looked to the gay press for how to live 'a gay life'.

Ford Hickson is a gay man who works at the London School of Hygiene and Tropical Medicine and is a researcher at Sigma, which for years has been one of the leading groups looking into the sex lives of men who have sex with men. We had lunch and discussed the gay press. He pointed out that gay publications originated in a grass-roots community reaction to tackle issues such as homophobia and inequality, and to fight HIV and AIDS, but today they are primarily businesses. The free papers in particular, he added, because they are more dependent on advertising from the gay scene, want to present a positive image of having a lot of sex partners. 'Most of the gay leisure sex industry wouldn't work if everyone were monogamous, so it is in their business interests for people to continue to acquire new sexual partners. The gay press normalizes high partner acquisition. It normalizes open relationships, it normalizes anal intercourse as the centre of gay sex.' He said that while gay magazines have their good and bad points, images of gay men that are portrayed by gay magazines – he cites *QX*, *Boyz*, *Gay Times* and *Attitude* – are all the same. 'What all of them do,' he explained, 'is portray a sexual life which doesn't give rise to harm.'

In other words, the gay press shows all the hotness and horniness but doesn't show the potential negative consequences that sex can have.

I went to meet Leigh Chislett, the clinic manager at 56 Dean Street. He has dedicated his professional life to helping gay people. One young man told me he loves the centre because it's like getting advice from friends. Leigh says over and over again that he is not judging anyone. He emphasizes that some people seem able to take drugs without it having a detrimental effect on their lives and health – but Leigh is worried by the growing number who can't.

He says that 'without a shadow of a doubt' there has been a huge increase in people coming in with sexualized drug problems. He has personally lost a friend to a G overdose, and talks of people who lived through the AIDS epidemic now being brought down by drugs. 'I've known some of these patients for over twenty years and I just started seeing these people come in who had lost their jobs, people destroying their lives, and it is becoming overwhelming, seeing more and more.'

In August 2014, Leigh says, Dean Street diagnosed fifty-six people HIV positive, more than double what it would have been in one month five years before. Gay and bi men are still the group most at risk of catching HIV in the UK. In 2014, the last year for which statistics are available, around 3,360 gay or bi men tested HIV positive in the UK, 54.6 per cent of the total number, just over nine gay/bi men every single day. This is the highest number of positive diagnoses of gay/bi men ever recorded in the UK. But it is not just happening in the UK. In July 2014 the World Health Organization reported that HIV infection across the world 'is exploding in gay men' and suggested all gay men use PrEP treatment, an anti-HIV drug that is believed to stop people catching HIV if taken every day.

When it comes to other STIs there are mixed findings. In England between 2010 and 2014, MSM (men who have sex with men) made up just under 5 per cent of all cases of sexually transmitted warts and genital herpes, but 51 per cent of all cases of gonorrhea and a staggering 80 per cent of all syphilis diagnoses. Leigh Chislett says it used to be that a case of syphilis was a talking point in the centre because it happened so rarely, but they are now diagnosing at least one case every day. 'I've been working in sexual health since 1986 and I've never known anything like this. The numbers are rocketing.' In June 2015 Public Health England issued a release about sexually transmitted infections. They said, 'We are particularly concerned with large rises in diagnoses among gay men. In this group we saw a 46 per cent increase in syphilis and a 32 per cent increase in gonorrhea. Gonorrhea in particular is becoming harder to treat as new antibiotic-resistant strains emerge.'

Hepatitis C also remains a disproportionate problem amongst men who have sex with men (around three times the rate in the general UK population, as of 2008/9), with rates rising, mainly in HIV-positive men in Europe, the US and Australia. Dean Street, Dr Sean Cummings at Freedom Health and the Hepatitis C Trust told me they are seeing more men coming in with recurrent infections. They contract it, clear it with medication and then catch it again. Dean Street has had patients who are on their sixth course of treatment.

Perhaps it would be less of a problem if we were having the sex we wanted. Again, Leigh emphasizes that he is not judging, but that often what the men he sees in the clinic say they want does not tally. 'I meet a lot of guys here who say, "Do you know, I'd love to meet a boyfriend. I really want what my brother's got with his wife." What I don't quite get is why these people are saying this and why it's not happening.'

Leigh tells me of a young man he met who was unhappy at the amount of sex he was having in saunas. 'He said, "I just want to meet somebody; to be in love." He was embarrassed telling me. I said, "I'm not quite sure what the problem is. You're a good-looking guy." And he looked at me and said, "I'm gay." That sort of startled me. It didn't seem an option to him that there was an alternative.'

He says he remembers a patient with HIV who was newly single who said to him, 'I've got to learn what it is like to be a gay man at forty.'

Leigh pauses. 'What does that mean? You have to "learn" to be a gay man at forty? Why can't you just be yourself?'

I talked with Leigh, as I have done with many people, about the way those organizations charged with looking after the health of gay and bisexual men in the UK have or haven't adequately addressed the problems. I pointed out that there seems to be a limp, wishy-washy approach where nobody ever seems brave enough to say that behaviour that is hurting people is a problem. There is, he says, a feeling that, 'You cannot tell the truth because it will upset people.' He tells me of an occasion when he was at a sexual-health confer-ence where representatives from all the different London boroughs enthusiastically reported back on the sexual-health education work they had been doing. The event concluded with graphs on a screen showing a list of things all going up – HIV infection rates, gonorrhea, LGV (lymphogranuloma venereum), etc. – and when they took questions Leigh gingerly put his hand up.

'I said, "Can we conclude from the figures that sexual health and HIV prevention has failed?" The audience appeared shocked by this and I got a very negative response. But what is the conclusion? Has it failed? Afterwards people said to me, "I think that too." There is some great work being done, but I think messages are often diluted for fear of offending someone.'

To say we need to take more care of ourselves and each other is sometimes considered to be 'slut shaming'.

In *Attitude* in September 2015, respected 1980s front-line HIV campaigner Simon Watney wrote, 'I get exasperated by gay men who invite us to look back to some supposed Golden Age of sexual freedom before the advent of HIV, and who argue that safer sex is somehow an assault on their imagined entitlement to limitless amounts of unprotected sex with limitless numbers of partners. Anyone questioning this fashionable new orthodoxy is instantly accused of "heteronormative" prejudice, and is roundly denounced as being "anti-sex".'

Watney wrote that he welcomed liberalized attitudes:

but we should not make the mistake of believing that this somehow magically erases centuries of internalised shame and guilt amongst gay men, and decades of accumulated anxiety about HIV. All of this however gets brushed away under the carpet by the new queer thought-police, by whom any questioning of our sexual behaviour gets angrily dismissed as 'anti-sex'. The implication is that it's somehow radical and edgy and 'pro-sex' to take huge risks with our own and our partners' sexual health. It also fundamentally and inexcusably trivialises what it really means to have HIV.

Ford Hickson told me, 'There's an almost militant individualization about sexual health. It's as if "It's your responsibility to look after your sexual health and it's my responsibility to look after mine. It's no one else's business what I do." But that ducks not only the issue that you're not just doing it with yourself, you're doing it with other people, but also that everything has an influence on other people. It arises very acutely in the debate about bareback porn. People say, "Bareback porn does not make me have unsafe sex", but at a societal level of course it does; of course the continual viewing of an activity that looks pleasurable and doesn't appear to have any drawbacks is an encouragement.'

Ford said that the gay media showing sex is not a problem in itself; the problem is that this is the *only* portrayal available of what it is to be gay. He says the cumulative effect 'of freely accessible, highly explicit images that portray the average gay sex life as being like a porn shoot . . . [means] porn stars become the aspirational models for [many] gay men.'

Think about it if it were the other way round. Imagine continually telling a heterosexual boy throughout his childhood that he was disgusting; that girls were disgusting, bad, evil people; that sex with them was wrong and not allowed, was immoral and would ruin his life, offend God, possibly kill him, may get him imprisoned and shunned by his community; and that he can never, ever find love or have a happy life – and then suddenly, overnight changing that message entirely to 'That was all wrong: girls are amazing, sleep with as many as you want, there are no boundaries at all', handing him copies of *Nuts* and *Zoo* magazines, dropping him in Magaluf surrounded by porn, prostitution, sex clubs, drugs and alcohol, with a load of women who've been told the same about men. It's probable that he'd be overwhelmed, confused and unlikely to express his sexuality in moderation, or that he'd find it easy to respect and fully value women rather than just seeing them as objects. You wouldn't expect those men and women to be able easily to form healthy, loving relationships with each other. It's a miracle that so many of us do.

Meanwhile, Jake in Patisserie Valerie tells me he is finding that Grindr is getting in the way of his recovery. Even when he puts 'no chems' on his profiles, men still ask him if he's sure and he relapses. It's affecting his ability to understand what it is he really wants. For the last year he has been escorting, during which, he says, he's met some nice guys but has also had unpleasant experiences, such as one guy who wanted to inflict pain on him by using sandpaper on his penis. He wants to stop and says it is affecting his self-esteem. 'My parents would give me money for food and I'd feel *so* guilty,' he says. 'If they knew what I was doing for money it would just break their hearts and I love them *so* much and they've done *so* much for me and given me the best upbringing.'

Grindr is also confusing him about what kind of guys he's interested in. 'When you're in a bar, when you actually meet someone, there's something different,' he says. 'So many times when I've found people really attractive I've thought if I saw your picture on Grindr I probably wouldn't go for you. But Grindr's like a drug itself. It's poison. It's a time-waster. Having it on tap so readily changes your relationship to sex.'

14

'Out of control and without care':
Rock Bottoms

'Catholic Schoolgirl Syndrome: A young person (not necessarily a schoolgirl) raised in a strict moral upbringing (not necessarily a Catholic) who acts completely opposite to the views they were taught in a way that is generally out of control and without care. Because they were taught that everything is equally sinful, they feel that any and all actions are morally equal (i.e.: kissing a guy is on a par with sleeping with the football team) and [are] not taught control, restraint, or moderation and instead taught only abstinence (i.e.: excessive uncontrolled drinking).'

Urban Dictionary

'ROCK-BOTTOMING' IS THE term for when people hit their lowest ebb, the point at which things have become so bad that they have no option other than to realize serious change is needed. Hopefully, it is also the point where they see that there is another way and ask for help. The term can be applied to individuals or sometimes whole groups of people.

It is important to say again and again, as I have done, that the vast majority of LGBT people are not doing the more extreme things described in this book. For example, the National Crime Survey figures quoted in Chapter 12 show that two thirds of gay/bi men in the UK do not take any illicit drugs at all. Many who are doing lots of these things will argue that it is not a problem. Even when someone does have a problem, often they take action and get their lives back together. But a phrase from the Urban Dictionary's definition of Catholic Schoolgirl Syndrome, quoted above, seems to be pertinent to the way a disproportionate number of us, myself included at times, live our lives: 'out of control and without care'.

Remember, at its root this isn't our fault. Those of us struggling did not ask for this. David Viney, who works at the Birmingham LGBT, told me, 'To reduce it down to its core, it's discrimination. If you imagine across someone's life course the plethora of places they can be discriminated against: from the moment they have an awareness of the world, they will be getting negative messages about being gay from family, from around school . . . into the workplace, into social situations with heterosexual friends when they're teenagers, into much later in life when they go into care settings and they might have staff who aren't gay friendly . . .; all those places will be places where they can be bullied or harassed for being gay. People carry that weight all through their lives. Everyone thinks it's easy to be gay now. It's not. There're still lots of problems. You have people that are carrying baggage from thirty or forty years ago when they have been spat at and punched in the street. You've got the stress of self-concealment, people living heteronormative lives. There's always that assumption that you are straight and there's the stress of coming out all the time. All of that internalizes.'

Ford Hickson agrees that despite all the advances it still isn't easy growing up gay. 'I think it might be harder now: you're so much more visible, you're under more scrutiny, people talk about it, demand things of it. I don't think it's any easier being a gay teenager. It's a fucking chaotic time.' He adds that, considering what we go through, 'it would be surprising if gay people didn't have more mental-health problems than straight people. It would seem like something was amiss.'

Leigh Chislett told me about a group of teenagers who came into the clinic at 56 Dean Street for a school visit and how he was impressed at how open they were – when they were talking about heterosexual sex. 'I said, "What about gay pupils?" and there was this absolute hushed silence. This was a really liberal school. They told me that a kid came out and as he used to leave school every day other pupils used to spit on him . . . and he had a breakdown.'

The irony of being told that in a sexual-health clinic is stark. It's not unlikely that, like me, that pupil will use sex as well as other things to cope.

David from Birmingham LGBT speaks the truth when he says that, with regard to gay people, 'The public health epidemic isn't solely HIV any more and it probably never was. It is drink, drugs, substance misuse, suicide ideation . . . it is mental health.'

Some readers may not believe me when I say I don't want to sensationalize this problem. Throughout the writing of this book I've looked for reasons to not write it. I've spent nights wrestling over the issues with friends, hoping to find an excuse to abandon it. But the main thing that convinced me to continue, as I've mentioned before, is what I was seeing amongst my friends. It's become not unusual to see a Facebook friend announce someone's suicide or overdose. Or to see a concerned boyfriend issue a desperate public plea to help find his possibly suicidal partner. Or another friend publishing goodbye messages on Facebook only to be found in time. Or hearing that a friend has got so far into the chemsex scene that he has made a decision to abandon condoms and has casually accepted he will catch HIV. Or another friend who meets someone he really likes but has to break off the relationship because the other man is so addicted to drugs, in this case injecting, that he has to leave London and move back to his parents.

You'll remember Lee, the young friend Tim and I made when we came out to our youth group in the early nineties and who emigrated to Australia in 2000. While I was writing this book, I heard he had returned to the UK and we met up for dinner. He'd had a great time in Australia but had also faced disaster. For a year he had dated a man he described as 'beautiful inside and out', but who was erratic, paranoid and, it turned out, was injecting steroids.

On the evening of his thirty-first birthday they had a major row and Lee's partner threw himself out of the window of their fifth-floor flat. Lee sat and held his hand the next day as they turned off his life-support machine. His entire story is too much to tell here, but now back in the UK he is in recovery for an eating disorder. He said he was finding it really difficult being nearly forty and back on the London gay scene, especially on Grindr with men who seemed to be all 'fucked up or wasted'.

It's easy to throw your arms up in disgust at some of the behaviour I have described in these chapters, but all I know for sure is that the men I have written about have one thing in common. They all grew up in fear, without adequate help, all dealing with a big, unacceptable secret on their own with zero support. This is our story.

Whilst I was writing this book I also noticed stories of attacks, such as that on eighteen-year-old Connor Huntley in May 2014, who was beaten about the head with a claw hammer by his homophobic flat-mate; or of three gay men who were called faggots and had ammonia thrown in their faces outside a Vauxhall gay bar; or an attack on two young gay men in Whitechapel, East London; or a twenty-one-year-old who suffered homophobic abuse and had petrol thrown in his face, blinding him in one eye. In that same month Catholic Cardinal Raymond Burke stated that homosexual relationships are disordered and that parents should keep their children away from gay family members. All of this is connected; one leads to the other. The dots join. They couldn't be clearer.

We need to look at the picture they make and do something about it. If we had done so before, Rob Goddard, whose story I told at the beginning of the book, might still be here today. Rob had one rock bottom after another, but because neither he nor his family had any real awareness of this stuff – how could they? – no one knew how to get him the help he really needed.

A year after his death I sat down with Andy to ask about Rob's life. Andy hadn't read this book, obviously, but described everything that I've written about – chronic oversensitivity, a codependent need to overdramatize, an inability to maintain boundaries or moderation, addictive tendencies and an experience of severe homophobia. Andy said that even as a child Rob was always oversensitive and would take offence at any little thing. When he came out to his family, he stormed off, slamming the door, because he didn't get the dramatic reaction he wanted. Although he was proud of being gay and would never ever hide it, Andy said, Rob didn't feel normal – he thought he was a failure, wasn't good enough, and he was always unhappy. He carried beer around with him in his rucksack like a safety blanket.

He had a lot of short, club-driven relationships. 'Sometimes he would find somebody, start a relationship with them, start feeling those feelings, then they'd talk about introducing someone else into the relationship,' said Andy. 'Those kind of things ate away at him.'

Rob was mugged four or five times and we know at least one incident was homophobic: a group of men attacked him and his boyfriend as Rob rested his head on his boyfriend's shoulder on the night bus home. One man headbutted Rob, breaking his nose, then the group got off the bus and came back to look for them with fighting dogs, which were set on them both. Rob said that the police made him feel it happened because he had 'flaunted his sexuality'.

Andy told me that Rob had unsafe sex willingly, multiple times, with the person from whom he caught HIV, despite knowing he was positive. He says that 'drugs, clubbing, being off his face' led to it. 'I do wonder,' he said, 'if there was a part of him that wanted to get it . . . self-harm.'

After Rob moved back in with his parents his drug taking got worse. In the early hours of one morning his dad was woken by terrible screams and found Rob grabbing his foot and smashing it repeatedly on the floor, shattering the bone. The ambulance team found he'd been drinking glass-cleaner. In the months before his suicide he had cold sores all over his mouth, worn-down teeth, scabs up his arms and over his face.

Rob Goddard was no different from Anthony Stubbs or Dominic Crouch or Ayden Olson or Mark Houghton, or the many other young lesbian, gay, bisexual or transgender children and teenagers who aren't with us because society failed to teach them that they did, in fact, have an inalienable right to be gay. Or straight or bisexual or pansexual or transgender, just whatever it is they were; and that they were as worthy of love and of being valued, respected, protected and cherished as anyone else.

Rob is no different from those men at bareback sex parties, from those of us addicted to Grindr or selfie 'likes', or terrified of letting our front down for fear we'll be rejected, or those of us bitching, judging or drinking ourselves silly, struggling to make sense of our lives. It is all the same thing.

It doesn't have to be this way. There is a way out of this mess. The great thing about rock bottoms is that the only way is up.

My rock bottom came, after years of hellish behaviour, back in 2009 when I was late for a photo shoot with Daniel Radcliffe. I'd spent years trying to get him for a shoot for *Attitude* and we had it, the world-exclusive first time the leading actor of the biggest family brand in the world had given a gay-press interview. We'd got him, flown in a prestigious photographer from Los Angeles and were due to shoot with a 9 a.m. start on a Sunday morning. I knew I needed to get to bed early to be up early. I spent the whole of Saturday at the theatre, anxiously avoiding alcohol; but when I got home I had one can of lager and logged on to Gaydar . . . and woke up at 10 a.m. with multiple missed calls and messages, surrounded by cans. I was so drunk I couldn't speak. My head spinning, I struggled to the studio and said I had food poisoning. Dan and his publicist were lovely about it and I went home sick. The shoot went fine and I met Dan later in the week and did a great interview. But I knew I was out of control.

Tim the compulsive overeater's rock bottom happened when suddenly he could see he was stuck. 'I became aware of the continual cycles,' he told me. 'I went to work one day wearing tracksuit bottoms, dirty with food stains – I had no other clothes that would fit me. At my desk, with my stomach bulging over the table, bending over to pick something up, one of the managers said, "Tim, I can see your arse, it's disgusting." I was so ashamed and embarrassed. I was on

222

antidepressants at that point. I went to the GP and burst into tears and told him I wanted to kill myself. That's when he suggested something I didn't even know existed . . .'

For Liam, who in Chapter 11 considered not taking PEP medication because he wouldn't be able to drink, it wasn't the risk of HIV infection that made him finally realize he had a problem, but the prospect of losing his relationship. After years of carnage he told himself he would hold it together on one occasion. He said, 'I was going for a Sunday lunch and I looked at myself in the mirror and said, keep a lid on it, just have a quiet lunch. And, of course, I went crazy. I got shit-faced. I left and disappeared while my boyfriend waited at home all night. I was so sick of the train wreck of when I drank and it suddenly became clear to me that if I didn't stop we would split up.'

For Jack, whom I also wrote about in Chapter 11 and who passed out on the South Bank, realization came at the end of a weekend's drinking after breaking up with his boyfriend. 'I'd gone into blackout again. Usual tale – lost loads of stuff, didn't know what happened. I woke up and I was in the kitchen, my flatmates were out, and everything was so quiet and still. In my head I thought, "I want to die, I've had enough." I realized I was so far removed from the man I thought I was going to become when I first moved to London and had all these hopes and dreams. I couldn't take any more. I'd lost all respect and love for myself. It sounds really crazy, but it felt like I had already died. I think I did die emotionally.'

You'll remember the story of Richard from Chapter 12 who had a severe problem with crystal meth. He had an extreme rock bottom. One of his dealers was arrested and police came to Richard's flat with a search warrant, believing he was laundering money, as the dealer had Gaydar and text messages discussing the £5,000 or £6,000 Richard owed. They found him high as a kite with a used needle, a crystal pipe, weighing scales and other paraphernalia scattered about. He was subsequently arrested and had to wait to see if he would be charged and face trial. In that time he tried to stop taking drugs and stay stopped, but he couldn't. He got pneumonia and was dealing crystal from the disabled toilet in the hospital.

Richard believed he simply had a problem with one drug and that if he could just control that he would be fine. 'I didn't realize the problem wasn't crystal, it was me,' he told me. 'I've got quite an intellectual brain, but nothing intellectual helped. There was no way of thinking myself out of this. I had no spirit. No lust for life or interest in it. There was nothing there and no way out. My weekends would be from Thursday to Tuesday. Crystal meth come-downs are horrendous. Absolutely awful, torture, abject depression. My flat is near the river. I used to wander up to Waterloo Bridge and look down into the water and think no one would miss me.'

It seemed things couldn't get any worse. And then Richard got another visit from the police to tell him he was going to be charged with possession of drugs.

'I got to my flat, dug up a quarter of a gram of crystal, was smoking it . . . And then the phone rang. It was an old friend. He was in recovery and he asked me if I wanted to go into recovery too.'

Part Three

Recovery

'I could have sworn we were all locked in,
Ain't that what you said?
I never knew it could hurt so bad,
When the power of love is dead.
But giving into the nighttime,
Ain't no cure for the pain.
You gotta wade into the water
You gotta learn to live again.'

Elton John and Bernie Taupin,
'Healing Hands', 1989

15

Coming Out of Denial

'We are addicted to our thoughts.
We cannot change anything unless we change our thinking.'

Santosh Kalwar, *Quote Me Everyday*, 2010

RICHARD HAD HIT HIS rock bottom. Like an animal struggling to escape the constrictions of a snake, every move he made that he thought would help him just enabled the addiction to tighten its grip. It was only when things could get no worse that he admitted defeat. He accepted his friend's offer and went with him to an LGBT Narcotics Anonymous meeting and then to a gay Alcoholics Anonymous group.

'The first meeting I walked into, everyone was incredibly welcoming,' he said. 'I didn't really get it at first, but I stuck around for the first month. I didn't understand why I couldn't have a glass of wine but everyone else could smoke. I didn't really want to connect with it until a few months later when I found some crystal in my flat, injected it, went out clubbing for the weekend, took loads of drugs, woke up and something inside me clicked: it's got to stop. I thought if they [at the meetings] can get it, so can I. I better just shut my ego up and listen to what they have to say and follow their suggestions [because] I've got no better options.'

Richard went on trial, where he pleaded guilty to possession of crystal meth. He has a very respectable, 'professional' job and this could have ruined his career, but it was a first offence, being in recovery helped and he was given a suspended sentence with community service. He described it as a horrendous time, but with the support that the groups offered him he got through it.

Getting emotional, he told me what recovery had done for him. 'NA and AA and the fellowships have saved my life, certainly. And they have given me a life back,' he said, adding that he has come to realize that the drug taking wasn't really about the drugs. 'In a way, it's like being addicted to self-harm. I thought I never cut myself so I wasn't self-harming, but if sticking needles in my veins isn't self-harm then what is? It's anger and frustration turned in on ourselves. I did all this because what I really craved was intimacy. Yes, rampant, dirty, filthy, sleazy sex is lovely. But I'd like it to come with cuddles, please. And that doesn't seem to happen very often, does it?'

You can get better

In terms of this book, we've got here. From now on the only way is up. Clearly not everyone has a serious problem that needs serious action. But for those who do, know there is a way out of this and it isn't the no-fun, misery-laden dull-fest you might think. This isn't about cutting out all the fun and making your life sober but miserable; it's about making it bigger and giving it a shine you might not be able to imagine at the moment.

If you need it, the first, most important thing to know is that there is hope. There *is* a way out. If Richard can do it then so can you. You might not have a major addiction like he did; you might just find yourself getting a bit down more often than you'd like and want to do something about it; or you might be worse than Richard. Whatever the situation, if you want to you can make real change in your life.

I remember, about a decade ago, standing in the shower thinking that I couldn't face another day feeling the way I did. I believed I was so completely screwed up that I couldn't even bear to think about it, let alone express these thoughts to another person and address them. I'd asked for help in the past and no one had got anywhere near making any difference. I thought I was a lost cause, that inside my head was a huge, tangled rubber ball of fucked-upness, so entwined that it couldn't ever be unpicked.

Was I right?

No, I was completely wrong. Once you pull the right piece of rubber, the ball starts to untangle on its own. Every piece of effort you make propels it along. This is the best news in this book. I'm here to tell you that if you need to and, crucially, if you *want* to, then you can change. You can stop any dangerous behaviour and you can also change the issues that caused you to feel bad and behave problematically in the first place. You can begin to feel better about yourself at a core level: have more confidence, reduce anxiety, have better, more relaxed relationships with other people. If you put the effort in, recovery won't just remove the problems, it will enhance your life beyond all recognition. I've seen it happen in many, many people and it's begun to happen in me too.

Right now you might not believe me. Part of the consequence of being so toxically shamed as children is that our head tells us that we are the worst case, the most screwed up, the one it won't work for. We've got so used to thinking in a certain way that we literally don't know what it's like to think differently. You may say, 'He might be right about other people, but he's not right about me. He doesn't *know* me.' I might not know you, but I do know we share, on some level, a similar experience. I hope by this point you trust me and know that I wouldn't tell you this if I wasn't certain it was true.

No matter how bad it is, you *can* get better, you *can* improve your life, and you *can* change in ways that, at the moment, you simply cannot comprehend. Trust me, put in the effort, reach out for help and your life will change.

I want to acknowledge that not everyone needs this drastic course of action. But a lot of people do. Collectively we need to make some larger systemic changes, which I highlight in Chapter 19, but what follows first is for people with a problem. If you are bored of feeling like crap, then listen up. There are answers here and they work.

In the following chapters I use language such as 'illness', 'condition' and 'getting better': these are terms that have been employed in a homophobic context in the past so, just to be certain, I want to make it absolutely clear once again that this isn't in any way about trying to stop you being gay or turning you straight or any of that nonsense. The 'condition' and 'illness' I refer to is not being gay, but the pattern of anxiety, fear and negative thinking instilled in us through being made to feel 'less than' other people and through the defence mechanisms we've used to cope. If anything, this is about making you more gay, by helping you become more comfortable with yourself and who you really are, helping you love yourself and, if you wish, love someone else – in short, helping you live the life you were meant to have.

Nor is this about magically finding you a boyfriend who will make everything all right. I want to make it clear that I'm not saying that being in a relationship is the key to happiness, though I make no apologies for recognizing that most of us, like the vast majority of people, do want to be in a happy, loving relationship. But this is far more than that. It's about being centred in your life and coming from a place of mental, emotional and spiritual health which will allow a whole range of positive things to happen, things you might not be able to comprehend at the moment.

Reach out for help

First, I again want to stress that I am not a doctor or a therapist. This book is based on my experience, on discussions with therapists and people in recovery, and on what I have learned about being in recovery and from many years of working with gay people.

My first piece of advice, **especially if you have a problem with alcohol, drugs or an eating disorder**, is go to your GP and seek professional help. If you can't face your GP try a sexual-health clinic or call an LGBT or related helpline to ask for guidance. This is especially important if you have a physical dependence on drugs or alcohol: **it can be incredibly dangerous to stop abruptly**, so you absolutely **must** seek medical help in the first instance.

Also remember that if any of what I'm going on to say brings up unmanageable feelings, then please ask for help. Use the support numbers on pages 349–54. Don't listen if there's a voice inside your head saying you aren't worthy of taking up their time. You are. That's what they are there for. **You don't have to do any of this alone**. In fact, not doing it alone is the second most important piece of advice. This isn't just because I want you to feel warm and fuzzy, but because being fiercely independent is part of the problem. Sometimes we become cynical about and uncomfortable with other people; we become the kind of person who won't take part in anything and acts like they are above it. Or we become nihilistic and angry at the world and don't let other people in.

Life isn't about being on your own. It's about connection, helping and being helped by others. I don't mean being in a relationship; I mean allowing yourself to be vulnerable and accepting help and support from other people. Accepting help is a fundamental part of getting over all this. It can seem hard. Don't listen to that voice. Reach out.

It is about helping you to live the best life you can – the life you want.

'Apricot answers'

Whilst huge change is totally achievable, it's going to take effort. This doesn't work by osmosis and there are no 'apricot answers'. I'll explain what I mean by that. When I was looking for help I would read magazine articles about depression and anxiety, which gave very simplistic answers: eat this, do that, try this. One magazine said you could fight depression by eating apricots because of the beta-carotene they contain. Rest, sleep, relaxation, exercise and diet are all genuinely very important parts of getting healthy, but if you have serious childhood trauma that is causing problems, then most likely you need more significant help to deal with it than just eating healthily.

So by 'apricot answers' I mean quick fixes that we jump on, thinking they will work. I've seen people waste time trying them all:

changing friends or jobs, moving to a new home, moving to a new country (what is called 'doing a geographical' in recovery language), getting a boyfriend or girlfriend. I'd go through phases where I'd get fit or start dating someone new and feel really great, as if I'd grabbed hold of a life ring. Then I'd put the weight back on or the dating would stop and I'd feel like the life ring had slipped out of my hand and I was drowning again.

Reading this book will not magically dissolve your problems. Maybe it will be a life ring, but you still need to kick your feet and swim. This is about getting to shore, on to dry land and making sure you stay there, build a house and thrive. I need to make it clear: reading this book is not enough. It will give you awareness and I can point you in the right direction, but if you want to move forward then you have to put in the hard work. Simply put:

If you want to change your life, *then you have to change your life.*

From where you are at the moment, it may seem overwhelming. But don't try to do everything in one go. One of the most important recovery sayings is 'Progress not perfection'. Let the perfectionism go. Give yourself a break. If you become overwhelmed or slip up or even ignore this book for a year or five years, that's fine. It's here when you are ready, just like all the help on offer. No one is perfect. Everyone falters. Coming back is the important part.

Open your mind and be honest

To begin with, you need to make a couple of commitments. First of all, you need to lose some of the judgements and know-it-all attitudes you have. Over-analysing everything is part of the problem. Life should be more about feeling and experiencing. There's another recovery saying: 'Quit the debating society', which means stop over-thinking, just listen and do the right thing. This goes against the grain of Western culture. We're all encouraged to believe we know best. But that gets us into trouble on a micro and a macro level. Even world leaders don't really know what they are doing. If they did, we wouldn't have financial crashes or wars or climate change. If you are certain you know everything, close this book now and don't read any further. But you don't know it all. Neither do I. No one does. Doing things the way you have always done them is why you are here now. **It's a very real choice and yours alone to make: carry on that way and get the same results – or try a new way of thinking.**

Keep an open mind and drop your cynicism. You have the opportunity to embark on literally the most enriching, substantial journey you will ever make. If you set out on it wholeheartedly, then it will be the most rewarding thing you ever do in your life. I mean that 100 per cent. It is a winding path that will lead you back to the person who has always been there deep inside that Russian doll. It might sound patronizing or melodramatic but it is true – and I couldn't be more excited for you.

The second commitment you need to make is to take an honest look at yourself. The easy course of action is to believe there is no problem and forget about all this. That might happen. If you don't want to change yet, then that's your prerogative: **know that you can come back to it at any time.** But you must understand that serious problems can have potentially serious consequences. Lots of us have reached crunch points, so try to be honest about what is going on. I promise it will be worth it and **you can do it**.

So, if you are ready, it's time for the most difficult part: getting over the denial and accepting that there is a problem.

Recognizing you have a problem

Addiction and depression are the only illnesses that tell you that you haven't got them, and for many they have to be self-diagnosed. Our head often says 'I feel shit because I am shit. It's just what I am.' But that's not true. Your head has been lying to you for a long time. You cannot have an addiction problem without some denial – otherwise you wouldn't have allowed your behaviour to get out of control in the first place.

No one likes the idea of being labelled with the word 'addict'; it comes with so much cultural baggage. If 'dependency' works for you rather than 'addiction', that's fine. Some people prefer putting it as 'I have an addictive personality'. Also fine. Do not let labels stop you from seeking help. I interviewed Sean, you'll remember, who caught HIV at a sex party high on drugs and found himself running through the streets accusing people of trying to 'get him'. He has sought help but told me he doesn't want to go to Narcotics Anonymous because he thinks that means he's got a serious problem. Can you see the flawed logic? He clearly does have a serious problem. He crossed that line long ago. The label is the least of his worries. What he needs now is to put down his pride and seek serious help. There is nothing to be ashamed about. You didn't ask for this to happen, but it is your responsibility to ask for help. Only you can do it.

Remember how this all began. Your subconscious mind coped with trauma by doing everything it could to get away from those feelings that were heaped on you. Just reading this book will have brought you closer to those feelings, so it's likely your mind will be in overdrive trying to stop you from coming out of denial, because it knows that will take you one step closer to the feelings – the last thing it wants. Remember, these feelings are strong enough to make you damage your health, ruin relationships, lose jobs – so the feeling-denial mechanisms do not give up easily. They may be telling you I'm an idiot, that you should fling this book in the bin, that you can't change, that you don't need to, that you use drink or drugs normally; or maybe you believe that gay life is all about excess and it's not a problem. Your head might be telling you it's the gay scene's fault, or your boyfriend's fault. Or that not having a boyfriend is the root of the problem: if you could just meet the right man everything would be fine. You could also put it down to where you live: you might convince yourself it will all be OK if you move flat/town/city/country.

It's not your fault; you didn't ask for this. But your problem isn't anyone else's. Making life changes can help, but until you fundamentally address what's going on inside you it's unlikely you can live to your potential.

If you've been living these patterns for a long time, then they will likely stay with you until you sort them out.

In some ways you've already begun your process of recovery just by reading this book because you now have some awareness. You might be feeling elated because you've been trying to find out what's wrong for so long, or you might be feeling scared about what all this means. All of these reactions are OK. Do not worry about what you are feeling. And if you can't stop worrying, don't worry about that either!

The next piece of advice is to try to stop thinking you are a bad person because of the way you feel and just accept **it is what it is**. Just take a deep breath and know that it will be OK.

A really important thing to remember is that **these are just feelings and feelings always pass.**

Again, I can't stress enough that if any of this becomes too intense, then please make sure you see your GP or use the helplines listed on pages 349–54. If you have any suicidal feelings then call the Samaritans straight away.

If you're still unsure whether you have a problem, then there are some questions that various Twelve Step fellowships ask in order to determine whether you do. You can find more details on their websites, but I've adapted some of them here. Grab a pen or pencil and a piece of paper and mark '1' for every point that applies to you. These are not definitive, but they will give you some idea of whether you have been acting in a way that might indicate a problem.

Problem with overeating?
1. Do you eat when you're not hungry, or not eat when your body needs nourishment?
2. Do you go on eating binges for no apparent reason, sometimes eating until you're stuffed or even feel sick?
3. Do you have feelings of guilt, shame or embarrassment about your weight or the way you eat?
4. Do you eat sensibly in front of others and then make up for it when you are alone?
5. Is your eating affecting your health or the way you live your life?
6. When your emotions are intense – whether positive or negative – do you find yourself reaching for food?

7. Does your eating behaviour make you or others unhappy?
8. Have you ever used laxatives, vomiting, diuretics, excessive exercise, diet pills, injections or other medical interventions (including surgery) to try to control your weight?
9. Do you fast or severely restrict your food intake to control your weight?
10. Do you fantasize about how much better life would be if you were a different size or weight?
11. Do you need to chew or have something in your mouth all the time – e.g. food, gum, mints, sweets or beverages?
12. Have you ever eaten food that is burned, frozen or spoiled, or directly from the shelf in the supermarket or out of the rubbish?
13. Are there certain foods you can't stop eating after having the first bite?
14. Have you lost weight through a diet or 'period of control', only to follow this by bouts of uncontrolled eating and/or weight gain?
15. Do you spend too much time thinking about food, arguing with yourself about whether – or what – to eat, planning the next diet or exercise cure, or counting calories?

Problem with undereating or bulimia?
1. Are you obsessed with the shape of certain parts of your body?
2. Have you ever made yourself sick to get rid of food in your stomach?
3. Do you have a powerful need to keep your body in shape?
4. Do you think you are fat when others think you are underweight?
5. Do you avoid social situations because there might be food present?
6. Have you tried breaking the cycle of bingeing, purging (vomiting) and dieting but been unable to do so?
7. Do you lie about what you eat or don't eat?
8. Do you feel guilty about what you do or don't eat?
9. Do you feel scared of foods you believe are fattening?

10. Do you ever fast to get rid of the food you have eaten?
11. Have you used laxatives to expel food?
12. Do you find yourself obsessing over food?

Problem with alcohol?

1. Have you ever tried to control your drinking?
2. Have you ever worried you may have a problem with your drinking?
3. Do you get angry or emotional when you are drunk?
4. Have friends ever expressed concern about the amount you drink?
5. Have you ever had a blackout?
6. Have you drunk to the point where you were sick more than three times in your life?
7. Do you worry about what you do when you are drunk?
8. Do you do things drunk which you later regret and would not do sober?
9. Do you drink alone?
10. Have you ever had unsafe sex under the influence of alcohol?
11. Have you lied about your drinking?
12. Have you taken time off work because of your drinking?
13. Do you find yourself scared at the thought of going out to a social event without alcohol?

Problem with drugs?

1. Do you use drugs alone?
2. Do you avoid people or places that make you feel bad about your drug taking?
3. Have you ever 'gone under'?
4. Have you ever taken a substance without knowing what it was?
5. Have you been arrested for drug use or possession?
6. Have you broken your own sexual boundaries under the influence of drugs or been sexually assaulted?
7. Does your drug use interfere with your sleep patterns?
8. Have you ever thought you needed drugs to fit in with another group of people or social situation?

9. Have you ever prioritized buying drugs over other important financial commitments, like paying bills, money for food, etc.?
10. Have you ever injected drugs?
11. Does the thought of running out of drugs scare you?
12. Have you ever used crystal meth?

Problem with sex?
1. Have you ever worried about your sexual behaviour?
2. Have you ever felt guilty or ashamed of some of your sexual behaviour?
3. Have friends expressed worry about your sexual behaviour?
4. Have you ever had unsafe sex without intending to?
5. Do you find yourself lying to friends about what you are doing when you are pursuing sex in some form?
6. Do you find yourself leaving social events early to spend time chasing sex (or watching porn, etc.)?
7. Have you ever spent money that you cannot afford on porn or escorts?
8. Do you think sex is the most important thing in your life?
9. Do you find yourself needing more extreme things in order to get a sexual high?
10. Do you find yourself lying about who you are online?
11. Have you ever thought there could be more you could do with your life if you weren't so preoccupied with sex?

Problem with love addiction?
1. Do you fall in love with people quickly and easily?
2. Do you assign magical qualities to people and believe they are special, exceptional and the thing that will make your life better?
3. Do you find yourself wasting time obsessing about people?
4. Do you find yourself attracted to people who treat you badly?
5. Do you find yourself attracted to people who are unavailable – they could be straight, unable to speak English, or too young to commit to you?

6. Do you find it hard to be single and always pursue relationships?
7. Does your romantic/sexual behaviour affect your reputation?
8. Do you only feel comfortable if someone wants or needs you?

Problem with codependency?

1. Do you try to control other people?
2. Do you often think you are better than other people?
3. Do you often strongly think you are less than other people?
4. Do you criticize other people a lot?
5. Do you think you always put other people before yourself, neglecting your own needs?
6. Do you feel uncomfortable when you are not in a relationship?
7. Do you believe you are unlovable?
8. Do you have problems admitting you have made a mistake?
9. Do you think in a very black-and-white way?

Problem with emotional, sexual or social anorexia?

1. Do you often feel separate from groups of people and switch between wishing you could be part of the group and looking down on it?
2. Do you tend to push people away when they get too close?
3. Do you have casual sex to stop any one person from getting emotionally close?
4. Do you sabotage your relationships?
5. Do you find that you have not had an emotional and/or sexual relationship for a long period of time?
6. Do you use pornography or prostitutes instead of having a substantial relationship?
7. Have you ever been paid for sex?
8. Does the thought of going on a date terrify you?
9. On dates, do you find insignificant reasons to not see the person again – like a brand of clothing they wear or a minor opinion with which you disagree?

10. Have you told yourself relationships are 'not for me' but find it difficult to examine the feelings underneath?

Only you can decide what applies to you, but if you've answered yes to three or more of these questions then there is a very strong chance you have a problem that you might wish to do something about. In the case of anorexia and bulimia, if you have answered yes to any of the questions you should seek help – most importantly medical help, as anorexia is extremely dangerous. If you are a man, try the website Beat, which has a 'Service Finder' page that gives you the nearest support groups: http://helpfinder.b-eat.co.uk

Two different approaches to recovery: 'harm reduction' and 'abstinence'

If you have recognized that you need some serious change and you are ready to stop using your drug of choice – and it would be by far the best thing, as you'll save yourself a whole load of grief – then act on it. Skip to the next chapter.

But you might not be ready. You might be adamant that you can control your use. If that's where you are, don't feel bad about it. It is what it is. Recovery is about accepting where you are and giving yourself a break. Many people are determined to see if they can control their drinking or drug use so that they can indulge in it without it being a problem.

This highlights a fundamental difference of approach in treating addictions. Some groups believe in an **abstinence**-based approach, which means you stop altogether (unless it's food or sex, which isn't practical; we'll come to this). Twelve Step groups (Alcoholics Anonymous, Narcotics Anonymous, etc.) follow an abstinence-based programme and this is also what, on the whole, rehabs offer.

Others believe in a **harm-reduction** approach, meaning you try to limit your use but are still able to use sometimes. Groups like Antidote, 56 Dean Street and some parts of the NHS often go for harm reduction. This is because they believe that using words like 'addiction' and 'addict' or telling someone they need to stop will put some people off getting help. Antidote and Dean Street will help people stop using if that's what they want, but if not they will help them try to control and cut down on their using and to do it more safely.

One example of harm reduction would be the NHS prescribing heroin addicts with methadone (very different from mephedrone) as a substitute; they carry on using but are provided with the drug, which is taken as a liquid, in the hope they don't have to go out and steal to feed their habit, don't inject and so on. The idea is that the amount of harm done is reduced – but the problematic feelings underneath that drove the destructive behaviour are not addressed.

Another harm-reduction example is clinics that give out free, clean needle packs.

The 56 Dean Street clinic takes the view that they will help the client achieve what they decide they want. If they want to give up, they'll help them do that; if they want to use once a month or every six months, they'll help them do that. It might involve educating people on how to use the drug more safely, how to make overdose less likely, and so on.

An abstinence-based approach is the one I favour, combined with harm reduction where necessary, because I believe unless you stop the addictive behaviour it makes it very hard to deal with the problem underneath. Abstinence-based programmes believe that controlled use is not possible because people with 'addictive personalities' cannot stop using once they start and this will always lead to troublesome behaviour. They believe that the only way to achieve recovery is to stop (abstain). But they won't force you. It's your choice. They just support you until you are ready. More on this later. I do believe people should be given access to clean needles, etc., but that they should also be encouraged to become free of drugs or alcohol.

However, the most important thing in the first instance is getting your foot in the door. No one will ever judge you or force you to do anything you don't want to do, so I can certainly appreciate the approach that Antidote takes: just helping people cut down and manage their use works for many, especially in the first instance.

Some people reading this book will just need to cut down their drinking or drugging. Others will need more drastic action. Only you can know. You are free to try a controlled-use approach if you wish to see if you can do it, but please be aware of how serious the problem potentially is.

Moderating your behaviour

If you want to try controlling your behaviour, go back to your answers to the questions above and write down what's working and what's not working. Whatever the problem is, write down why you want to stop the negative consequences: e.g. I don't want to catch STIs; I don't want to be late for work; I don't want to miss family events; I want a serious relationship; I don't want to lose my keys and phone again; I don't want to feel tired and down all the time.

Now set some relevant boundaries that might prevent these things happening – they are up to you, but I've suggested some below.

If alcohol is the issue, then perhaps you could set a boundary of having two nights a week when you don't drink at all and on other week nights restricting yourself to no more than two drinks. Maybe allow yourself to get drunk on one night a month and set a limit for what time you go home to bed. Or maybe decide not to drink Monday to Thursday nights, perhaps with the exception of special events like birthdays.

If you want, try to scale down your drinking over two weeks. Then see if you can do it for a month with your new boundaries in place. Tell a close friend you trust what you are doing and ask them to monitor your drinking when you are out together.

Some people find this thought process helpful: when you are deciding whether to have the first drink, try to project what will happen when you've had it. Will it lead to two, to three, maybe more? How will you feel? Will that euphoric, relaxed feeling last or will it go very quickly and will you need more and more, then end up doing something you don't want to do, like texting an ex or getting into an argument or, at the very least, having a bad hangover in the morning?

How will that feel? Sometimes we can use that projection to stop us having that first drink and to override the 'fuck-it button'.

If you want to change your Grindr use, make a rule of only checking it for half an hour every evening at a set time. Or make a rule that you tell people within ten messages that you should now take the conversation into the real world and meet in a public place like a coffee shop. If you wish, you could make a rule of never sending explicit pictures. If it's all too much, then try deleting Grindr and committing to not using it for four weeks and see if you can manage that. You can always come back to it.

If you are concerned about your sexual behaviour, recovery is not about stopping you having sex. So set some boundaries, such as not letting strangers into your home, or not sleeping with someone till you've had two dates with them in a public place. Set a boundary that you won't have anal sex without a condom.

Try to work out what triggers behaviour you're not comfortable with – alcohol, drugs, whatever it may be – and put a boundary round that: maybe 'I won't go on Grindr after I've had alcohol.' It could be that you immediately block anyone who talks about drugs on Grindr. For people who waste hours and hours compulsively masturbating, try cutting out masturbation for a period of time, like a month or a week. Or have a rule that you will only masturbate if you are aroused, that you will not start the process just to pass the time. See if you can stick to the boundary.

Again, be very careful. If you have a serious substance problem I don't recommend controlled use; this is just an option for you if you do not want to make that big leap to abstinence. So my serious advice is that if you are using crystal meth, G or mephedrone, then seek professional help to stop. These drugs are just too dangerous, too unpredictable and too addictive, as well as illegal. If you are injecting then you have a very serious problem and you need to get help to stop; there is no doubt about it. You are gambling with your health and there's a very real possibility that these drugs will get you into legal trouble too. But I am realistic that many people won't want to stop. If you are not ready, then at the very least you should learn about harm-reduction methods and make sure you are using equipment that is clean and sterile. Call a local sexual-health clinic and ask if they provide clean needles. Learn about how to use more safely if that is your decision, as hard as it is.

If you are adamant you cannot or don't want to stop your drug use but you do want to cut down, then get a piece of paper and work out what your triggers are. Is it going on Grindr? Is it sex parties? Put boundaries round those things – commit to not going to them for a period of time, or maybe to going only once every three months. Are Friday nights a problem for you, or is it Sunday afternoons when you have a stretch of time? Or bank holidays? Work out in advance new things to do at these times, like arranging to see a friend or family, or book cinema tickets – anything that gives you some way of having something else to do in the potentially dangerous period. Are there websites that are triggers for you? Is it porn? Commit to not going on them.

Maybe chat to a close friend to decide what your boundary is. Call one of the drugs support lines and get some advice on how to try to control your using.

Be aware too that the nature of addiction is that when you stop one behaviour another often comes up. It's like that game 'Whack a Mole' that you might see in arcades. One mole pops up, you bash it down then another one pops up, bash that and another jumps up. So if you stop drinking you might find your sex drive goes crazy. If you stop having casual sex you might find yourself overeating or smoking or even obsessively cleaning. If you cut down on drugs you might start drinking more or maybe going to the gym obsessively. Some of these are more harmful than others: obviously cleaning is not as bad as drinking too much, but be aware, set boundaries where need be and take it easy. Remember, this is about progress not perfection.

When you are trying to control your behaviour, be aware that your head may make excuses and tell you it's OK to indulge because it's someone's birthday or a Saturday night or a bank holiday. If this is within your boundary, then that's OK, but if not you need to recognize that you've broken it. Again, don't give yourself a hard time if you break a boundary. Don't think you are weak or a bad person. You are not. It is just a warning that you need to address this more seriously.

Maybe you do have some control over what you are doing; that will be true for some readers. That is great. Now try to keep it up for the next month. It's common to manage it for a short period of time and then slip back into old habits.

What I've written above sounds simplistic. And that's because it is. In reality, people with the most serious addiction problems usually can't stop for more than a day or two, if at all. Others can stop at first, which convinces them they have no problem; but they soon slip back across the boundary. Be aware that just stopping for a period of time doesn't mean you are out of the woods. Sometimes people control their drinking or drugging for a few months and then disaster strikes and they end up having an accident or getting hurt.

It's tempting to play this down and make excuses: 'I'll do it next time'; 'I'll just have one more binge'; 'I'll have one more weekend of chemsex'; and so on. 'I'll stop after the next time' is the national anthem of people with dependency problems. But next time never comes.

If you have tried to moderate your behaviour and have failed to do so safely, then it's time to accept you must take serious action. It's time to defeat the problem before it defeats you. It may seem like the last thing you want to do, because you can't imagine any life without alcohol or drugs or Grindr, or because it seems scary or downright impossible. It isn't. That is just part of addictive thinking. No one is going to force you to do anything. Changing does not mean a boring, dull or holier-than-thou life. It's the opposite. It's a better life than you have now, one where you get more done, achieve more, have more fun and have better relationships. There are hundreds of people to help you, all of whom have been in the position you are in, all of whom know what it's like inside your head because they've been there and they came out the other side. You can too.

16

Getting Serious Help

'The moment I let go of it was the moment I got more than I could handle,
The moment I jumped off of it was the moment I touched down'

Alanis Morissette, 'Thank U'

OK, LET'S PRESUME YOU'VE already taken the hardest and most important step: accepting that you have a problem. The next step is doing something about it and asking for help – and this too can be difficult. Addiction keys into patterns of secrecy. Take a deep breath, stop fighting and make the leap.

So I've told you I don't believe in 'apricot answers'. You can't wave a magic wand and make your life better overnight. But you can start making real change that *will* happen, perhaps quickly or perhaps slowly, but will happen. The most important thing is that you can see a glimmer of hope.

You have lots of options. Some I've mentioned before. Let's go over them again.

Medical help

If you have a problem with depression, bulimia or anorexia, or a problem with alcohol or drugs, then I recommend you go to a doctor and get help. You can discuss this with any of the helplines first if you wish. Anorexia is exceptionally dangerous and kills many people. You must take it seriously and get yourself medically assessed. There are also helplines to call if you are too scared to go to your doctor.

There is a potential problem here, though: as we saw in Chapter 12, not all GPs and doctors have much experience with some of the drugs that have emerged in recent years, such as G, mephedrone or crystal meth. If you have this problem, then the following organizations will correspond with you and offer advice:

Club Drug Clinic Advice on physical addiction, and psychiatric support.
http://clubdrugclinic.cnwl.nhs.uk
69 Warwick Road, Earls Court, London SW5 9HB
For confidential advice call 020 3315 6111, or email clubdrugclinic.cnwl@nhs.net

Antidote Part of London Friend, for general drug/alcohol use.
http://londonfriend.org.uk/get-support/drugsandalcohol/
Telephone: 020 7833 1674

56 Dean Street Chemsex issues and psychosexual support.
http://www.chelwest.nhs.uk/services/hiv-sexual-health/
clinics/56-dean-street/56-dean-street
Appointments: 020 3315 6699

I am asking Switchboard to compile a list of helplines and support services for anyone in need of help or support for these issues. They can be contacted via www.switchboard.lgbt; 0300 330 0630; or email chris@switchboard.lgbt

Rehab

If you have an extreme problem and are exceptionally lucky your GP might send you to rehab. This is the best thing you can do, but also the most expensive, and it's rare for the NHS to pay for it.

There are different types of rehab, but primarily what they do is take you in for a substantial period, from one month to six months or more. They manage any physical detox that is needed, remove all your access to phones, TV, internet, etc., as well as all addictive substances and processes, and give you intense therapy. The coping mechanisms are stopped and the buried feelings come up. I spent a week at the famous Priory as an outpatient doing one of their 'Trauma Reduction' programmes, which is not the same as rehab, but I saw some of what went on.

Rehabs are usually in very calm, peaceful, rural places, normally with big grounds. Everything is designed to look after, nurture and hold you. Often there will be a range of programmes, including one-to-one and group therapy, and others such as arts-based therapy and even equine therapy (working with horses); many rehabs also start patients on Twelve Step programmes.

Rehabs are amazing but incredibly expensive. Some of them cost tens of thousands of pounds because the care is so comprehensive. This means that for most they are not an option. There are some NHS places available, but they are hard to get because there are relatively few of them. Some private health insurance companies will pay for rehab. Talk to your doctor or therapist about this.

Antidepressants

If you have anxiety or depression your doctor may suggest a course of medication such as antidepressants. Many people swear by them, but other professionals don't like them. My experience with them was that they reduced my anxiety but meant that I couldn't feel my feelings and so couldn't deal with the problematic ones. Because they often reduce sex drive, I did find them helpful in calming some of my behaviour. However, sometimes people can be going through extreme distress and depression, and antidepressants can be helpful for when they can't cope.

There are a variety of antidepressants and some are good at low doses just for anxiety. Talk with your GP about their potential benefits and side-effects. If you are severely depressed and your doctor seriously thinks you need them, then listen to him or her.

Therapy

Your doctor may refer you to an NHS therapist but you may have to wait for a number of weeks to see someone. You will normally have an assessment, after which the therapist will decide which type of therapy is best for you. Be warned that some therapists are better than others and sometimes it can be pot luck. Ask specifically if a therapist has an understanding of LGBT issues and shame. I've already mentioned that my experience of NHS therapy unfortunately wasn't great. I have friends who really benefited from it, but I also hear a lot of people in recovery say that their therapists did not understand addiction – so it is important, if that is your issue, that you ask about their experience of addiction.

Another option is private therapy. Paying to see a therapist means you can pick and choose to find one who specializes in working with alcohol/drug dependency/food or sex issues or whatever you need, as well as making sure they are LGBT-friendly. The high cost, however, means many people cannot take this option.

Private therapy can be anywhere from 'pay what you can' to between £20 and £150 per hour, and psychiatrists can charge more. Many therapists, however, charge around £60 per hour and some see a limited number of clients at very low rates, sometimes even for free. Think seriously, though: keep in mind how much you spend on booze, drugs, porn or sex, and so on, and understand that this is a far more important way to use your money because it will benefit you. If you are in dire need it is worth emailing and asking if a therapist offers the possibility of reduced rates, explaining your income and need for therapy.

Again, check that any therapist you are thinking of seeing understands addiction and working with LGBT people. Pink Therapy has a listing on its website of LGBT-friendly therapists: www.pinktherapy.com

Be aware specifically that even LGBT-friendly therapists may not all agree with the concept of sex addiction. Some may even try to talk you out of seeing extreme sexual behaviour as problematic. Remember that therapists are people too and have been shaped by their own life experiences and opinions. If you believe your sexual behaviour is a problem, then make sure you find someone who works with sexual addiction or compulsion.

CBT (cognitive behavioural therapy) is often recommended by the NHS for people with depression, anxiety and addictions. This is a 'talking therapy', where you work out with your therapist what is causing your problems, what the triggers are and learn new ways to deal with them.

CBT is the therapy of choice in the NHS. I have met many people who have found it helpful. Everyone is different, however, and it did not work for me. My problems were far more deep-seated and I found CBT frustrating; for me, it didn't touch the sides. I have also heard many other people say that CBT didn't help them. It tends to be a therapy of the thought processes, focusing on retraining the mind, while addiction, I believe, being an illness of the mind, body and spirit, is more complex. I'll explain this in more detail below.

Gay support groups offer free or very cheap LGBT-specific therapy depending on your need, such as the Lesbian and Gay Centre in Manchester. I've listed these on pages 349–54. London's 56 Dean Street offers psychosexual therapy. Antidote in London offers one-to-one therapy, group therapy and mini-rehab programmes that run over a series of weekends. All of this can help.

Twelve Steps for addiction are free groups that run every day all over the country offering help and support, first to stop using and then to address the underlying problems. You'll have heard of Alcoholics Anonymous, but there are countless other groups for different types of addictive behaviour, including overeating, gambling, sex addiction, compulsive spending, work addiction and so on. I would highly recommend these groups, and in the next section of this chapter I will explain why.

Twelve Steps

Twelve Step programmes have been exceptionally successful in helping people conquer addictions. They are based on the original **Alcoholics Anonymous** group that was founded in 1935 by two men, Bill Wilson and Dr Bob Smith, in Akron, Ohio. Both of them were alcoholics who had tried to stop drinking with no success until they devised their own course of action, which involved going through a programme of twelve stages that helped them get and stay sober. They found that it worked for them and helped others too, and, quickly, the programme expanded across their home city, then across America and the world.

Today there are millions of people attending AA meetings. There will be one very near you, wherever you live, and many if you live in a big town or city. Lots of people attend AA, but because the programme is anonymous and addiction carries stigma, most don't tell many people. You can download an app to tell you where your nearest one is, check online or call their helpline. For details, see www.alcoholics-anonymous.org.uk

As AA became successful, people used the Twelve Step model to help with other addictive problems, using the same principles but replacing 'alcohol' with other behaviours. In 1953 the first official **Narcotics Anonymous** meetings for people with drug addictions were held in Los Angeles and these too spread across the world. **Gamblers Anonymous** began in LA four years later. In 1976 an AA member in Boston realized that his patterns of cheating on his wife seemed to be very similar to the compulsive need he had to drink, so he started **Sex and Love Addicts Anonymous**. **Overeaters Anonymous** has also become very popular, as has **Anorexics and Bulimics Anonymous**. Wikipedia has a list of the many groups that exist around the world, which include everything from **Underearners Anonymous** (for people who have a problem accepting that they deserve a good job) through to **Smokers Anonymous**, **Workaholics Anonymous** and even **Clutterers Anonymous**. Groups focused on a particular problem are called **fellowships**.

All these addictions are the result of the same things – fear, anxiety and low self-esteem – but manifest in different ways. It's very common for people to be cross-addicted – that is, they have more than one addiction. My personal belief is that everyone with an addiction is cross-addicted in some way.

Twelve Step groups are unique in that they are run by the people who attend, do not have leaders and are not run for profit. They meet in rented rooms such as community centres or church halls. There are no fees, though the groups are self-supporting so members contribute what they can – 10p, 50p, £1, whatever they are able to afford – to pay for the hire of the room and to buy the explanatory AA books and pamphlets. Usually they pay by popping change into a pot or cup that is passed around. If you have no money, that is fine too.

Meetings are informal and are essentially discussion and group-therapy sessions. You don't need to book or give your name; you just come along and sit and listen. It's great if you turn up on time, but you are welcome to pop in, arrive late, leave early. There are no registers. You come and go as you please. Everyone is welcome. If you want to speak you can, but you don't have to. No one runs the group – members put themselves forward if they wish to be the 'secretary' of their group and take responsibility for opening, setting up and locking up; someone will do so for a set period (though they are free to give up the commitment at any time) before another member takes the position. Groups are absolutely democratic.

You are encouraged – though it's not obligatory – to go for tea or coffee after the meetings and to make friends with people. This is a really important part of recovery, because opening up and sharing your story with other people is a way of combating shame. But again, you don't have to. No one will force you. As with all aspects of Twelve Step groups, you do things as you wish.

AA encourages members to complete the 'Twelve Steps' when they are ready. No one will force you and not everyone does it, though they are hugely beneficial and I would strongly advise it. You are encouraged, in your own time, to ask another member who has completed the steps to buddy up with you and help take you through them. These people are called 'sponsors'. You and your sponsor decide between you how you will work the steps and you do so at your own pace. Again, no one holds you to it. You are free to drop out or change sponsors whenever you want. Everything is completely up to you. It's not school. There is no pressure.

The Twelve Steps help you define what your problem is, what boundaries you want to set, how to stick to them, and how to identify and deal with the causal issues underneath. Doing the steps can be emotional and draining, but people report a profound unburdening as they go through them. The idea is that you are left a happier and calmer person, able to face life's challenges without having to rely on your drug of choice in order to cope. The theory is that once you have stopped doing what you have been doing, the negative feelings come to the surface, start to lift and your life begins to transform and improve.

The good news is that if you do the steps, the programme works. No one is entirely sure how or why, but AA has helped literally millions of people to get sober and to live happier lives, and I cannot recommend it – or other Twelve Step groups – strongly enough.

I believe Twelve Step groups are the most beneficial way to enable and achieve a far-reaching, long-lasting recovery because they offer a whole range of things in one go:

They are inexpensive Unlike paying £60-plus for a therapist once a week, you can go whenever you like – five times a day if you wish – and pay what you want towards the running of the meeting. It's entirely up to you.

They are local There are meetings all over the country and there is most likely one very near you. In London there are several meetings within ten minutes' walk of my front door. If there isn't one where you live, once you have some recovery you can find other people and set a new one up.

There are no waiting lists and you can go as regularly as you need You don't have to wait months to start. Go today if you want. This is better than waiting from appointment to appointment.

No one forces you With therapy you have to commit to the sessions and be on time or you will lose the money or risk being dismissed from the service. No one from Twelve Step groups will check up on you or ask you where you've been if you don't go. It's recommended you go to a minimum of six meetings to get a feel for it, but no one will make you. It will work best if you commit and go to at least three meetings a week, but ultimately it's completely up to you. The good thing is that even if you drop out you can go back at any time. No one will judge you for it.

You are welcome even if you carry on using Do not worry if you aren't ready to stop drinking (or whatever it is you do): you are still welcome to go to the meetings. They usually make an announcement at the beginning of every meeting requesting that if you have drunk or used drugs on that day then you refrain from speaking in the main meeting, but they are happy for you to listen and to talk to other attendees afterwards.

They are the same wherever you go There are Twelve Step groups in most Western countries and you can walk into any of them any-where and be welcomed. This is helpful for many reasons. Let's say you have a drink problem and have stopped with the help of a ther-apist in Bristol. What if one day you have to go to another city for a work event or on holiday? Holidays, work or family events can be stressful things; they can cause you to feel anxious and start thinking about drinking. But if you are in AA then there will be a meeting somewhere nearby. Simply download an app, check the website or call the helpline for whatever fellowship you need and they will tell you where your nearest meeting is. Once you find it you will be welcomed and you will get a top-up of all the positive things that the meetings give you.

Some other methods of recovery just focus on the immediate problem I'm not convinced the medical profession completely understands that addiction is about far more than just the problem behaviour. Twelve Step meetings are as much about helping you deal with the underlying issues as they are about the compulsive behaviour. They are like going to a good dentist for a filling – he stops the pain, drills out the rot, then the tooth heals and you start a regular cleaning programme. The AA saying goes 'Come for the drinking, stay for the thinking', which means a problem with drinking may be the thing that brings you to the meetings, but once you've stopped you realize you need help with what's underneath, the emotional problems that caused the problematic drinking in the first place.

They make you feel less alone Addiction makes you think you are the only person with the problem. Twelve Step groups connect you to people who have been through – and are going through – the same thing as you. Whereas a doctor or therapist may not know personally what it is like, Twelve Step groups operate on the principle of a person who has been through it helping others go through the same thing.

They reduce shame Addiction is a shame-based illness. Hearing other people say they've done the same thing as you, or have done things that are even more extreme, reduces your sense of shame.

They give you a support network You are encouraged – but again, no one forces you – to make friends. This means that if you have a craving you have a whole group of people to call to ask for advice and support. You'd be surprised, but having someone on the other end of a phone who understands, who won't judge you or try to convince you to act in a certain way – as even your most well-meaning friend might – can be immensely powerful.

They get you out of the house This sounds flippant, but actually it's important. Shame wants you to stay alone in your home, miserable and suffering in isolation. Getting out and not just wallowing is incredibly important. The illness is about living small – staying drunk or high or in anonymous sexual situations; meetings get you back into real life and open up the world.

They reduce anxiety Meetings get you out of your head. The very process of going to a meeting and listening to other people talking honestly of their deepest fears and feelings takes the focus away from yourself and relaxes you without you even knowing it. When you attend regularly you remember other people's stories, and this too subtly builds your capacity to be interested in others. Bit by bit it starts to reduce the amount of obsessing about yourself that you do.

They give you confidence If you want to, you can sit in a meeting and listen without ever speaking. It's completely up to you. But even if it seems like the worst idea in the world right now, most people eventually feel confident enough to speak in meetings they become familiar with. It is a *huge* unburdening and begins to build self-confidence you might not think you have at the moment. Remember: no one will force you. You can take part whenever you are ready. If that's never, then that's fine too. Just sitting and listening has a powerful effect on its own. You will surprise yourself.

There are LGBT-specific groups Mainstream meetings are heavily attended by LGBT people and there are also specific LGBT meetings. Both types are helpful. Some of us feel understandably alienated from or intimidated by straight people. In mainstream meetings, however, all sorts of people will trust you with their innermost thoughts and feelings. You will build relationships with them and learn that sexuality isn't a big deal to most people – in my experience groups are entirely supportive of LGBT people. You'll also realize that it's not only gay people who have troubles in these areas.

LGBT-specific meetings do the same for you with gay people. Many of us have only really interacted with LGBT people in pubs and clubs and in the context of trying to meet sexual or romantic partners. Gay meetings help you build, perhaps for the first time, friendships with other gay people based on personality and deeper connections, not on sexual attraction.

In London there is at least one LGBT AA meeting every day. Brighton has several and so do large cities like Manchester. As I write this, there is an increasing number of LGBT meetings for other fellowships, such as Narcotics Anonymous, Sex Addicts Anonymous, Sex and Love Addicts Anonymous, plus two very quickly growing gay Crystal Meth Addict Anonymous groups in London. You can Google these UK groups and search for the LGBT meetings; I've listed details on pages 350–52. There are also other specific meetings for women, people of different backgrounds and ethnicities, young people's meetings, etc.

Anonymity It's important that members know they will be anonymous. You probably won't know anyone when you first go, but there is always a chance you will. You shouldn't worry about that. If you do see someone you know, they are seeking help for a problem too and wish to be anonymous like you do. Members are specifically asked to respect fellow attendees' privacy. Don't let this stop you from going.

Members of Twelve Step groups are encouraged to remain anonymous in public media. The idea is that the fellowships are about 'principles, not personalities', and that no one should be a public figure representing the group. If they were to relapse, as sometimes people do as with all methods of recovery, other people might use this as a reason to tell themselves it doesn't work and they shouldn't bother trying. However, more and more famous people are 'out' about being members of Twelve Step groups and my own belief is that it can be beneficial, as it means more people know help is available.

Misconceptions about Twelve Steps

It's worth looking at a few problems that some people have with Twelve Step groups and common misconceptions about them.

The G-word

OK, this is the big one and the thing most likely to put you off, but it's important you read on. One of the main reasons some people don't like Twelve Step programmes is because they involve talk of God or a 'higher power'. The reason for this is that Bill Wilson, one of the founders, was a religious man and credited God with helping him overcome his alcoholism, something he hadn't thought possible on his own. He and the original founding members understood correctly that addictions are not just physical or mental problems but spiritual problems as well.

So the Twelve Steps *are* a spiritual programme of recovery – but they are *not* Christian or religious in any way.

When I said earlier that you needed to put your intellect to one side, this is the moment to do that, and to keep an open mind and trust me. I believe organized religion is one of the root causes of evil and of the persecution of LGBT people, so I wouldn't recommend Twelve Step groups if they were religious or about brainwashing you in any way.

In Twelve Step programmes the concept of a 'higher power' is about accepting that you need something bigger than yourself to get better – you need something outside yourself. That's not as dramatic as it sounds, just that you've tried before to stay on track and the fact that you still need help means that you haven't been able to do it by yourself. This is simply about realizing that human beings need to be connected both to other people and to a concept of something bigger than themselves. That 'higher power' can be whatever you want. It can be your friends, your family, your dog or cat; I've heard people say their higher power is the sky, or nature, or, commonly, even the group as a whole. It is completely up to you. You can absolutely be an atheist and be a member of a Twelve Step group.

It's very common to hear members say they hate the part about God – but despite that they still attend and it still works for them, often after years of trying all other options. Gay people have been bludgeoned by religion and many of us are naturally hostile to anything involving it. That's the way I feel too. If this was about convincing someone to be religious, I would tell you to run a mile. I'm telling you the opposite.

Spirituality and religion are two different things. Spirituality is not about rules and dogma and feeling guilty. Neither are Twelve Step programmes: they are about helping you **remove that guilt and shame**, which has often been put there by religion. You might not understand or like the concept of spirituality, but you are already living a spiritual life whether you like it or not – we all are. Your spirituality is simply the positive, loving side of yourself, the energy of joy and togetherness. It's the feeling you have when your dog bounds up wagging its tail, or the biggest laugh you have with your best friend. Or that feeling in a concert when sixty thousand people sing along in unison to a song you love, or the moment when you are looking into the eyes of someone you love, or when you feel at your most confident and happy, as if you can do anything. It is all the most positive aspects of our existence. In short, it is love.

We don't talk about love, especially in the UK, because we are painfully self-conscious and embarrassed about our feelings, but this is about love for yourself, for the people you care about, love for other people, for the world, for the whole of existence. It sounds happy-clappy and crazy, and your head may be telling you 'What rubbish', but it is not as insane as telling yourself everything's shit and getting to the point where you are so depressed you want to kill yourself. It doesn't have to be that way. Ultimately it is a choice. Reconnecting to that innate spiritual joy in yourself is essentially what the Twelve Steps are about. And they work. Keep going and you will slowly start to reconnect to these feelings.

A good way to understand the concept of higher power and spirituality is something simple a therapist told me: an acceptance that what you can't do alone you can do with the help of other people. It might just be one person or it might be a whole group of people, but that in itself is a power greater than yourself. If it helps, think of it simply as 'two heads are better than one'.

The word 'God' does come up in the literature for Twelve Step groups. It helps some people to think of the word 'Good' instead. Or sometimes people use it as an acronym for 'Good Orderly Direction'. There is an expression in Twelve Step groups: 'Fake it to make it'. That means even if you don't believe it, just go with it, pretend. Have faith in the process. In other words, get over it and it will work.

If you have an addiction problem I cannot emphasize enough how strongly I would urge you to join a Twelve Step group, even if you just use it as a way of getting into recovery and you see outside therapists, etc., along the way. The next sentence is one of the most important things you need to take away from this book:

Do not let the God thing put you off Twelve Step groups!

'It doesn't work'

Some people say Twelve Step groups don't work. But that's because there is no quick fix. If you go to the meetings, work the programme and commit to it, then it *will* change your whole life for the better.

Some people stop using the first time they go to a Twelve Step meeting, others take longer; sometimes people remain sober for ever and some people fall off the wagon then get back on again, or don't. It's up to them. That doesn't mean it doesn't work, but that addiction is a deadly serious, powerful affliction. If it wasn't, then you wouldn't need any help with it. You might find recovery easy or you might need to work at it for a long time. Don't stress about that. If you commit to the group, things *will* start getting better.

'It's for losers'

Some think 'Me? An alcoholic? A sex addict? A drug addict? How very dare you!!' But it's not a question of winners or losers. In fact,

I would argue, if you make it into a group you are a winner, one of the lucky ones. To put it frankly, what's better – being dead like the people I mentioned at the beginning of the book, or going to a group with lots of other supportive people who help you live a healthier, happier life?

The people who attend Twelve Step meetings are from all walks of life – doctors, lawyers, bankers, students, nurses, housewives, artists, people in the media, young people, old people, gay, straight, bi, pan, trans, cis, of all different ethnicities. Across the world many high-achieving people have been or are in recovery. As already mentioned, anonymity is key, but occasionally – for various reasons – some famous names have gone public about turning their lives around through Twelve Step programmes: Betty Ford, former First Lady of the United States and founder of the famous Betty Ford Center in California for the treatment of substance dependency; Buzz Aldrin, the second man on the moon; the bestselling author Stephen King, who's spoken a lot about it; actors Anthony Hopkins and Robert Downey Jr; comedian and writer Russell Brand; writer-performer Harvey Fierstein; scene DJ Fat Tony; musicians Eric Clapton, Robbie Williams and Boy George are just a few of them. Princess Leia herself, Carrie Fisher, has spoken a lot about being a member of AA and NA. In 2015 Elton John celebrated twenty-five years of being sober from alcohol and drugs with the help of AA and NA. They have all spoken about it publicly.

In February 2015 TV presenter Davina McCall spoke in an interview with the *Daily Mirror* about being a member of Narcotics Anonymous. She credits going to NA and AA meetings with getting her life back on track after heroin and alcohol addictions. She told the *Daily Mirror*, 'I do still go to meetings because I just think that NA is brilliant – a very, very clever system . . . I've always been really nervous talking about it though, because obviously it's an anonymous thing . . . But it really does work and I've had an awful lot of support from NA over the years . . . It's not some weird cult – it's just a place where people get help and support . . . I get a lot from it.'

Many creative people with drink or drug problems believe they will be boring and won't be able to create without drink and drugs. Davina McCall's career took off, Stephen King has written more books since he got sober, Robert Downey Jr became the highest-paid actor in the world, and after Elton John got sober he wrote *The Lion King* and *Billy Elliot*, found the love of his life and had children.

Singer John Grant wrote his best songs and found success and fame after getting sober. In summer 2015 he told me that it was when he was at his lowest ebb and was diagnosed with late-stage syphilis (which can be terminal) that his nurse told him she went to AA and recommended he try it. He said, 'I've had amazing experiences there with people. Going there is a great time for me . . . I get a great perspective there, I get great advice [from] listening to other people's experience and I hear shit there that resonates with me. I hear stories that help me understand more about what I'm going through and help me feel like I'm not alone. You can get what you want out of it . . . I hear people say all the time, fuck that shit, I will never be a part of that club, and I get it, I do. I do understand that, but I've met incredible people there and I do notice it helps me get away from myself. And not in an escape way, but the bad part, the selfish part where you have your head up your own ass and you go oh poor me, me, me, me, me. That doesn't do anybody any good and it really helps me get away from that.'

The vast majority of people in Twelve Step groups aren't famous; they are just normal people. They are often the most inspiring people you will meet, especially if they have come from places like those mentioned in this book, both gay and straight, and have built their lives back up.

The right programme for you

I would strongly suggest you look at your most pressing problem and go to the fellowship that is most appropriate and urgent for you – see the list on pages 350–51. However, I have included here some advice about particular problems, which I hope may be helpful.

Codependency

What if your problem isn't any of the addictions we've been discussing but is codependency – being too needy, people-pleasing, putting others first all the time? CoDA (Codependents Anonymous) is a group that uses the Twelve Steps, which can help you work through the issues, and it is also worth seeing a private therapist if you can afford it (be sure to ask them if they understand codependency when you are looking for someone). See www.coda-uk.org

Sex addiction

There is not much understanding or treatment of sexual compulsion issues, so I would highly recommend reading Robert Weiss's book *Cruise Control: Understanding Sex Addiction in Gay Men*. If you can afford a private therapist you can search online for someone with experience working with sex addiction or compulsive sexual behaviour. But again, I would suggest the best possible course of action is to go to a Sex Addicts Anonymous or Sex and Love Addicts Anonymous meeting, even if just because it will get you into some structured support. In London at the time of writing there is one LGBT-specific Sex and Love Anonymous Addicts every week, and there are two LGBT-specific Sex Addicts Anonymous meetings weekly. I would hope that more begin around the country after this book is published. All the mainstream SAA and SLAA meetings are LGBT-friendly. See www.slaauk.org and www.saa-recovery.org.uk

Recovery from sex issues with a Twelve Step group essentially involves defining with a sponsor what boundaries you wish to live by – perhaps not going to saunas, or maybe not going on apps, whatever you decide; you then have someone to whom you can speak and be accountable and who can give you support. The aim is not to stop having sex but to have the sex that you want to have. You may decide to abstain from all sexual activity for a period of time, sometimes a month, just so you can reflect and get clarity about what you do want from your sex and romantic life. If you are living in a city with a big gay scene you might want to refrain from going to gay clubs and pubs for a time, or not drinking or watching porn, or anything else that triggers you – i.e. if you are someone who gets drunk and then goes to saunas it might be an idea to not drink for a while. It is completely up to you and no one will force you. Again, you'll be able to listen and talk to other people who have been through it.

Sex and Love Addicts Anonymous meetings differ from Sex Addicts Anonymous meetings in that they tend to focus more on the emotional side of relationships. Members are encouraged to abstain from their bottom-line behaviours (problematic behaviours that they agree with their sponsors to avoid) early on and then to work on the emotional aspects of addiction. Sex Addicts Anonymous meetings, on the other hand, can be more helpful for those with very intense and specific sexual addictions. They tend to be more male-orientated. Both can be helpful.

Sex and love addict meetings help you work out what is real and appropriate and what is obsession and addiction. People, love addicts especially, will automatically go, 'Ah, but crazy, fiery love affairs are the only ones worth having.' Passion is great, but grown-up relationships aren't about screaming and shouting and flinging things at each other so that you can have passionate make-up sex; they are about intimacy and mutual respect. Dealing with this helps you manage relationships so that you are not sacrificing yourself to the whim of someone else, or letting people treat you badly, or falling in love with every second person who smiles at you. Dealing with love addiction, which is very closely related to codependency, helps you have more balanced, adult, long-lasting, respectful, serious relationships.

It may be very intimidating to think of going to one of these meetings, but everyone there is in the same position. If you want, go and sit at the back and just listen. Sometimes people imagine sex-addict meetings are places to pick up sexual partners, but nothing could be further from the truth. There is no place less sexy than a sex-addiction meeting with a group of people seriously trying to address their problems. Don't go there thinking that you will find sexual partners, because you will be disappointed. The people attending do so because their sexual and romantic behaviour has caused them problems and they are looking for serious recovery. I'm sure there are occasional slip-ups, but these are strenuously discouraged for the benefit of all the members.

Crystal-meth addiction

There is a growing network of CMAA meetings in London and, I hope, soon in other cities too. Crystal-meth use can take people to such intense, dark places that many users feel comfortable speaking only amongst men who have had this specific problem. I will be starting a website with information on this and other issues.

Food and eating issues

Without wanting to sound like a broken record, if you have anorexia or bulimia you must immediately go and see a medical professional. Making yourself vomit starves your body of nutrients (dangerous in itself), bulimia causes changes to chemicals in your body that can result in serious damage to your heart, and your doctor needs to make sure your health has not been permanently affected. Again, use the helplines and websites I've listed.

It's important to remember that these problems are as serious as drug or alcohol addiction and must be treated as such. Many people find that the group Overeaters Anonymous helps, as does ABA – Anorexics and Bulimics Anonymous. Some people find it useful to go to both. Again, I've listed details on pages 350–51. Eating disorders tend to come with such excessive shame that it can take a huge effort to get someone to accept they have a problem. Talking about it is the most important first step. The helplines listed have people you can speak to.

Overeaters Anonymous and Anorexics and Bulimics Anonymous follow the same principles as other Twelve Step groups: with a sponsor, you set the boundaries you want and then work through the steps.

Body dysmorphia

All the things already listed in this chapter are recommended for body dysmorphia – cognitive behavioural therapy in particular – but I believe that this will be one symptom of an underlying problem and won't come on its own, so recovery will come alongside looking at the other issues.

Creating the conditions for recovery

A word on sex and eating disorders

Stopping alcohol and drug use, for many, is often easier than gaining sobriety from problematic sexual or eating behaviour. This is because sex and food are essential parts of life. If addiction is a problem of control, then it is harder to have sex or control your eating without going berserk. But it can be done and people do get sobriety in these areas.

With food problems, success often comes through having a food plan, working out what are reasonable portions and sticking to three meals a day with support from your sponsor and friends in the fellowship. Some lines of thinking are excessively strict, suggesting you cut out major trigger foods like sugar or white flour, but this is up to you to decide with your sponsor. It is possible to re-establish healthy relationships with sex, food and your body; many, many people manage it. You can too.

A note on drinking

Even if you don't have a problem with alcohol, it is wise to stop drinking or at least severely cut down while you work on codependency or anxiety or depression problems. Alcohol is a depressant. We often use it to take the edge off anxiety without understanding that it is itself one of the main causes of anxiety. It makes anxiety disorders and/or depression worse.

If you are depressed, stop drinking – at least for a period of time while you focus on getting better. Is your recovery worth the effort of not drinking? Yes it is. You may want to do this instead of beginning medication for your anxiety, or perhaps alongside it. If that prospect is too daunting for you, then stop and listen to the message: if you can't stand the thought of not drinking for a while, then maybe you have a problem with alcohol and *need* to stop. Think very, very carefully about this. Alcohol is one of the most socially acceptable and reinforced drugs but it is extremely damaging and dangerous. An awareness of your intake should be something you think about very seriously. *Nothing is more important than getting access to your feelings and dealing with them.*

Keeping it in the day

It can be terrifying to think you are giving up something on which you are dependent, so it is of huge importance that you don't think of it in this way and, instead, just focus on the day. Just today. Not tomorrow or the day after, just getting through this day. No one is forcing you to do anything and there are no set rules.

If you are trying to give up Grindr – which will be very hard for some people – or whatever your drug of choice is, then just focus on getting through each day without using. Work out what your triggers are and keep a diary. If it's being bored or in that period before bedtime, then work out ways to deal with these times, like reading a book or trying a new social activity. Have a friend you can call who knows you are trying to do this and will support you. All of these things are easier in the context of a Twelve Step group. If you get a craving you are encouraged to call another member and chat to them about it. Just talking about it alleviates the desire to use, which soon passes.

In early recovery just focus on getting through that one day and to bed. That's all that matters.

Friends and family

I know that many people reading this will be wondering what they can do to help a friend or family member. The bad news is that it is exceptionally hard to force someone into recovery. A man I know is deep in the chill-out sex-party scene. I and another friend have tried to help, but he does not believe he has a problem and, no matter what we've told him, he hasn't yet stopped or taken control of his using. Some experts believe you cannot force people but must just leave them to hit their own rock bottom; sometimes they have to ruin their lives before they wake up. This approach suggests that you let them do so and don't dive in to save or help them get out of sticky situations, because this stops them from seeing how severe their problem has become and helps them avoid the consequences of their actions. This is very hard to do if you care about someone: the trouble is that, frankly, some people die.

Sometimes when a problem is very serious, friends and family members come together to confront the person firmly about the problem in the hope of getting them to go into some kind of recovery. This is called an **intervention**. The loved ones calmly tell the person how they have seen them change, how it has affected their relationship with them, how much they love them, what they hope the person can do and how they will support them. Hopefully then the person can be helped into recovery. As with everything, this is easier if you have money and can pay for the person to go to rehab but that's not practical for most people.

It sounds harsh, but it is also important not to let the person's behaviour drag you down and damage your life too. Addiction experts will often say it is important to not be an **enabler**. This means not making light of what's happening, not making excuses for it or joking about it or acting like dangerous behaviour is OK. If you are worried about someone it is important you tell them in an effort to help them see the reality. If they text you late at night high or drunk, don't let them come round or act like it's a joke. Reply 'You are drunk/ high and I'm worried about you. I care about you so please go home and let's speak tomorrow.' Don't lend them money. Give them a copy of this book and tell them they should read it.

Tell them you know they are going through a hard time underneath it all, and that you love them and are there for them and are ready to listen. Find the details for a local Twelve Step meeting and suggest you take them to it, or offer to go to the doctor with them. It's a truly important thing to do for someone. If you are in London take them to one of the events such as 'Let's Talk About Sex and Drugs' or 'A Change of Scene', which may help them get into a place where they can start hearing a healing message. Or take them to a local LGBT centre to see a therapist.

This is a hard place to be, as you may think you will lose the friendship – and that is a possibility. But the person may be causing themselves the most serious harm.

Another aspect of getting better is what to tell your friends and family if you go into recovery. You don't have to tell people anything and if you do so then it should be in your own time. Good friends will understand and it is helpful to have their support. Sometimes you can experience a kind of euphoria, called 'pink clouding', at being able to stop your drug of choice and you may want to tell everyone. Think very carefully, because although some people will be fine about it, it's human nature to gossip and judge people. Some people won't be supportive.

One problem with addressing problematic behaviours is that other people start reflecting on their own behaviour. If they are drinking the same amount as you they may feel judged or threatened and try to convince you that you haven't got a problem or don't need to stop. Be aware of this. It is another reason why Twelve Step groups are so effective, as they help you make friends with people who will support you.

It is recommended that you do not make any major life decisions like starting new relationships or leaving your job for the first year of recovery while your emotions take time to settle.

Tackling anxiety

As you get further and further away from the fog of your coping mechanisms or other repetitive behaviour, you start to see your life more clearly, including all your own patterns of behaviour. Another recovery saying: 'The best thing about recovery is getting your feelings back. The worst thing is getting your feelings back.' All of those feelings you have been running from will start to reappear. This can be wonderful and it can be painful, but it is also a valuable and rewarding time because you start to re-learn who you are, to be responsible and adopt boundaries. You might find yourself crying or that your emotions are all over the place. Some people can suffer depression, so watch out for it and take steps if it happens. This can be confusing, but keep going and your feelings will settle. The support of Twelve Step groups, professionals and/or friends helps you get through this period. Crucially, you learn how to deal with life's ups and downs in a healthy, responsible way.

So there are several goals: getting enough clarity to see your patterns, understanding them and slowly changing them; and then reducing anxiety.

As people make progress in therapy or work the Twelve Steps in one or more of the various fellowships, anxiety levels change. They may go up and down at first, but gradually – especially if you are moving away from your drug of choice – they will begin to reduce and settle. All the issues you have will start to change as the anxiety levels change. To reduce anxiety, though, you need to do as much as you can to avoid over-exerting yourself and to take it easy.

Remember the recovery acronym HALT. This stands for 'Hungry Angry Lonely Tired'. Being any of these things will make you more likely to indulge in self-destructive or compulsive behaviour. Especially in your early days of recovery, try to be conscious of not allowing yourself to be any of these things.

There are ways of helping yourself:

Don't try to do it all at once

I'm giving you a lot of information here in one go. For most people, stopping one addictive process is incredibly hard work. Those who are cross-addicted usually find stopping all of them in one go too much. Identify the most urgent problem and focus on that first.

It would be great if we all lived completely stress-free lives and ate nothing but healthy food, but that's not realistic. Some people believe they have to cut out all stimulants, such as caffeine, sugar and anything else they can think of. If you want to look at these kinds of things in the long term, great, but for now this is about small, manageable, achievable steps. Do what works for you. The short-term priority is to get safe. The long-term aim is for recovery to be 'a bridge to normal living', not to becoming superhuman.

Take it easy

When you are trying to reduce anxiety the following things are really important:

Get enough sleep Most people need eight hours. Scientists have shown that every hour you sleep before midnight is the same as several hours after midnight. Aim to get to bed at 10 or 11 p.m. This needn't be rigid, but the more often you can do it the better. If you can't manage it all the time, aim for three times a week as a start. Switch off phones and laptops at least an hour before you go to bed so that your brain activity can settle down. A banana or a cup of camomile tea is helpful an hour or two before you go to bed.

Eat properly You need to make sure you have three meals every day, with a balance of carbohydrate, protein and vegetables. It sounds simplistic, but not eating properly affects your mood. Make sure you eat breakfast. Try to have sensible portions. It mustn't be about obsessively eating to look perfect; this is about giving your body the fuel it needs to function properly. Again, as with your spiritual and mental health, what you put in is what you get out. If you have an eating disorder, then food plans and support with diet will be something you work out with a therapist, your GP or with a Twelve Step group such as OA or ABA.

Exercise Keeping active releases endorphins and other chemicals that make you feel better. Be on guard: don't let it become compulsive. It's not about making you ripped. It's about getting fit, being healthy and getting a chemical boost from a good workout. Do not overdo it. Even a brisk twenty-minute walk on as many days as possible will help.

Meditation

One of the main things you can do to help your recovery is to sit calmly without speaking for a short period of time – anything from a few minutes to fifteen minutes or more – and focus your attention inwards on to yourself and your breathing.

There are different types of meditation, such as **transcendental meditation** where you chant a phrase called a mantra over and over again to take your mind into a place of deep peacefulness. You need to be trained to do this, but most meditation is very simple and can be learned from looking online: there are millions of websites, apps and YouTube videos to help you. Many people find it hard, but with practice anyone can do this. Stick with it and don't give yourself a hard time.

Mindfulness is a form of meditation focused on connecting you to and making you aware of your emotions and where in your body you are feeling them. It is the direct opposite of addiction, which is about getting away from your feelings, so it too can be difficult. Mindfulness has become very popular in recent years and many people believe it is going to become one of the dominant weapons against anxiety and depression. Again, Google more about it.

Start meditation by sitting peacefully on a cushion with your phone, TV and radio off. Simply sit for five minutes with your eyes shut, just being aware of your breathing. Some people use a timer but others suggest you judge the time yourself intuitively and don't worry if you are over or under. If thoughts come in, don't stress; learn to observe and acknowledge them but bring your attention back to your breath, always focusing on it.

Do this in the morning and evening. You can build on it as you go. The more you do it the easier it becomes and it is one of the best things you can do for long-term relief of anxiety.

Deep-breathing exercises

Your fight or flight system affects your breathing. For years I complained to doctors that I had asthma; only much later did I realize it was just shallow breathing as a result of anxiety. Working on breathing correctly, as done in Eastern spiritual practices, is a helpful part of recovery. There are many programmes online – you will find some on YouTube – which teach you how to breathe deeply and properly.

Panic attacks are a result of not breathing deeply and slowly enough. They make you feel as if you can't breathe and are having a heart attack, when actually you're breathing too fast or too shallowly and not exhaling enough carbon dioxide. If you are feeling light-headed and suspect a panic attack is coming on, the simple method is to breathe out as much as you can, then breathe in slowly, then out again. Sometimes people breathe into a paper bag. Breathing deeply stimulates your sympathetic nervous system, reducing your blood pressure and helping you to calm down.

Yoga

This is an incredibly effective way of getting light exercise and facilitating relaxation by, again, working on your breathing and focusing on establishing a relationship with your body. Yoga classes are held everywhere: go online to find one near you.

Acupuncture and massage

Both of these help with relaxation. They can be costly, obviously, but are worthwhile if you can afford them. Some health centres offer low-cost or even free acupuncture. Antidote in London offers free acupuncture sessions to clients.

Learning to feel good about yourself

Recovery is about fostering a sense of self-esteem and a feeling that you are a good person, worthy of love and kindness. Anything you can do to help this along is a good thing.

Affirmations It might sound like hokey rubbish, but affirmations can be helpful. For years your head will have told you that you are awful, ugly, stupid, unlovable and other nasty, untrue things. Write down the opposite, perhaps on cards, and keep them in your home, even on your phone. They could be simple: 'I am a good person', 'I am good enough', 'I like myself', or 'My life is full of love'. Say them like you mean them, even if you don't. Repeating them ensures your brain takes in some of the meaning. Scientists have shown that just the process of smiling, even if it is forced, makes you feel better. Again, 'fake it to make it', which means pretend you believe it, do it with enthusiasm and it can have an effect. Louise Hay, the author of a popular book called *You Can Heal Your Life*, also publishes sets of affirmations. They are worth trying.

Creative visualization This is where you imagine good things in your life, focusing on what you want to happen rather than what you want not to happen. In other words, positive thinking. I don't know if it works, but it has been used in some forms of Buddhism and some of the world's top athletes use creative visualization before they compete. Don't beat yourself up for negative thinking, but recognize you do it. Try to focus on what you *do* want: to be healthy, to be happy, to be calm, to be with friends or family, and so on.

Esteemable acts I have a fun app on my phone, a shark game. As the shark swims round it depletes its energy levels. If it encounters a diver who stabs it or if it gets bitten by a crab, its energy levels drop. If it eats the crabs, divers or fish it builds its energy up. There's a little graphic, which goes down when it gets attacked and up when it feeds itself. I believe self-esteem is the same. If you do things you don't feel good about, then your self-esteem levels dip. To get the levels back up you have to do things you feel good about.

I'm not dictating to you what is morally acceptable and what isn't; you have to decide your own moral code. But there are some things which are blatantly not good for you. Missing friends' birthdays because you are watching porn all day with the curtains drawn, or cheating on someone you care about even though he may have no idea of it, isn't going to make you feel good. You may think, 'What he doesn't know won't hurt him', but it does have a payback. This is like the shark in my game being constantly attacked. If you keep going without replenishing the levels, eventually you crash. If, for instance, you can have casual sex without it making you feel bad, great. But if it does make you feel bad afterwards, or lonely, then think about stopping or calming it down or investigating what lies behind those feelings. Being bitchy and judgemental is a defence mechanism that may have served us well, but it has a payback too. We may not feel it immediately, but subconsciously we know it isn't nice and it will always come out in some way.

So, decide what is esteemable for you, but make sure that these are things that aren't based on external esteem, such as people 'liking' your shirtless selfie or your new shoes – not that there's anything wrong with those things from time to time, but they're not what your self-esteem should be based on. Esteemable things might be taking up interests, hobbies, visiting museums or galleries, going to the cinema, for walks, or simply taking an interest in or learning something you haven't done before – in other words, things that give you a sense of purpose and achievement, that stretch your horizons. Even just meeting a friend for a coffee.

John Grant, on his album *Grey Tickles, Black Pressure*, has a song called 'Voodoo Doll'. It isn't about hurting enemies but being kind to a friend with depression who can't get out of bed. He feeds the doll chicken soup and hot chocolate, puts it in a corduroy jumpsuit and takes it to the zoo. The song is about how when you have depression you don't want to do the things that help you feel better, but you must because they really do help!

One of the most esteem-boosting things is doing something to help other people. Get involved with charities, take an interest in other people, send a friend a postcard congratulating them on a work achievement, listen to friends (without butting in and talking about yourself), help an old person across the road, whatever it takes. Again, this sounds like meaningless fluff, but even though you won't feel it straight away, it all adds to your self-esteem levels. Volunteering at LGBT charities can be extremely useful, as it helps you to interact with gay people outside clubs and gives you a sense of gay community.

Be nice

Getting into recovery is about connecting to yourself and other people. Part of healing and getting better is treating people well and enabling them to treat you better. Letting love into your life means you have to keep it going and emit it too. Accepting that you deserve happiness and to be treated well means you have to treat other people the same way. This isn't easy. No one's perfect, but you have to come to the understanding that you must treat people the same way you want to be treated. In the end, none of this works without it.

Of course some people treat us badly too. Often, as people with low self-esteem and codependency, we allow it. But we can find the strength to not allow people to walk all over us. This isn't about being nasty; it's about having boundaries with other people, saying 'It's not OK to treat me badly.' If they continue, you can find other people to surround yourself with. Nobody deserves to be treated badly. The answer is not fighting and screaming back, but rising above it and, if need be, removing yourself from the situation.

The trauma connection

For some people, doing a talking therapy and unpicking unhealthy patterns and/or doing a Twelve Step programme is enough. It deals with their past issues, reduces their anxiety and helps them move forward with their lives. For many of us with deep-seated childhood trauma, though, we also need outside help in the form of a more intense therapy to go in and seriously focus on the deep problem. For some of us, if we don't do this, that childhood trauma can keep raising its ugly head to fuel our anxiety and other unhealthy behaviour.

It feels to me that there's growing belief that 'experiential therapy' as opposed to 'talking therapy' is the way to deal with deep-seated trauma. **Talking therapy** – most commonly CBT – is about talking through your feelings and issues, understanding them in your head and trying to take different courses of action. This works for some people. **Experiential therapy** is when you actually physically and emotionally connect to or experience the trauma in order to process and release it or physically change the way your body deals with it.

I've been lucky enough to try the programmes below. Most of them are very expensive, which frustratingly means they are out of reach for most people. All of them had some positive benefits but none succeeded in erasing my anxiety completely.

The Trauma Reduction Programme This is a course based on the trauma work of author and therapist Pia Mellody. I did the Trauma Week at The Priory, which costs around £2,200 for the outpatient programme. You work in a group and also alone with a therapist to dig out specific childhood trauma and 're-parent' the child inside you. I found it incredibly powerful and had a real breakthrough. It was very emotional and something within me shifted. However, once back at work, my patterns of intense anxiety returned – partly, I'm sure, because I was still drinking.

The Hoffman Process This is an eight-day, residential, multi-disciplinary programme that started in the US but is now also run in various locations around the UK. They recommend you are not using recreational drugs and have drunk no alcohol for at least a week before you embark on the process. You give up your phone, etc., and have no access to the world for eight days while you go through a very hard-core structured programme, which has been described as a lifetime of therapy in eight days. It costs more than £2,700 but it is very powerful. When I did it I had one of the most positive weeks I've had in my recovery, and if you can afford it I would recommend it as part of the arsenal of things you can use in your recovery process. It might sound ridiculous, but as someone who has found it hard to relax and enjoy holidays, this was like a holiday for me.

More details at www.hoffmaninstitute.co.uk

The Lightning Process I have suffered from Chronic Fatigue Syndrome since I was fourteen. No one knows exactly what causes CFS. Sufferers passionately believe it arises from a physical illness, but some professionals suggest it may be a psychological problem. How it feels for me – and I could be completely wrong – is that it is both psychological and physical, as our fight or flight system, fuelled by negative thinking, constantly attacks us, setting off a cycle of physical problems. I have a gut feeling that LGBT people will have higher levels of this and other illnesses caused by stress. A controversial technique called the Lightning Process claims to treat both the syndrome and negative thinking by interrupting the fight or flight system through retraining and redirecting the impulse to attack ourselves. I did the Lightning Process and it definitely had a powerful emotional effect, but I couldn't keep it up. I did it early in recovery and I would try it again. See www.lightningprocess.com. The Gupta Programme claims to have a similar effect on negative thinking. See www.guptaprogramme.com

Trauma therapy What has worked best for me is a new approach to trauma. American therapist Peter A. Levine is the author of a book called *Waking the Tiger* about reducing trauma through experiential and body-based therapy. He believes that trauma is stored in the body and to release it you have to work with the body as well as the mind. Again, it's just my opinion, but my instinct is that this is the future of trauma therapy.

This tallies with a new study by Rachel Yehuda of Mount Sinai Hospital, New York, and Elisabeth Binder of the Max Planck Institute of Psychiatry in Munich. They studied the children of Holocaust survivors and found that trauma had been physically handed down to the children, who had a higher likelihood of stress disorders. In these people the accessibility of a gene associated with a person's ability to deal with stress had been altered. Their findings suggested that trauma actually affects the cells of people's bodies – not just their minds. They too believe trauma is stored in a person's body and not just their brains.

I have been seeing a therapist called Sheryl Close, who practises body-based trauma therapy based on the work of Peter A. Levine. I've alleviated more of my anxiety through this than through any of the other things I have done. Working with her has really shifted something and given me the greatest relief I have had so far.

Drama therapy My friend Simon Marks, who runs 'A Change of Scene', has spoken to me about the healing power of arts therapies, especially drama therapy, in which clients are encouraged to replay and act out aspects of their selves and experiences in an effort to heal trauma and work through issues. I haven't tried it myself, but Simon has been working with gay and bi men during his training as a drama therapist and is extremely passionate about its potential to help heal this kind of developmental trauma. Contact details for the British Association of Dramatherapists can be found in Appendix 1.

All in all there are many ways of dealing with these problems. I would recommend going into Twelve Step programmes if you can, because they mean you plant yourself firmly in the soil of recovery. Even if you use other methods too, it means your life starts to shift from being about addiction and/or depression to being about recovery and hope.

The people in the next chapter did it and so can you.

17

A Change of Scene: Positive Experiences

'When I was growing up I was taught that I should be ashamed of myself simply for being who I am. That was drilled into me to such an extent that it took me decades, and coming out of alcohol abuse and cocaine abuse, to realize that becoming myself was exactly what was needed for me to achieve the things I wanted to . . . I suppose what I set out to do in my music was simply to say the things I was always unable to say in the past, because being exactly who I am and saying exactly how I feel is the only way for me to survive. A lot of what I do is very selfish too. I talk about having HIV because I felt I should be ashamed about that too. Whenever I have that feeling now then I do exactly the opposite and talk about it. I'm seeking connections with other people who have been through this and can help me get through the difficult times . . .'

Singer John Grant in his speech accepting the Man of the
Year Attitude Award, Royal Courts of Justice, 14 October 2013

CHANGE IS HAPPENING. THE word is getting out and more and more people are dealing with their issues. I wanted to include some of their stories to show you that it *is* possible. All these people have come from terrible places and are rebuilding their lives.

The story of this book really begins with Tim and his recovery. Without it you wouldn't be reading this now. In 2007 Tim walked into his GP's office and told him about his yo-yoing weight, said he wanted to kill himself and burst into tears. Unusually, his GP suggested he tried going to an Overeaters Anonymous meeting. Tim went along, didn't get it at first and decided not to go back. But his eating problems continued, so he tried it again. He has now been in recovery for seven years and goes to both OA and AA. In that time he has lost nine stone and, for the first time ever, has kept it off; he has also had an operation to remove the excess skin that was left. After a few years in recovery what he wanted from life started to change. He quit his career, which was an exciting one but which he was finding unfulfilling and too stressful, and is now retraining to do something that he is passionate about. Having grown up hating his body, he told me that, fundamentally, for him recovery was about acceptance.

'When you start clearing your mind of all the crazy obsessions, you get to see yourself how you really are,' he said, 'and it's never as bad as you think. A lot of my problem was having an absolute distorted image of what I looked like. But I've realized that physically I'm OK. My mind wants to play tricks on me and tell me I'm not and I just need to be vigilant about that. I'm never going to be a Muscle Mary and have the perfect body, and that's OK. Sometimes I have moments of feeling bad about it and that's OK too. I've learned bad feelings pass. Today I don't hate my body like I used to.'

I've known Tim for a long time and have found the difference in him absolutely staggering. I literally would not have believed it would be possible. The emotional change in him has been even more profound than the physical. He is calmer, kinder to himself and others, and his relationships with friends and family have dramatically improved. He has gone from being a self-absorbed person to one who is concerned with others. His feelings about being gay have also changed. He used to be someone who often raged at other gay people, blaming them for the fact that he didn't feel attractive or lovable, but now he is a volunteer for an LGBT charity and marches with them at Gay Pride.

'I used to hate Pride,' he said. 'I'd hate myself, feel judged, I'd slag everyone off and get pissed to get through it. I'd feel isolated and end up going to a bar and trying to sleep with someone. I used to feel like I wasn't relevant or good enough as a gay man, because I didn't have the body or the lifestyle, but I suppose recovery has allowed me to see that all of that stuff is external, even my body is external. It doesn't represent my spirit and my mind and my emotions . . . These days I'm more aware of other people and more connected to them.

'There was a time once, years ago, when I left work. I was in Soho. I felt frozen to the spot. I was so unhappy. I remember thinking I could go and get shitfaced and end up in some sleazy bar, or I could go home and binge on food. Either way it would end in complete and utter oblivion and I just hated myself. Today I have a relationship with gay men, and everyone else for that matter, where I feel equal. I think a big part of that is the gay AA meetings that I go to regularly, absolutely. It's like I found my place, my vision of what I always hoped the gay community would be – a group of men and women from all different walks of life being kind to each other and looking out for each other. I can feel challenged and insecure sometimes, that's a human thing, but I absolutely don't feel the need to run away any more.'

Jack, who passed out on the South Bank in the chapter on alcohol, is now thirty and has been in Alcoholics Anonymous for three years. Working the steps with his AA sponsor, he went back to look at how growing up had affected his behaviour years later.

'It was like someone had to hold my hand and take me into the past to see it again properly, what really happened,' he explained. 'I realized I wasn't responsible for that bullying. I was a child. I could see what led to me feeling certain things about myself and the way that had led to dysfunction in my thinking and behaviour and relationships. The gay scene fed into all the shit I had. The reason I was so emotionally unstable was because I was in a battle with myself. There was a voice inside me that said, "You're not good enough, you're never going to meet anyone, you're not masculine enough, you're a poof, fag, queer," and on and on and on. But in recovery, I had this lightning-bolt moment where I realized that, shit, that voice isn't actually my voice. It is other people's voices from my childhood. That was a breakthrough for me.'

Throughout his life, Jack has obsessed over how attractive he is to other men. Gradually, despite his new friends making nice comments about the way he looked, he realized that no number of compliments could ever make him feel good about himself. In reality the only thing that could was doing the work to develop a real sense of self-esteem. His relationship with himself is getting better every day. 'I feel I do love myself now, which is the biggest thing. I couldn't even look at photos of myself before. Being able to say I think I'm an attractive guy was a huge milestone. It takes time. I literally had to stand in front of the mirror and tell myself I was good-looking.' Today Jack has a new career, is happier than ever and is gradually starting to date again.

I asked David from the alcohol chapter, who grew up in the 1950s and was married to a woman, what recovery has meant for him. Remember that this was a man who nearly killed himself through drink-driving and, in his own words, hated himself entirely. He told me when he first went into recovery at thirty-six he was in denial about his sexuality, had no ambition and thought the best that could happen was that he would get another job as a salesman. Now sixty-three, today David Smallwood is one of the UK's leading addiction therapists and author of the book *Who Says I'm An Addict?*

'I would never have believed I would have gone on to do a Masters degree,' he told me, 'to be treatment director of a national company, to have written a book, to have twenty-seven years of recovery, to have friends, to have taught at national conferences and gone around the world and met amazing people, to have the depth of knowledge I have about lots and lots of things. It's absolutely incredible. If I died tomorrow I can say I've actually achieved something that I would never have believed was possible. That feels wonderful.'

Towards the end of writing this, I met up with Richard, the man whose crystal-meth addiction nearly killed him, for a coffee at Waterloo station. By strange coincidence, it was the very day of his sixth anniversary of giving up alcohol. Some readers might suspect recovery is all about sanitizing gay men and 'heteronormalizing' them, but Richard is still into leather, still into the harder side of the sex scene. It's for him to decide what is OK in his life. I asked him if the Twelve Step programme had been positive for him.

'Absolutely,' he said. 'The way of living that the programme suggests speaks such common sense. I think more people should look at it. A lot of people get turned off because it comes from 1936, it's very Judaeo-Christian in its wording, talking of God, God being a him, talking of praying, this, that and the other; that turns a lot of people off. But I would say look beyond that, look at what it asks of yourself and how it asks you to connect with other people, which is the thing I'm bad at. For me it's the only thing that works.

'I've always been so codependent,' he went on, 'always wanted to be liked by everybody. It's helped me unravel the parts of my personality that cause me problems and then put it back together. My relationships with my friends are more honest because I'm more honest. I'm very awkward in myself and I've been brought up with lots of masks and veneers to hide it. But I am getting less awkward in myself. You go to a meeting and listen to some bullshit [*laughs*] but in amongst that there's so many things that resonate so closely. For me the whole thing is a work in progress. Sometimes I love it, sometimes I hate it, but I would rather recovery be the constant in my life than active addiction.'

Not everyone I know or have included in this book has used Twelve Step groups.

Ramesh is a friend who hit rock bottom and posted a social-media message that made it clear he was going to take his own life. Two years later we met for a coffee in the café at Foyles on Charing Cross Road to talk about it. I'm glad to say he told me he was in a much better place now. He said he had always been prone to depression;

eventually stress at work and mounting financial issues tipped him over the edge and he took himself off to a hotel with the intention of killing himself. Friends found him and got him to hospital, where he was given serious psychiatric help and, crucially, accepted support from those closest to him. He told me that since then he's had counselling, went on antidepressants for a few months, sorted out his finances, changed job and put some significant effort into working on his self-esteem.

'Asking for help was the biggest turning point for me,' he said. 'I found that there were loads of people who cared and wanted to help. My dad came in and helped me get on top of my financial issues. Just going through my direct debits, practical things like that, helped. If I'd done this five years ago I wouldn't have got into this situation. Moving out of my job really helped, accepting that I was working too hard.'

He explained he'd learned to hide his sexuality as an adolescent because his mother didn't approve of it, and that learning to talk has been a major part of his recovery. 'Growing up I was so used to not talking about how I was feeling. That probably contributed to getting ill in the first place, but certainly not talking about how down I was getting and internalizing everything contributed to getting to the point where everything got on top of me.'

Ramesh loves his new job and is enjoying life again. He sees this low point as something that is most definitely in the past. 'My self-esteem has always been very low, but now I'm able to see a bit more of what other people see when they see me,' he said. 'It's not easy but it is possible. Whereas before I was very ill with moments of lucidity, it's the opposite now. I feel whole in a way I haven't for a long time.'

I met up with a man I know through London life, Chris, a black guy who decided he needed to quit drink and drugs but hasn't used Twelve Step groups. We met for a coffee and he explained why he stopped – because he was raped at a sex party when he had 'gone under' after using G. He came round to be told by one guy that another, who was in the toilet, had had sex with him without a condom while he was unconscious. 'I thought is this where we've got to as gay men?' he said. He went straight to A&E and went on PEP treatment. 'I called my best friend and told him what was going on and he didn't get back to me until twenty-four hours later. At that moment I decided to cut off a lot of those friends on the party scene.'

Chris realized that drink was his gateway drug to other substances and he hasn't had a drink since then. That was two years ago. 'I saw things from a new perspective,' he told me. 'I didn't want my weekends to be forty-eight-hour binges. I thought I will never get myself into that situation again. The drugs stopped easily. I don't miss it. My nicotine addiction continues, but I love waking up on a Saturday or a Sunday morning feeling fresh and awake. It sounds cheesy, but I love going for walks by the canal and meeting my friends in Brick Lane for coffee. That means more to me than coming home at 3 a.m. regretting who I've sent a text to, who I've been a bitch to or being still awake and wondering whose fucking squat I'm in.'

Just before we met, Chris had a relapse on G after a date with someone attractive he'd met. He ended up spending the night nursing the guy, who became unconscious. He says he sees it as a timely reminder of why he gave up and, although he's had a slip, it has made him realize this is it: he is going to try never to take drugs again. 'The happiness I feel now compared to how I felt then . . . I feel like a completely different person,' he said. 'I feel good, you know?'

Another friend I've known for a long time, Ed, has addressed some serious anxiety and self-esteem issues through CBT therapy alone. He had a series of life events that made him evaluate everything and eventually led to him quitting his career, which was stressing him out, and moving into something less well paid that allowed him to have more free time to pursue things he loves.

He told me that recently he 'took a deep breath', asked for help from his GP and had ten weeks of CBT therapy, which really helped him get on top of his 'internal bully' – that voice in his head that was always criticizing him. 'Throughout my twenties I felt such excessive amounts of guilt over so many unnecessary things and it's definitely a lot better now,' he said. 'The sessions helped me engage that voice that was continually bullying me, criticizing my every move, to learn to get a better relationship with it. It's never going to go away but you can kind of strengthen the more rational response to it and just be aware it is present and that it is not an accurate interpretation of who I am.'

He said he still has bumpy moments but has things to help him cope. 'I've been given some strategies to help me. It's continual work to have good mental health. Recently my boyfriend and I have tried to meditate every morning. I'm rubbish at it and we don't do it every day, but we try and I hope we get better at it.'

Ed's relationship began after many one-night stands and other relationships that didn't work. After years of partying he decided to cut down on the drinking and clubbing and started hanging out with an old friend with whom he shared a love of art-house films. They spent more and more time together, not taking drugs or chasing men or sitting online rowing with people. 'There was one day when I was at his flat, washing up, and I just realized I was in love with him,' he said. 'It sounds a bit cheesy but I had managed to get to a place where I felt safe with him and I could be myself and he with me, and he really got me and I got him. It evolved and it happened on that level. He's someone who totally gets me and understands me and makes me feel safe, and that's the best thing really.'

The conflict between homosexuality and religion seems to be a terribly difficult problem to overcome. But there is hope. The complexities of being LGBT and from black, Asian and minority ethnic communities are being aired more and more. Channel 4's *Muslim Drag Queens*, in which Asifa Lahore told her story, and Reggie Yates's *Extreme UK: Gay and Under Attack* in December 2015 created a dialogue which enlightened people from all sides.

Minhaj, an Asian man we heard from in Chapter 5, had a difficult time during which he couldn't get out of bed. But an attempt to take his own life was his rock bottom and turning point. 'The minute I did it,' he said, 'I got a very strong message that it wasn't the right thing to do. It was such a wake-up call. I made a decision that I had to take positive action. It took me about a year before I saw a counsellor and immediately I realized how scared I had been about who I really was. I couldn't and didn't want to live the lie any more. I called my brothers pretty much straight away and told them the truth, and they were supportive and shocked I had gone through so much alone.

'In the last six years I've rebuilt my life and nurtured my self-esteem. I've had some great boyfriends and some not so great ones! I started feeling more confident about myself and my looks. I've begun to feel more attractive. I still practise my faith and have found a place where my sexuality can co-exist with it in peace. I can finally be true to myself.

'Recently, this new strength led me to finally tell my parents the truth. It was one of the worst weeks of my life. There were big arguments and in their anger things were said to me that no child should hear from their parents. I'm open-minded and believe things will change in my relationship with them, but it will take time. I still believe in my faith. I know God loves me for the person I am, judges me on the actions I take.'

I wrote earlier that I believed the LGBT community was rock-bottoming. As I said, the flipside to a rock bottom is that the only way is up. More and more individuals and groups are responding, so far primarily to the drug problem. In London, 56 Dean Street has been the major hub of activity; the LGBT Foundation in Manchester is fostering a sense of community; the Birmingham LGBT Centre is doing great work with scant resources; while the Leicester LGBT Centre is struggling to meet the needs of service users, as are smaller gay charities all over the country.

David Stuart and the team at Dean Street have started a new initiative called the Wellbeing Programme to talk about these issues, to educate and inform the public, the media and the healthcare system, and to provide other spaces for LGBT people to meet. Patrick Cash's monthly open-mic night called 'Let's Talk About Gay Sex and Drugs' is facilitating conversation and the 'Change of Scene' group which I co-founded, run by drama therapist Simon Marks who aims to work with gay men when he qualifies this year, is doing the same. These groups have been incredible, with men expressing their struggles about some of the issues discussed in this book, often getting emotional just because they have the opportunity actually to speak and relate to other gay/bi men. The Vice film *Chemsex* will have started a bigger discussion about some of the problems and I hope it continues after the publication of this book.

There are also fun things happening. DJ Fat Tony, now nine years clean and sober from drugs and alcohol, still plays in clubs. Performance artist Johnny Woo no longer drinks or takes drugs and has opened a very trendy new pub in East London, bucking the trend of gay-venue closures. He's not preaching abstinence but giving people a place to go, fostering a sense of community based in creativity.

Also in the alcohol chapter I told you about another friend of mine who is in recovery: Liam, who went to AA because he thought his drinking was going to destroy his relationship. Giving up booze didn't save the relationship, but he sees now that his recovery has been about so much more than that. It has enabled him to start treating that little boy inside him, who was bullied and alienated at school, with love.

During the writing of this book Liam announced that he was going to make a big move to another country he'd always dreamed of living in. When we were both drinking we weren't very good friends. Today he's someone I am so grateful to have in my life. I was really sad that he was leaving and met him for a coffee on Old Compton Street the day before he left. As the cleaners put the bins out from the previous night's performance of *Miss Saigon*, we reminisced about our wilder days. He said that recovery had changed every single aspect of his life for the better. For a start, he said, there was no way he would have got the visa to live abroad, as he was always in debt. A few days earlier he'd gone home to say goodbye to his parents and had turned down £350 that his mother had offered from her pension for his trip.

'That's her money,' he said. 'Before recovery the only reason I'd go home was to ask my parents for cash to pay off credit-card debts I'd racked up.'

His father, with whom he had frequently been impatient and in-tolerant, hugged him at the station and told him he loved him. 'I have enough recovery to see my part in that relationship now. Having a gay alcoholic son might not have been the thing he would have chosen, but he has always loved me unconditionally.'

He said he has learned to have better relationships with other gay men. 'Because I have a smidgen of compassion for myself these days, I have some compassion for other people too. I think all of us are quite brittle when we are drinking and drugging on the scene. That doesn't mean I didn't meet some fucking fantastic, fabulous, magnifi-cent men, but I was totally out of my depth with the people I was hanging out with. It was about being wrapped up as a gay man in London, trying to present the image I thought I was meant to have, but I became less and less sure of myself. I thought I was being wild and crazy, but looking back the reality was incredibly conformist. The people I tended to migrate towards were not very kind. For me, drink and drugs were a quick fix to the pressures of the unobtainable standards that the gay world inflicts on itself.'

Ramesh, who nearly killed himself, also told me he has learned to get a perspective on what the gay scene really is. 'It was easy for me to accept I wasn't going to be part of the scene because I had worked in it,' he said. 'Today, you can walk into a bar and mentally you can see people swiping left. It's tough. I got to see the meanness and the bitchiness of Soho first hand, but I saw that the scene isn't everything and once you recognize that . . . if they don't like me, it doesn't matter. You realize you can take it or leave it. I can still go to gay bars but it's about who I go with rather than where I'm going.'

In Liam's case, controlled, moderate drinking was not some-thing he could do, and when he realized this the prospect was terri-fying for him. I asked him what he would say to someone reading this who was equally appalled or frightened by the idea of making major changes to their life. 'I felt that life without booze and drugs would be no life at all,' he admitted. 'I projected into the future and it seemed empty, like a wasteland. But the truth is that when I was using, life wasn't actually that great. What I'm trying to say is: the easier, softer way is to live a life free of these dependencies. There are different ways to do it, but I don't think I would be able to stay stopped without the support of AA. A lot of my friends, people I was drawn to at 4 a.m. in my old life, are also in recovery now. If you think you have a problem, why not give it a go? Because there is another way of living.'

Today Liam's life is, in his words, beyond his wildest dreams. 'It had to be a viable alternative,' he said. 'If it was just equal, then the pull of the old life would be very strong and I probably would have started drinking again, but as time has gone on the scales have tipped. It's not like "It's a bit rubbish because you can't drink but there are a few benefits" – it is a better life than the one before. There are benefits beyond what you can even imagine. By the simple act of putting down something that is causing damage and swapping it for a new set of habits that are life-sustaining, it is amazing what benefits come to you without you doing anything. It's like putting your money into a mortgage instead of splurging it on a corrupt landlord.'

As I prepared to say goodbye to him, he told me that when he got settled in his new city he was planning to look at his issues around sex and love, something which, he said with a laugh, were for him the final frontier.

'I don't just mean getting a boyfriend,' he explained. 'I'm talking about being fully comfortable in my own skin so I potentially can have a better relationship with someone else – be they friends or romantic, whatever.'

David Smallwood, a man who helped me massively in my early recovery, has the final word here. He has now gone to take up a senior position in one of the world's most prestigious treatment centres in Switzerland. Popping his hat and scarf on as he walked me to the door of his office in Harley Street, he told me that, though he has great affection for his ex-wife, getting sober and well has given him the biggest benefit of all. 'Without recovery I wouldn't have the partner I have now,' he said. 'He is absolutely the love of my life. We've been together for seventeen years. He is the nicest person I have ever met. I love him completely. I wouldn't have him without recovery and I wouldn't have him without being gay. For me, that's the joy of recovery and the joy of being gay.'

18

We Are Family: Calling Straight People

'You cheated me out of your life then blamed me for not being there!'

Mother to Arnold in Harvey Fierstein's
Torch Song Trilogy, 1982

THE BRILLIANT TORCH SONG *Trilogy* was the first gay-themed play
to make money on Broadway and then became an equally brilliant
film. The line quoted above comes at the climax of the play from the
mother of the main character, Arnold, as he challenges her homophobia. It used to jar with me because it suggests that we play some
part in our own isolation. But I've come to realize that there is an
element of truth to it.

I've met so many different inspirational people in my career at
Attitude and while I was writing this book. One of them was Roger
Crouch, whose story was told in Chapter 6. After their fifteen-
year-old son Dominic took his own life, the pain that Roger and
his wife, Paola, felt was immense. Yet Roger would not be silent. He
campaigned to raise the issue of homophobic bullying, speaking at
the Stonewall Education for All conference and talking to anyone
who would listen.

You will also remember Mena Houghton, whom we also met in
Chapter 6, whose son Mark died of an unintentional heroin overdose in May 2010. She fought to get her son into a rehab and is now
fighting for schools to be more proactive in combating homophobic

bullying. Mena contacted me to ask for a donation from *Attitude* for the Space Youth Project, which helped Mark and for whom he wanted to work. The service they provide to kids is failing because they have no money. She calls me regularly to ask if I've finished this book. She won't let it go and she is exactly what we need. We gave her the very first Attitude Pride Award in June 2015 and dedicated the ongoing awards to Mark.

It's time to bring straight people in out of the cold. As LGBT people, we have had isolation inflicted on us. We've been separated from the concept of society and family: not acceptable, not part of real life, we've been effectively outlawed. Thatcher expressed this when Section 28 described us as 'pretend family'. As a result, we retain a complicated relationship with 'family'. The word has been used to hurt us. Many of us have, sometimes literally, been kicked out of them. But we've played a part too. Often we've reacted by sticking two fingers up at the entire concept. We've said, 'You don't want us? Fine, we'll do without you too.' Sometimes we've worn this as a badge of honour.

But that is a fear-based reaction and it is also part of the problem. The truth is, Mrs Thatcher, the Kelvin MacKenzies of the world, and the ignorant and religious nutcases don't get to decide what families are. All of us do. The reality is we *are* part of families. Lesbians, gay, bisexual and transgender people are brothers, sisters, sons, daughters, aunts, uncles, cousins – and nothing anyone does can change that. And that means this isn't just our fight.

Enlisting the support of straight people does not mean they set the terms or determine our lives, but it's not our right to exclude them from this movement. I sometimes see us attack straight people who are trying to be supportive because they express it in a clunky way or get the words wrong. We have to get over it. It is victim mentality. We need to remember: we don't exist on another planet or independently of other people around us. The aim of gay liberation is not – as much as it might sometimes seem desirable – to live on a gay island on our own; it is about society working for everyone. LGBT rights are human rights.

Similarly, it is an abdication of responsibility if straight people do not get involved – especially in the issue of school bullying and sex and relationships education. I want them to read this book. I want mothers and fathers to download the Stonewall School Report and to know exactly what young LGBT people are going through in our schools. The media needs to step up too. Journalists in the mainstream media need to make the public aware of the stories of Mark Houghton, Dominic Crouch, Ayden Olsen, Anthony Stubbs and the other kids who are out there, unsupported, right now, today. There are more in the pipeline. They need to speak out: to challenge schools and religious institutions and political parties regardless of how their own kids identify. The media also needs to start telling LGBT stories in a better way. It has begun, but it has a long way to go. It's crazy that we have to wait fifteen years between major gay TV shows, for instance.

We have a war to win between sanity and extremism, against people with their own childhood trauma and subsequent damaged mental health – extremists, the religious right, etc. – who wish to imprint their own trauma and sexual shame on to more generations of young people. Straight people can no longer be on the sidelines; they need to stand up and fight for their children. There's no excuse for heterosexual people not to get involved, nor for us not to welcome them and call out those who don't support us.

And it is happening. I went to my old school, Wilson's in Croydon, to discuss with the headmaster what they were doing to help LGBT students. In the foyer, a place where I felt utter loneliness as a teenager, there was a Stonewall 'Some people are gay, get over it!' poster, permanent and framed. The school now has a strong anti-homophobic bullying policy, and the deputy head, Mr Burton, a straight man – along with his wife, who is a teacher at another school – has made it his mission to help support pupils who may be LGBT or questioning.

As mentioned in Chapter 6, in 2013 I invited the then leaders of the three main parties to meet the parents of some of the children who had featured in the anti-bullying article I wrote for *Attitude* in 2012. Ed Miliband agreed and on 5 July 2013 we visited Blatchington Mill School in Hove, which won a Stonewall award for its work fighting homophobic bullying. (Brighton and Hove Council, run by the Green Party, received a Stonewall award in July 2014 for being one of the councils that best deals with homophobia.) We had a private meeting in which Ed Miliband met Mena Houghton, and we heard how the school makes it explicitly clear to pupils, parents and teachers that homo- and transphobia is unacceptable. There are three student equality commissioners to whom pupils can talk if they have any issues. Ed Miliband spoke in a special assembly about combating homophobia. Boys and girls – including tough-looking boys one might not expect to be concerned about gay equality – spoke firmly about respecting gay people and of instances where they had defended their gay friends against bullying. One young man asked Ed Miliband why the Archbishop of Canterbury was allowed to be against same-sex marriage, which was being discussed at the time. Miliband said he disagreed with the Archbishop's position but could not force him to change it, but this young man insisted that it was not acceptable. He was adamant and fired up. It was exciting and moving to see.

On two occasions over the last few years I have visited the Brit School in South London, which is also doing exceptional things. A fundamental part of its ethos is to teach people to respect one another and this begins before students even join the school. When prospective pupils and their parents attend open evenings, the headmaster spells out to them that if you are racist, sexist or homophobic then this is not the school for you and you should not apply. It isn't a piecemeal add-on; it is a major part of the fabric of the place. When pupils begin they are required to sign a contract that forms part of their school diaries and includes their commitment neither to tolerate nor express prejudice in any form. Tutors, parents and new pupils all sign it.

During the year the school actively celebrates Black History Month, Holocaust Memorial Day and LGBT History Month. To mark this they have a special assembly where pupils, if they wish, can perform a piece of work – a poem, a monologue, a piece of music or anything they want – that expresses support for equality. I went to two of these assemblies. Nothing could have prepared me for the energy and enthusiasm of seeing these kids all allowed to support and explore the concept of respecting each other. Some pupils were gay and some were not, but this was an issue for all of them. Two young men performed a dance piece inspired by Tennessee Williams. A boy and a girl sang a version of 'I Know Him So Well'. It might sound a bit drippy and like a Conservative commentator's worst nightmare come true. But it wasn't wet or naive or indoctrinating: these were tough South London kids of all different ethnicities who were in a school that made them understand that if they treated other people with respect they would get it too. And they took to it with enthusiasm.

A young straight lad who wants to be a stand-up comedian wrote and performed a monologue about an occasion when he had risked his own safety to stop a gay friend from being homophobically bullied in the street. One of the two assemblies I saw ended with a girl with a beautiful voice singing 'I Wanna Hold Your Hand', with all the audience joining in and then invading the stage. The other ended with a video on a big screen of a group of blokey straight lads re-creating, shot by shot, Queen's 'I Want to Break Free' video in comedy Queen drag, with hoovers and so on. Towards the end of the track the video stopped and the boys, with their hoovers and mops, entered the hall to finish the song, as all the other pupils roared. It wasn't inappropriate or strange or indoctrinating; it was supportive and one of the healthiest things I have ever seen in my life.

It isn't just in performance assemblies that the Brit School ensures it develops mutual respect. Meeting staff afterwards, I was told that at the school there is a special member of staff whom pupils can email confidentially if they have personal issues they wish to speak about. She holds private lunchtime meetings for LGBT pupils to come and get support if they wish. Two teachers, Mike Offen and Rachel Penn, were also helping set up a more social club for LGBT and supportive straight students to discuss issues of diversity and hear from outside speakers. They both enthused about the way the Brit deals with these issues.

Mike, who is gay, told me how he had felt restricted and pressured at previous schools he had worked in. He was told by one member of staff not to disclose his sexuality to a certain teacher because she didn't like gay people. It affected students too. 'I knew of gay students who were being bullied,' he said. 'Certain students didn't feel they could come back to the sixth form because of it.' Sometimes he himself felt self-conscious about even going out in the local town with his partner in case pupils or parents saw them together. When he began teaching at the Brit School that fear disappeared. 'I was wowed by the assemblies when I first came here,' he recalled, 'and I realized there wasn't a conflict between me being a gay man and a teacher.'

Similarly, Rachel, a straight woman, told me of a fellow teacher friend of hers at a previous school who wanted to start a blog for LGBT students after a young pupil came to her in distress. The idea was blocked by the headmaster, who didn't want to upset parents or attract media attention. Rachel told me about the low-level homophobia she'd witnessed and the constant use of the word 'gay' as a derogatory term.

'When I started here,' she said, 'one of the first things I saw in a classroom was a big poster that said "There are no gay pens in this room, there are no gay chairs or gay computers – but there are gay people and this is a safe space".'

Mike tells me that it's not perfect; there are pockets of homophobia in the school, as there are everywhere, but they are stamped on immediately and kids are referred to their contract and the values they signed up to. Mike is conducting a piece of research supported by the school for which he interviewed more than seventy students: 97 per cent said they had frequently heard homophobic language in their previous schools; 30 per cent said they heard it at the Brit; 73 per cent said LGBT issues were talked about positively at the Brit compared to 5 per cent who said this was the case at their previous schools.

I asked Rachel why, as a straight woman, she cares about the issue so much. 'I just care about people and I want people to be nice to each other,' she said, with a 'why are you asking me this question?' kind of smile. 'I think everyone's important and we need to celebrate that. I've been surrounded by heterosexual and homosexual role models growing up, and I've got so many people in my life who are gay that I love and are important to me, and so I feel a responsibility and a duty to do something about this and not to ignore it.'

Straight people, gay people, trans people, cisgendered people, black, white, brown – none of us can afford to accept this medieval situation any more. We have a choice and it lies in the hands of all of us, but especially of the mothers and fathers of this country. The choice is between an increasing number of families being destroyed by the devastating effects of homo, bi- or transphobic bullying – the Crouches, the Houghtons, the Olsens, the Stubbs and the many more that don't get reported – or the experience of a young man I met at the Brit School.

Ethan is a fifteen-year-old straight, working-class lad who was homophobically bullied solidly for two years, despite the fact that he isn't gay, just because he wanted to be an actor. He's a tough guy but had been severely affected by the bullying. Mike and Rachel saw him going past the classroom we were chatting in and asked him to come in to speak to me.

'Because I was exposed to the arts, people said I was gay,' he told me. 'I was repeatedly called a poof, bender, queer, just because I did acting, singing and dancing. I got the whole nine yards, I got called everything. It got so hard.'

Over time Ethan became depressed and his schoolwork suffered. 'Because I was being called gay all the time, I thought I must be,' he explained. 'And I'm not gay – I love women too much! It got to the point where I didn't even want to go into school. I thought, "I can't be bothered to do well because I'm going to get called all these names. What's the point?" I couldn't cope. I'd be fighting not to flip my fist. I wanted to fight them and I had to learn to walk away no matter what.'

He didn't always walk away. Ethan became angrier and angrier and sometimes started random fights, as he put it, 'just to prove how masculine I was'. He got arrested three times and things started to look bleak. 'I thought I couldn't change this. It was bad because it was affecting my relationships with other people.' He paused and I asked how badly it had affected him.

'There were a few suicidal thoughts going on,' he said.

Ethan auditioned for the Brit School and was accepted. Their progressive policies have had a huge effect on him.

'Coming here has changed my opinion on a lot of things. I had started to think that being gay was wrong. I was getting called all these names. I came here being a little bit homophobic, because I knew it was the arts [so] there's going to be a fair few gay people. [But] I've made some brilliant friends who are gay and it's shown me how immature people can be when they're not exposed to things they need to know.

'The people here don't care if you're gay, straight, or an alien. They just don't care as long as you are being you. Everyone here is so nice, and because everyone has the same passions they couldn't care what your attractions are. My views were changed in about a week. This guy [names a schoolfriend who is gay and appeared in the LGBT assembly I saw], you can tell, obviously, and at first I kept my distance – but he's one of the nicest lads . . .'

It's affected his attitude too when he goes back home and sees the same kids who used to give him abuse. 'Now if I see someone at home and they shout something, I laugh at them. They don't know what I've had to go through to realize what's actually right and what's wrong. They can just go on like they are because they're not going to get anywhere in life with their views . . . and you need to change them. And if you don't, don't bother me 'cos I've got my views and I know they're the right ones.'

As I sat on the train back to Central London from Croydon, thinking how so much can change and how there is still much change that needs to happen, it struck me that Ethan represents the choice that straight people have. There are thousands of kids who need our help and support. We all need to make that choice now and actively coerce the government to enforce not just anti-bullying policy but also mandatory sex and relationships education so that all young people are taught to respect themselves and each other. If we don't, we must be prepared to sacrifice more of them now and in years to come.

It doesn't have to be this way. There is a choice and we cannot make it quietly. The time to be vocal is now.

19

Towards a New Way of Living

'I am larger, better than I thought,
I did not know I held so much goodness.
All seems beautiful to me;
I can repeat over to men and women,
You have done such good to me,
I would do the same to you.
I will recruit for myself and you as I go;
I will scatter myself among men and women as I go;
I will toss a new gladness and roughness among them;
Whoever denies me it shall not trouble me;
Whoever accepts me, he or she shall be blessed and shall bless me.'

Walt Whitman, *Song of the Open Road*, 1856

WE NEED CHANGE. From outside the LGBT community and from within too. We've all got a part to play. Our thinking, like that of wider society, needs a reboot: how we express ourselves, how we relate to each other, how we portray and treat each other. This isn't about becoming less gay or conforming to a heteronormative narrative – whatever that means exactly – but about looking after ourselves and treating each other with respect.

Below are some suggestions of things I think need to happen in society to ensure that we break out of the cycle of self-destruction that affects so many of us. You may not agree with all of them, but what is clear is that the way we're doing things now is not tenable any longer. I want to acknowledge that I'm by no means perfect and I'm saying this to myself as much as to anyone else. My aim is to start a discussion.

Creating a better society

The NHS must start monitoring sexual orientation – and we must disclose this information when asked

So many of those working with LGBT people told me we urgently need to monitor sexual orientation at the point of contact with the NHS. We need to see more clearly how the inequalities manifest.

NHS service users are asked to declare ethnicity. We know black people have a genetic difference that puts them at greater risk of developing diabetes and so services are tailored to them. We know, for instance, that people from some countries have a higher risk of vitamin D deficiency or of sickle-cell anaemia. It's clear that gay people have statistically higher levels of alcohol and drug misuse and there is a strong probability that this will result in higher levels of certain cancers and diseases related to stress. We know that rates of suicide in men in the UK are huge, but we don't know what proportion of those are gay or bisexual. I was disturbed by something that Dr Sean Cummings told me. He is also a part-time coroner, and he said that other (heterosexual) coroners have suggested they believe that there is a disproportionate number of deaths, either from suicide or overdosing, of young, healthy men whom they suspect may have been gay or bisexual. We need to find out exactly what's going on. We also need to look seriously at the problems faced specifically by LGBT people from different cultures.

This is a role for the mainstream NHS, but it's equally important that LGBT people cooperate with it. Some of us are nervous about giving this information: it is vital we do so.

A revolution is needed in the professional understanding of the mental-health implications of growing up LGBT

Most healthcare professionals seem to have no idea that being LGBT can correlate with mental-health and self-esteem issues. Dominic Davies of Pink Therapy told me that the standard of training potential therapists receive on sexuality is appalling and that many trainers and trainees are embarrassed to spend much time on the subject. That urgently needs to change.

A societal revolution is needed in the understanding and treatment of mental health and addiction

I find it baffling that the leading rehabs in the world, which put people (who can afford it) through the gold standard of addiction treatment, understand that addiction is trauma-based, what causes it, how it manifests and how it's treated – yet the medical community does not. A serious inquiry is needed into the effectiveness of the NHS approach, which seems to focus on treating the symptom but not the cause. Intense, long-lasting trauma therapy to fix the actual root cause means more expense, but it's got to be done.

The therapeutic community needs to understand that compulsive drinking, drugging, spending, debt, sexual behaviour, and more can all be destructive, destroying people's relationships with those around them and their health. The obesity crisis is a mental-health problem fuelled by unrestrained capitalism which allows fast-food and sweets companies to keep us all hooked. The same goes for alcoholism. The UK has a drink problem. We all know it. It's worse than in most countries in the world and it is because we have problems owning our emotions. We need to understand that emotional problems are at the root of most of the dysfunction in our society, made worse by inequality, lack of opportunity and unfairness, which puts more strain on everyone. We need to stand up to the drinks and food companies and tackle these issues at a societal level.

Schools, teacher training, sex and relationships education

The current situation where teachers get barely any – sometimes no – training on LGBT issues/experiences doesn't make sense and bears a huge weight of responsibility for what is happening. Dealing with the welfare of all children should be a fundamental part of what teachers are taught. Likewise, I believe the next LGBT rights campaign, with the help of straight people, should be to force the government to bring in mandatory sex and relationships education – for teachers as well as all children at an age-appropriate level, with no exceptions.

Some people have expressed to me a belief that the current way that schools are categorized and carved up is intentionally to make it difficult to change the system and bring in advances like this. But it has to change and the people to do it, I believe, will be parents. Young adults need to be taught about HIV and other sexually transmitted infections. Young people need to be taught more than just what makes babies; they need to learn what relationships are, what consent is, that pornography is not realistic or a template for sexual relationships. Young people need to be taught to respect their bodies and those of other people.

The mainstream media need to give a better reflection of LGBT lives and issues

We pay the same amount for a licence fee, for media and we buy the same products advertised on TV and billboards. The media needs to reflect gay lives as more than just soap-opera characters. For instance, every year BBC London news covers the Notting Hill Carnival: the build-up to the event, its politics and leadership. The same should happen with Gay Pride and other relevant events. Why are the Attitude Awards not on TV? Why aren't more gay dramas commissioned? It is outrageous that our stories and lives are not reflected too. There is a BBC Asian network. Why is there not an LGBT one? Because we are so diverse no one's quite sure what it should be, but quality content can be produced. It doesn't have to be just disco music and fluff. There could be call-in shows, discussions, help and advice. This should also reflect all skin colours and cultures, as well as trans and non-binary people, not just stories about white gay men.

People in media companies – film, theatre, publishing, newspapers, radio, TV, online – need to think in a different way and make renewed efforts to feature gay content. Some do it. Channel 4 has often been at the forefront, but there is room for improvement. The *Independent on Sunday* does a great job with its Rainbow List every year but this is a rare example. It's inexcusable that the media do not highlight homophobic bullying. Employ more staff. Employ gay staff like BuzzFeed has. Why do newspapers not have LGBT sections? I hear time and again that broadcasters refuse to commission gay content because they 'did a gay drama a few years ago'. If we are maybe 5 per cent of the population, then we should be represented in at least 5 per cent of media content. In my experience gay media staff are often too scared to push gay content for fear of being labelled 'the gay staff member', or they aren't interested because of their own issues. Why aren't publishers publishing more gay fiction? Progress is being made with the creation of the Green Carnation Prize for fiction, but there is still far more to do.

LGBT events and initiatives need to be more mainstream

Laws may have changed, but culture lags behind. I am proud that the Attitude Awards and the Attitude Pride Awards give an opportunity for the nation to see people in public life – Ian McKellen, Daniel Radcliffe, Tom Daley, Jonathan Ross, Ellie Goulding, Nigella Lawson, Naomi Campbell – supporting and celebrating gay people. If this kind of thing gets seen by the country, it becomes part of its DNA. Plenty of gay or gay-friendly people are in positions of responsibility at major companies that could support events like Pride and other initiatives similar to the old Stonewall Equality Show, which was a great rallying point and fundraiser. Major companies need to be more creative.

Understand wider society matters. Inequality hurts us.

In the 1980s, when the right were so viciously homophobic, I could not countenance any gay people supporting anyone but the left. Since then, I have met many decent people I've liked and respected who argue the importance of having LGBT voices within the evolving Conservative Party.

It remains a controversial subject, but, wherever you stand politically, one thing is clear: when public services falter, the more unfair society is and the harder life becomes for everyone but those at the top – especially those of us battling these issues. In the PACE RaRE study one of the key factors, for straight people as well as gay, in suicidal ideation was poverty and financial worries. In other words, money worries can be the thing that pushes someone over into feeling suicidal. On top of this, the less money you have, the harder it is to get good help.

In some ways capitalism (and the perhaps dubious concept of the pink pound) has helped us, but it has also diminished us. Gay-themed films, plays and books don't always make much money, and so get made or published less often. Market forces are why many gay venues are shutting and others are becoming sex clubs – not through a libertarian commitment to sexual liberation, but because, in this climate, it is the only way some venues can make money.

David Cameron made equal marriage a reality, but his austerity agenda cut NHS funding, mental and sexual health provision, and many other crucial services. After years of cuts, the police now claim they are being used as a mental health service. Violent crime, as well as homophobic hate crime, is rising. Being able to get married is clearly not much use to someone if they are seriously depressed or using drugs because they cannot cope with financial stress and health problems for which they can't get good-quality, timely help. We need to make society fairer for everyone – regardless of gender, skin colour and orientation. It's in all our interests.

We need to demand more of the people we support

There are certain celebrities whose careers literally would not exist if it wasn't for the LGBT community. These relationships are often take-take-take – they give nothing back. Doing a PA in a gay club or a gay-press interview when you have a record out is not enough. Some artists have been massively impressive and gone the extra mile: Daniel Radcliffe does more to highlight homophobic bullying than most gay celebrities; Beverley Knight actively supports rucomingout.com and its events; and Lady Gaga started her Born This Way Foundation and speaks at political rallies. These are few and far between.

People can be very cynical about artists who actively support the gay community – and yet we continue to richly reward those who don't lift a finger for us. Most 'gay icon' celebrities couldn't even spare a tweet on the days when the UK or Ireland legalized gay marriage, for instance. It's appalling. We need to ask more of them. Days like Pride are really important cultural events for young people, especially those who are trying to find their identities. Most of the time these events don't have a great line-up because they can't afford the huge fees for massive stars. If pop stars aren't prepared to give up an afternoon to perform at a major Pride event here and there, then they don't deserve our support.

Gay writers: give us happy endings!

You might think this an ironic statement in this book, but more gay stories – whether books, TV, theatre or film – need to be upbeat and have happy endings. Especially after this book, we are in desperate need of positivity. One of the reasons that people love *Beautiful Thing* and *Torch Song Trilogy* is because they are romantic and uplifting. It's still rare to see two men or women kiss tenderly in a gay play or TV show. Where are the love stories and the lightness? How amazing would it be for a major Hollywood studio to make a mainstream film with an authentic, solid gay love story central to the plot – like *Brokeback Mountain* minus the tears, murder and depression? Where are the gay rom-coms? One of the reasons Tom Wells' play *Jumpers for Goalposts* was so popular was because it was romantic, funny and no one shot themselves. We desperately need more of these! They can only happen if executives in media companies commission them.

The gay media needs to change

The gay media need to show that we are more than usually white shirtless clubbers, escorts and porn stars. This means we need to support those publications and websites that do a better job. Does this mean that there can be no sexual content? No, but gay media need to show that we're more than our sex lives.

We are in the midst of an HIV and sexual-health/drug crisis. I think gay media – magazines and online – need to commit to publishing a full page in every issue, or a link online, of safe-sex and sexual-health information. Given that we all report that there's no same-sex education in schools, it's surely the very least we could do.

As editor of *Attitude*, the issue of how we present body image is the one that I struggled with the most. When I took over I made an effort to balance the sexual content. We ditched the chatline and porn ads. Other magazines still carry them, as well as escort ads. I stripped out the many pages of club listings and editorial, figuring there was enough club coverage in free mags. I scrapped the annual 'Porn' issue and said if we had to do the 'Naked' issue, the highest-selling of the year, then it would have to promote a safe-sex message.

I put out a string of non-shirtless covers, but – as I described in Chapter 10 – the sexier, fleshier ones always outsold them. A friend on the phone once said to me, 'I've got your magazine here. Why do you have to have a shirtless straight man on the cover?' and then added, 'That's why I bought it, I suppose.' The people who moan about the sexy covers simply don't support the magazine when it does anything else.

During my time at *Attitude* I also changed the content of the magazine. In 2011 MP Jo Swinson held an all-party inquiry in parliament to look at the issues of body image in the media, focusing on portrayals of women. The editors of many of the UK's glossy magazines were invited and every single one declined the invitation – except me. I went to the inquiry and pointed out that the issue was one of capitalism – it's human nature that people want to look at sexy people. I explained that we include lots of 'real' people in *Attitude*. Gay MP Stephen Williams said that real people in magazines were always easy-on-the-eye real people. In our case it was not true! As well as real people in general features, we had a dating page, a couples page (which had a long-term couple talking about their relationship) and a spread with a man specifically over fifty years old talking about his life. There was our monthly 'Real Bodies' feature showing a man photographed in his shorts talking about his body. We literally included anyone who applied: massively obese, underweight, average, on all levels of attractiveness. But it seems that not many people noticed this content; they just saw the sexy covers and the fashion models, of which admittedly there were a significant number because they were why the readers bought the magazine!

I am proud of what I did at *Attitude*. But it, the other magazines and all of us as consumers can do far better. All of us in the gay media need to look at the messages we are sending out. Black, Asian, South-east Asian and other 'ethnic minorities' should be better represented in the staff and output. This isn't easy. These are small companies, as I know well, and finger-pointing isn't helpful, but it needs to happen. And readers of these magazines should email the editorial staff. If, after this book, enough of you support *Attitude*, you can affect editorial policy. In other words: support magazines doing a better job. On top of this, we *all* need to be more conscious of how we present ourselves. Maybe when we do an ice-bucket challenge we shouldn't feel the need to do it in our pants . . .

Sex and objectification

We need to take the heat out of anal sex and, if need be, work through our personal relationship with gender

There is nothing shameful about being a woman, but because you like to be penetrated does not make you a woman. You are a man, a gay (or bi) man. Being penetrated is not a shameful thing and it should be treated with respect.

If you are hung up on the issues around penetrative sex and masculinity, then talk about it with a therapist, perhaps a gay-friendly sex therapist of whom there are many, or at a Sex Addicts or Sex and Love Addicts Anonymous meeting if that is appropriate. Part of accepting ourselves is accepting that many of us gay men are not what you would call traditionally masculine – and that's OK. What matters is how we feel about it. And if you decide that you don't want to have anal sex because it's painful, or for any other reason that isn't shame-based, then that's fine too.

We need to understand the link between constant casual sex, objectification, body-image issues and problems forming relationships

The Sigma Research study *What Constitutes the Best Sex Life for Gay and Bisexual Men?*, published in 2013, showed that many gay men wanted to be in a relationship with someone they loved and to have a sex life free from harm and sexually transmitted infection. For many of us that's not a reality. I've heard so many gay men complain that other men treat them without respect – whilst they do the same thing themselves.

No one's going to thank me for making this next point, and I want to acknowledge that I do this myself and have also done so through my work at *Attitude*. It's easy to do and difficult to stop. None of us is perfect . . . But the way we sexualize our culture so heavily and the way many of us (including myself again) have sex so casually leads to us treating each other as objects. It's then that physical attributes – the best body, biggest chest, biggest penis and so on – become someone's most important values. The person inside – their thoughts, feelings, emotions – is less important. That's OK if it's all you want. But most of us say that's not all we want. Objectifying people makes it hard to build connections and meaningful, respectful relationships whether they are friendships or romances.

Our language plays into that objectification too and comes from that inbuilt disrespect we've been taught about each other: 'tops', 'bottoms', 'bears', 'otters', 'cubs', 'twinks', 'cock', even the word 'queen' – 'This queen did this', 'That queen over there'. Does that sound like a respectful term? The word 'twink' implies a young, passive, weak man purely as an object in our jungle-like pecking order of fuck-ability. Describing other men as 'cock' or 'trade' is objectifying to the greatest extent possible. I'm sure we'd all scorn straight men acting as if they were on *Magaluf Uncovered* and referring to women as 'pussy'. What would you think of women who referred to themselves, in all seriousness, as 'bimbos'? What would you say to a girlfriend of yours if she said, 'I'm going out to a bimbo bar, for men who like bimbos. I'm really hoping I meet someone special there.' We'd think she was crazy.

As I say, it's fine if sex is all you want from other people, but then you must accept that your own value is just that of 'a fuck' – and that your value will diminish as you get older. This is where the 'gay men don't get old' mentality comes from. Our internalized homophobia has affected our view of gay people so much that we believe we and others have no value other than our attractiveness, and that soon passes as we age. If we want to hang on to this objectification then we have to accept that we all have a limited shelf-life. I don't believe this is conducive to us truly valuing ourselves or each other.

If we wish to have serious, loving, tender relationships, we have to treat others and ourselves as meaningful, vulnerable, *valuable* human beings. Not as 'twinks' or 'tops' or 'bottoms' or 'cock'.

Let's get real about Grindr

One of the ways we do this is by getting off Grindr, getting out of the bars and meeting and talking to other men in the real world without drugs or alcohol. I understand that some people love Grindr and have a great time on it. Brilliant. But if that's not your experience, then let's be realistic about the situation. Most men I have spoken to say they find Grindr brutal, harsh and depressing.

Let's talk about it. If it doesn't work for you then delete it. If you can't keep it deleted then you may want to try a Sex and Love Addicts meeting. Unless you want to spend the next thirty years going from one crap Grindr shag to the next, you have to understand this is serious. Don't sit there moaning about all the men on there – make sure you are not one of them. We need to find other ways to meet. If you want a relationship, get real and don't be surprised if you are having trouble finding one on Grindr. Ask yourself why you are still on there if it's not working for you.

We need to look at body-image issues, vanity and physical self-obsession

This doesn't mean not caring what you look like or not going to the gym, but it does mean you can begin to examine what really lies beneath your feelings about the way you look. The constant extreme e-vanity of posting shirtless images at any opportunity is exhausting. You are more than your body. We need to commit to finding a way to value ourselves that is based on who we are and not the way we look.

If you have a serious problem with body-image issues, then go into therapy. Don't let it fester. You can start by reading the book *The Adonis Complex: How to Identify, Treat and Prevent Body Obsession in Men and Boys* by Pope, Phillips and Olivardia.

Body image is an issue that comes up time and again at the 'A Change of Scene' events. We as a community need to work on it.

We need to talk about porn

Watching people have sex is hot. We've celebrated it a lot at *Attitude*. I could tell you I'm never going to watch it again. I wish it were true, but I doubt it will be. As I've grown up I've become increasingly uneasy about the values of porn. It is the most powerful fount of objectification and body insecurity bar none, and ignores the fact that these are real people with real lives. We can tell ourselves men in porn are all enjoying themselves with no consequences, and it may be true for some, but not for many. I've heard many porn performers speak of mental-health issues, drug issues and loneliness; Chapter 1 looks at this. Often these are young, naive men who have launched themselves down a path they can't escape.

We need to stop glamorizing porn, and young people especially need to understand the consequences of taking part in it. Pre-internet, magazines would come and go, never to be seen again; but if you take part in porn today those images are for ever, out there for the rest of your life. You need to be prepared for your friends, siblings, parents (and even, perhaps, your future children), new boyfriends, in-laws and possibly prospective bosses to see them. It's all very well to take a 'sex-positive' approach to this, but, rightly or wrongly, in the real world porn carries stigma and will always do so, gay porn in particular. Several recent cases highlight this: a straight, married Irish football player appeared on a gay porn site after developing a gambling addiction; a young straight man was dumped by his soap-actress girlfriend after his gay porn career was revealed; and another young man was fired from his job as a teacher after one of his pupils saw his videos online.

Porn sites pay pitiful money. I have been told of some companies where the models sign release forms and are paid a few hundred pounds, but if they wish to remove the photos at any future time they have to pay a fee of tens of thousands of pounds to buy them back, something which they can't afford. You are very unlikely to be able to make a career out of porn. No doubt the 'sex-positive' lobby will go berserk at this suggestion, but I would say to them: look at the obscenely long list of porn stars who have either killed themselves or died from drugs overdoses.

I think it's perfectly reasonable that a law should ensure some cooling-off period in which people can buy their pictures back at a more reasonable price; and, perhaps, an age limit, also by law, preventing people under the age of twenty-one taking part in porn.

We need an honest discussion about sex culture

Again, I can't tell you I will not have casual sex in the future and of course I'm not demanding it of anyone else. We all have to decide what is right for ourselves. But we need to be honest about the obvious fact that the normalization of extreme sex culture – saunas, sex clubs, etc. – has played a major part in the worryingly high levels of sexually transmitted infections, including HIV.

It's not enough to dismiss concerns about this. We now have a problem with hepatitis C infection and with previously uncommon sexually transmitted infections like shigellosis and LGV (lympho-granuloma venereum). There is also the frightening prospect of infections like gonorrhea becoming harder to treat as they become resistant to antibiotics. What happens then? Alongside this, we need to discuss the fact that STI levels contribute to the community risk of HIV infection. As Ford Hickson explained to me, passing on STIs increases the pool of risk of HIV transmission for everybody because HIV spreads more easily if the person has another STI.

In 2014 the Terrence Higgins Trust criticized a call from campaigner James Wharton to shut saunas by saying that they were great places to disseminate safe-sex information. They should also have said that it would be entirely reasonable to have a discussion about the extremely high rates of sexually transmitted infections, the record high levels of HIV transmission and the many drug-related incidents that happen in saunas. If Fiez, the man from the A&E of a London hospital to whom I spoke in Chapter 14, is right and hospitals are receiving such large numbers of casualties from saunas, then we need a serious discussion about how safe they are. It's not homophobia or heteronormativity to want to stop people dying or getting raped in gay saunas.

It's time to admit that our approaches to tackling STI and HIV rates have failed and that we need a new approach.

I agree that of course it's important not to shame people. I suggest we use the term 'with care and control' and that sexual-health centres talk about these principles. It's not shaming to ask people if they have control and are taking care in their sexual lives, and if they don't think that's the case then we should discuss what they are doing. Let's have a more in-depth conversation about the risk of sexual harm, consent, sexual compulsiveness and addiction.

56 Dean Street's template for bright, young, shame-free sexual-health centres should be a model that is rolled out up and down the country for all the population but especially, as a priority, in places with high numbers of LGBT people.

We need a complete rethink about HIV

Stonewall estimates that 5–7 per cent of the population are LGBT; despite this, according to aidsmap.com:

- 44 per cent of people living with HIV in the UK are men who have sex with men.

- Statistically, in 2014, just over nine gay or bi men tested HIV positive in the UK every day. Five of those are in London – every single day.

- In 2014 it was estimated that 103,700 people were living with HIV in the UK. Of these, 18,700 were unaware that they had it, and an estimated 6,500 of these were men who have sex with men.

The HIV prevention campaigns of the last fifteen years have not worked as they should have. I'm disturbed by the number of young gay men who do not understand that they are more at risk of HIV infection than straight people.

We need a major inquiry to look into the experience of LGBT people, to work out what is happening with HIV and other diseases like hepatitis C, and how mental health, poverty and inequality play into this. We need to pay special attention to the experience of black, Asian and minority ethnic (BAME) communities.

We then need a new national HIV campaign. I'm not confident that the Terrence Higgins Trust has been as effective as it might have been; HIV and other STI rates have all climbed higher and higher, and the growing drugs problem, in my opinion, has not been adequately addressed.

A new campaign should educate the entire population about the facts of HIV, a virus that can affect anyone but, in the West, disproportionately affects men who have sex with men, especially men from BAME groups. If you are HIV positive, you can live a healthy life by getting on to medication as long as you begin it early enough. But it isn't an easy ride: HIV medication needs to be taken every single day at the same time for the rest of your life. People can have reactions to the medicine, but the biggest problem my friends who are HIV positive have is the psychological impact of living with such a serious condition.

You'd think gay men would understand HIV and be compassionate to those who have it. Many are. But, sadly, people with HIV are still treated badly by many gay men. On apps some people refer to positive men as 'dirty' or 'not clean'. This is not acceptable. Gay people are a minority group that has faced prejudice, and it is not fair that we then face more prejudice over something that could affect anyone who is sexually active. We need to check ourselves and call out people treating others this way.

We all need to pledge to take an HIV test at least every year

What does need to be stigmatized is not regularly testing for HIV – at least once a year, and more if you are having unprotected sex. We need to ask friends whether they are being tested and talk about what risk they may or may not be taking.

There is information on page 355 about safe sex and how to avoid catching HIV.

We also need to accept the fact that a significant number of gay/bi men catch HIV in relationships. That's painful to discuss, but it is not uncommon. You need to think very carefully before you stop using condoms, even in a relationship.

Much has been made of the new protective treatment, PrEP, which doctors believe will radically decrease the risk of catching HIV, possibly completely. It requires taking a daily pill of an HIV medication called Truvada. We need PrEP, but alongside an honest discussion about sexual compulsion, other STIs, responsibility and an understanding that it should not be used as an opportunity to ditch condoms.

Support for positive people

It seems much discussion of HIV focuses on keeping people HIV negative and ignores the needs of HIV-positive people as if they aren't worth worrying about any more. We need to re-evaluate how we look after positive people and their needs.

An HIV/AIDS memorial

HIV and AIDS have devastated us and have directly altered the lives of so many people. It is crazy that there is not a national memorial statue and event to commemorate what we have been through. I believe this lack contributes to so many people just acting as though HIV is not an issue. I suggest a memorial statue somewhere and a candlelit vigil, on the Friday night before London Pride, in Trafalgar Square, so we can acknowledge and process the immensity of what we continue to go through with HIV.

Helping ourselves and each other

Remove the stigma from self-loathing

We fling the term 'self-loathing' around in an accusatory and judge-mental way as if it is a crime committed by choice, when in reality it's an excruciating, life-diminishing thing which has been thrust upon us.

Whilst it's important to call people out when they attack us, even anti-gay politicians who are outed deserve some level of compassion. They are damaged gay people too. If people feel bad about being gay we need to be able to talk about that and try to help them and ourselves. Let's get it out in the open and offer people help, support and understanding.

We need to understand the concept of treating ourselves with esteem

As I explained earlier, I believe self-esteem is directly affected by our actions and behaviour. We are responsible for our own self-esteem. Crucially, nurturing your self-esteem also means actively avoiding things that don't make you feel good and understanding that the way you treat people has a direct effect on the way you feel about yourself.

Understand that being a mean girl is not cool

Being nasty to people isn't clever or funny or a game. It's a defence mechanism we employ when we don't feel good about ourselves – and it has consequences. It's so common in our culture that we've come to think of it *as* our culture. It's time that we all moved away from thinking it's OK to be catty and behave in an unpleasant way to people. We're not mean girls, we're grown adults.

Sometimes we're so addicted to putting people down that we try to dress it up as witticism or something else. Examples would be putting 'Expect sarcasm' on a Grindr profile, or saying things like 'I tell it like it is, so if you can't handle the truth . . .' Being unpleasant is just a defence mechanism. It's a signal we are in pain. Putting other people down to make yourself feel better is not OK. Although it might seem fun in the moment, somewhere inside we know it's not nice and, whether we acknowledge it or not, the feeling will come back to bite us. On top of this, it's totally unattractive.

It may also be that you gravitate to people who like putting others down, leading to a toxic mess. If people bitch *with* you it is likely they bitch *about* you too. Get out of the toxic pot. It may sound obvious, but treat people as you wish to be treated.

Oprah Winfrey gave a great tip on *The Jonathan Ross Show* when she talked about what she calls 'the nine-second rule'. If she thinks she is going to say something nasty she counts to nine before speaking and usually, by that point, she realizes that it's wrong and doesn't say it.

Think too about how you behave online. We can't complain about homophobic bullying in schools but be happy to slag people off on Facebook or Twitter – sometimes celebrities, sometimes people we know. Bullying is never OK. Rowing and arguing is a waste of your time. Confrontation is usually a sign something isn't working. Don't continue aggression online: it doesn't achieve anything. Step away from the computer. We each get only one life. Don't waste it rowing with people online.

If you have trouble with this, or issues with anger (as many of us understandably do), then you need to seek help for it. It's a drain on your self-esteem and it gets in the way of making solid relationships. If you are in recovery, then you'll very likely find a lot of this begins to subside and dissipate as you progress.

Young people: show your elders some respect . . .

Ultimately, we all need to treat each other with respect. Many older LGBT people have fought so that younger people can have the lives we have today. Many of them have not had as easy an experience as the younger generation has. Respect them and that experience. This doesn't mean you have to sleep with them, but respect their experience, what they have been through and done. There is a huge amount that younger men can learn from older men.

. . . and older people: show young people respect back

Older men need to treat young people with respect too. I often hear older men moan that they aren't welcome in bars full of young people. I understand this and I think it's important we all feel welcome in communal places, but it's also true that often young people, gay or straight, want to be around other young people. There's nothing wrong with that.

I know this will offend some people, but I myself fit into that older generation now, and there are plenty of bars where older people can feel welcome. It is important that young people have gay spaces where, when they want, they can mix with people of their own age the way all young people need to and the way most of us wanted to when we were their age.

Racism

I can never fully understand the experience of racism, but there is clearly a devastating fault line of unfairness that runs through society – both mainstream and LGBT. From the racism of online social media, to the lack of proper representation and staffing in gay media, to the direct racism experienced on the gay scene, there is a crisis in its own right that needs to be addressed. That black gay men have higher levels of HIV is an outrage upon an outrage. We must make this a priority now.

It's crass and embarrassing to say we all need to treat each other better, but it is true. LGBT organizations need to redouble their efforts to employ, engage and represent people from black, Asian and minority ethnic communities.

There seems to be some disagreement about levels of homophobia in BAME communities, but I would respectfully suggest this discussion must also be had – but not at the expense of focusing on the racism that BAME people face. I am proud to have put the first black gay man, first gay Asian man, first black gay woman on the cover of *Attitude* – but we can do more too. We all can and we all must.

Start caring about yourself more than about Madonna

I'm saying it as much to myself as to anyone else. As I explained in Chapter 8, I have been obsessed with Madonna since I was sixteen.

Often divas and people we love have saved our lives when we needed them. I want to say thank you to her for being that person for me. But now I'm a grown adult I need to focus on myself.

Madonna, Beyoncé, Kylie, Gaga and all other celebrities are not more important or worthy than I am or you are. Celebrities often do great things, but they are not more worthwhile human beings than the rest of us. I'm not saying anyone should abandon artists they love, but let's start living our own lives, rather than living vicariously through celebrities. Let's turn at least some of that passion towards ourselves, our friends, our emotional wellness, and towards living authentic lives.

There'll always be a place for idols. I'll still buy Madonna's CDs. I still love cinema, film, music, theatre. I will still go to concerts and still get excited about great music and art. But let's get it into an appropriate part in our lives. Enjoy them, love them. But when you are ready to, with love, put *your* life first.

Stop pointing and get well

All human beings have a tendency to blame. No more of that. The most important thing you can take from this book is to *be* the change you wish to see. When you work on your own issues and become part of the solution rather than the problem, you are contributing to a process of healing an entire community. Telling people what to do is a feature of codependency. It's one we need to stop. Heal ourselves and we help by becoming one of the role models we never had. Most of all, you're helping yourself. There is nothing more important.

Until you help yourself you cannot help other people.

How can we help some of these challenges along?

A new community

The absolute number-one problem that came up time and again while I was researching this book is loneliness and lack of a community feeling. Young people had nowhere to go to get support. People had nowhere to socialize apart from apps, bars and clubs. Older people had nowhere to go to feel part of a community. HIV-positive people feel left out. People from black, Asian and minority ethnic backgrounds feel excluded and objectified. **We need to re-install and reboot a new sense of community.**

To transform the experience of LGBT people in the UK, I believe we need a new national organization that runs a network of major and ambitious community centres. Instead of lobbying, they should at heart be about supporting the sexual, social, mental and spiritual wellbeing of LGBT people. New York, Los Angeles and Sydney all have their own centres. In London Jewish people have the JW3 centre, which the Jewish community itself made happen. We can do this too. I imagine a huge complex that provides free or subsidized office space to smaller organizations such as the Albert Kennedy Trust, which helps young homeless LGBT people, and London Friend and Antidote. Like Dean Street, it should provide sexual-health screening and offer a substantial amount of free or subsidized counselling, along with space for community groups and classes to meet.

But more than this, it should be a social space that provides somewhere for people to interact, to have coffee, attend events and meetings, see exhibitions, ideally a performance space and screening room. I met a man called David Robson who suggested an event called 'The Friday Night Project' which would offer a social place on Friday evenings – a time when many feel tempted to go out, take drugs and go off the rails – to meet up, have a meal and socialize, without alcohol. This could be a place where recovery meetings could be held, with social gatherings and support for positive men, support for people of differing ethnicities, support groups for friends and family of LGBT people and also, crucially, for older LGBT people. The sky is the limit.

In a dream scenario, I see a building that embodies the gay community. It should be a place that is buzzing, modern and equally welcoming to all types of people. Initially, there is no point in having this anywhere but Soho, because it needs to be in a place where people feel comfortable. Is this realistic? It is ambitious, but there's no point in not aiming high. If the LGBT Foundation in Manchester and other cities can do it, if Leigh Chislett can revolutionize sexual-health services in London, if the Jewish community can create a social centre, then why can't we do this?

This is going to cost tens of millions of pounds, and once we've done it we need to set up versions in Brighton, Birmingham, Leicester, Glasgow and other cities around the country. I see it as an organization that receives government funding for all the health work it will do, but also support from companies and private individuals. People would contribute to it with standing orders, donations and fundraising so that we have a sense of doing something for ourselves. I know for sure that, though there are many gay people in poverty, there are also many who have a lot of money.

We can do this because we need to. Anything is possible. We need it because, however much we may support people, unless we can provide them with an alternative to simply going to bars and clubs then this problem will continue. If we can't help ourselves now, then the problem is even bigger than I thought. Nearly fifty years after the Stonewall Riots and the (partial) decriminalization of homosexuality in England and Wales, this is our opportunity to prove once and for all that there really is a gay community. Individual recovery is really important and helping one another is part of that. We help other people and we help ourselves. This is the future.

20

Turning Point

'You don't need to be helped any longer. You've always had the power to go back to Kansas.'

Glinda, the Good Witch, *The Wizard of Oz*, 1939

'Love takes off the masks that we fear we cannot live without and know we cannot live within.'

James Baldwin

'But the wild things cried, "Oh please don't go – we'll eat you up – we love you so!"

And Max said, "No!"

The wild things roared their terrible roars and gnashed their terrible teeth and rolled their terrible eyes and showed their terrible claws but Max stepped into his private boat and waved goodbye.'

From Maurice Sendak's *Where the Wild Things Are*, 1963

FIRST PUBLISHED IN 1963 and now one of the most iconic, best-loved children's books of all time, Maurice Sendak's *Where the Wild Things Are* tells the story of a little boy, Max, who is told off by his mother and sent to his room without his tea. Feeling hurt and alone, he finds that there is a wood in his bedroom leading to a sea and a boat, which takes him far away to the land of the monsters. They seem fun at first, but they have gnashing, razor-sharp teeth and terrible tempers. He spends what feels like a year away from his family before finally sailing back to his bedroom, where, in fact, no time has passed and his tea is ready.

You might not be surprised to know that Maurice Sendak was one of us. He passed away in 2012 aged eighty-three, five years after his partner of fifty years, psychologist Dr Eugene Glynn. In a *New York Times* article in 2008 Sendak said, 'All I wanted was to be straight so my parents could be happy. They never, never, never knew.' His most famous work is about escaping from the real world – and, crucially, about the fact that, when all is said and done, we have to come back to reality in the end. When we do so, usually we'll find that things are never as bad as they seem. It is the ultimate, simple book – second only to *The Wizard of Oz* – about the human experience of fantasy as a reaction to painful feelings.

It's time. I know it, and I think you know it too. The way things are isn't working any longer. Something has to change. If not now, then when? There's no time to waste. Like Max in *Where the Wild Things Are*, it's time for us to leave the fantasy, the distractions, the monsters we've created to help us cope with what's happened to us, and to face life as it really is. Those monsters that were such great playthings at first have got too much power, their teeth have grown bigger and bigger and they are destroying us. They won't want us to leave them behind. They will kick and scream and do everything they can to keep us on their island. So will the people who are invested in them. But the drugs, the alcohol, the crazy sex, the self-harm, the bitching, the moaning, the attacking on Twitter and Facebook, the living in fantasy and attention-seeking – they've all served us well, but we've outgrown their usefulness. They are hurting too many of us. I know because they've been part of my story. Now it's time to step into the boat and sail away, back to ourselves.

In *City Limits* magazine on 31 December 1987, journalist and LGBT activist Brian Kennedy, who was to die of AIDS three years later, wrote:

> If every lesbian or gay man was open about their lives with a
> dozen or so heterosexuals we know, we could transform public

debate on the issue. All the indications are that the public is widely ignorant rather than fundamentally bigoted, and an encounter with an openly gay person can change perspectives . . . Unfortunately the flip side to this tactic is that our closetry, the times we cover or hide our lifestyles, is probably the greatest asset available to our enemies. The personal choice we make now between openness and the closet may well determine the shape of gay life into the next century.

Our LGBT lives have been defined by secrecy. At first we were just little kids, learning that to survive we had to pretend we weren't who we were. Society, too, denied our existence. Indeed, in many places around the world it still does. But in the West, in the1980s, faced with what felt like the threat of annihilation, we came out, showed who we really were, asserted that we *were* worth something and created change. Twenty years earlier that same spirit breathed through those black trans women and other queer people who started the Stonewall Riots. Today it's time for a new generation to be honest about our lives once again – this time not to others but, primarily, to ourselves.

When Rob Goddard killed himself he had more than fifteen hundred friends on Facebook – all friends with a man who, in pictures, was always smiling and happy. On what would have been his next birthday, hundreds of those friends posted birthday greetings on his page, not knowing he was gone. Those friends, like his happy, smiling image, weren't real. As LGBT people we are fantastic at putting a sheen on the surface, making everything look like it is OK, that things are 'fabulous', but we are not very good at acknowledging the pain underneath. We learned to hide it in order to survive when we were little. But as adults it's stifling our souls.

It's taken its toll. As I have said, at the beginning and many times throughout, there are many happy LGBT people leading brilliant lives. Many of us have come out relatively unscathed, making the most of our situations with a tenacity and strength that is almost unfathomable. When, occasionally, straight people question why there isn't a Straight Pride, it is because straight people do not have to find strength and courage just to be themselves. Take Ted Spring, aged seventy-eight, and Paul Pollard, seventy-seven, who are believed to have been together for longer than any other gay couple in the UK. They met in 1960 at the Lockyer Hotel in Plymouth. When Ted first met Paul he was engaged to a woman. For the first seven years of their relationship it was illegal to be gay. Ted told the *Plymouth Herald* in 2015 that he had always been frightened by 'the gay side of life' but that his partner had changed all that: 'He showed me that no matter who you love, or what you love, love is beautiful and, after being with Paul for 55 years, I can honestly say I've never been happier'. As I have endeavoured to show in *Attitude*, there are countless gay male couples like this and, I'm certain, many lesbian couples in the same position.

But, of course, there are walking wounded from what we've been subjected to, and some no longer walking. As we come to the end of this book I can't help but think of some beautiful people I have known, and some I haven't, who are no longer with us. I think of the terrible loss of Simon Santos, who inspired the earlier chapter 'Gay men don't get old'. That man should still be here. I think of my flatmate who died of AIDS at thirty-two; of Kristian Digby, a beautiful man inside and out; of the Crouch family – Roger Crouch, who hanged himself after his son took his own life as a result of homophobic bullying; of Mark Houghton, whose mum has been so brave; of Lucy Meadows, whom I didn't know, but whose harassment stands as a symbol of the appalling treatment of transgender people; of Rob Goddard. They should all still be here.

But there is hope. Back at the start of this book I wrote about my memories of Gay Pride on Clapham Common in 1997, which remains one of the most joyous, hope- and love-filled days of my life, a day when it seemed anything was possible. I remember how it felt to see all those people happy, interacting with each other. That day I spoke to a black lesbian who was painted white from head to toe. I high-fived a nun on roller skates. I smiled at people, men and women. I hugged strangers. I was young, it's true, but I felt that sense of community and I feel that energy beginning to bubble up again today. It is a twinkling point of hope.

I see it in the trans community through people like Paris Lees and those at All About Trans, like Ayla Holdom, an RAF search-and-rescue pilot outed by the *Sun* who went on to teach them that trans people should be respected; Suran Dickson of Diversity Role Models; Leigh Chislett at 56 Dean Street; the people of the NAZ project addressing the needs of black, Asian and minority ethnic men; the brave Asifa Lahore and her *Muslim Drag Queens* documentary; Monty Moncrieff and the team at London Friend; DJ Fat Tony helping people into recovery. I see Boy George seven years clean and sober, Elton John twenty-five years sober in 2015, and many other LGBT people living sober lives.

I see Wayne Dhesi and his rucomingout site, Patrick Cash with his 'Let's Talk About Gay Sex and Drugs' events, Simon Marks' enabling discussion at 'A Change of Scene' and David Stuart being brave enough to draw attention to what people do not want to see. I see therapists David Smallwood and Sarah Graham working to help gay people. I see others starting alcohol- and drug-free events, like at the Light Yoga Space Centre in North London, or the 5 Rhythms dance events; the hard work at the LGBT centres in Leicester, Birmingham, Manchester, Glasgow and Dumfries; the kindness and passion that has gone into relaunching Switchboard. I see brave young people like Danny Bowman talking about his recovery from mental-health problems, mothers like Mena Houghton doing what she can to draw attention to homophobic bullying. And I'm sure there are many more I don't know about. I saw the tears of a gay media audience, not used to hearing about our lives with emotional authenticity, when we held the first Attitude Pride Awards in June 2015, honouring not celebrities but real people in the community who truly embody the spirit of Pride.

In the last weeks of writing, a man whom I had almost forgotten I dated for several months about thirteen years ago sent me a message on social media asking to have a coffee so, he said, he could apologize to me face to face. He reminded me that, because of my drinking, he had just disappeared and stopped calling. I didn't know, but it turned out he was now in AA and working through the process of taking responsibility for his actions.

We can heal ourselves. When I originally met Jake from the sex chapter, I was really worried for him. He was in a bad place: he was regularly passing out on G, a man he liked died from an overdose, he was escorting. None of this is anything to be ashamed of. It wasn't his fault. When I met him a year later he was clean and sober, with a new job, and looked like a different person. His parents don't know everything, but they know he hit rock bottom and is working the steps. He told me, smiling, his eyes welling with tears, 'My dad said to me, "You're the person I'm most proud of because you've over-come so many things. You're smart enough to realize you had a problem."'

All of us, not just gay people, have been sold a pup. Life is not about being the best at school, about beating people, winning races or getting the best marks at university. It's not about being the best looking, or hearts for shirtless selfies, or sleeping with the hottest people, or getting the best job, or being on guest lists for clubs or hanging with cool people who aren't really cool because how can they be when 'cool' doesn't actually exist? No, life is about coming to terms with who you are, dealing with your demons and enabling yourself to love and be loved. There really is nothing else to it.

I am proud of the things I brought to *Attitude*, but I also want to say that if anything I did there has contributed to furthering those lies, then I apologize. I am sorry. I've come to see that the gay media, and indeed the wider media, amongst the most powerful forces of the modern world, are the blind leading the blind. In the last twenty years I have met so many people who have the things our society prizes: fame, money, power, looks. I have met models, politicians – including three prime ministers – celebrities and superstars and, often, they have all the same problems. It's a cliché, but success has not made them happy. Until we learn truly to treat ourselves and other people with love and respect, regardless of who we are, we cannot truly be happy. It is the human condition. The world needs to hear this. As Alan Downs said in *The Velvet Rage*, if we LGBT people, so famous for being early adopters, could get this down, maybe it could be the ultimate gift gay people could give the world.

Forgive me for being mawkish, but I want to remind you of *The Wizard of Oz*. It was only in recovery, when I'd stopped running from myself, that I realized why I felt such a connection with that film. In 1964, years after the movie was made, when he was an old man, Ray Bolger, the actor who played the Scarecrow, appeared on *The Judy Garland Show* and duetted with her in 'If I Only Had a Heart'. He said, 'I was brought up on the books of *The Wizard of Oz* and my mother told me that these were great philosophies. It was a very simple philosophy that everybody had a heart, that everybody had a brain, that everybody had courage. These were the gifts given to you on this Earth and if you used them properly you reached the pot of gold at the end of the rainbow. And that pot of gold was a home. And home isn't just a house or an abode, it's people, people who love you and that you love. That's a home.'

I used to feel annoyed at the end of the film when Dorothy learns that 'There's no place like home' – that, in fact, her aunt and uncle do love her and she loves them too. The Scarecrow asks why Glinda didn't just tell her. 'Because she wouldn't have believed me,' Glinda replies. 'She had to learn it for herself.'

And so it is. We *are* enough. You are. I am. We all are. But because of what's been done to us – to any child of any gender or sexual orientation who has been shamed – it can be hard for us to believe it. Really to feel it, we have to find out for ourselves, sometimes the hard way. And that's where we are now. It's time to learn it for ourselves: you and me too.

Earlier, I explained how codependency was sometimes about putting other people before yourself as a way of not feeling your feelings; in other words, helping other people as a defence mechanism against your own pain. Well, in some ways that's what this book has been for me. But I put my own recovery on hold to write it because I could see so much pain around me and I wanted to try to help. I hope I have, but it's been hard writing this, sometimes overwhelming. At the time of writing I am twenty-two months sober from alcohol and taking it, as ever, one day at a time. Who knows where it will lead me, but I am happy to tell you, if it helps, that I am a recovering alcoholic and working on my other issues too. I wouldn't say I am proud of it but, equally, I am in no way ashamed of it. It wasn't my fault. My five-year-old self did not ask to be so overly sensitive, to be not like the other boys, to be different in a world that does not understand difference. I could easily have been one of those names that didn't make it. But I coped in the only way I knew. Now it is my responsibility to deal with it. What I am proud of is that I am facing my own issues and working to heal myself from the past.

I did not decide to step down from the *Attitude* editorship because of my personal issues, but because of the conflicts of trying to produce a mainstream magazine with tiny resources when I want to focus on the solutions to a mental-health crisis. I thought for a long time that a magazine could change all this. But market forces demand that a mainstream magazine produce fun and froth and sexiness. The readers want hot, shirtless men. I did for a long time too, but I don't think that's what we need any more. Maybe that can change. It's in your hands. I did my bit, created two great awards events and raised some awareness; and, most importantly, I wrote and published the article that led to this book.

Now I need to put my money where my mouth is and focus on getting myself better too. If I can do this, then you can. And even if I can't, you can. We are all on our own journey and focusing on getting ourselves better is the most important and helpful thing we can do.

There is a saying from Twelve Step groups which is as true of life in general as it is of recovery: 'Only you can do this – but you cannot do it alone.' The time has come for us to help each other while we help ourselves. We can all finally reach out to that little boy or girl inside us who has always been there but, through no fault of our own, didn't get the help they should have back when they so crucially needed it. How nice, finally, to put a hand out to them, a hand that should have been there all those years ago. This can be our time. We can do it if we do it now and we do it together.

Afterword

Since Then: November 2017

It's been eighteen months since I signed off the final text of *Straight Jacket* and, by the time this paperback edition is published, it will be nearly two years since the hardback came out. Seeing the book out there has been incredible. I have received messages from people all over the world saying they saw themselves in the pages. Some have told me it saved their lives. Some said it made them face up to seriously problematic behaviour. Some told me they hadn't experienced anything extreme but could relate to the isolation of our teenage years. Others said they had given their parents a copy to explain their lives and past difficulties. I've been contacted by people inspired to write degree theses, to make short films and to create performance pieces related to the issues. Most incredible has been when people have told me they have gone into recovery or sought help as a result of reading the book. One man told me his parents sent their thanks because they had been so worried about him over the years and it was only through reading the book that he knew what help to get. I cannot express my sincere and profound gratitude. It is completely overwhelming.

The two years since publication have been tumultuous, with various events and changes – some specific to LGBT issues but others in the wider world that affect us all.

On 12 June 2016, just days before *Straight Jacket* was published, forty-nine people were murdered and fifty-eight injured at the Pulse nightclub, Orlando, Florida, by a twenty-nine-year-old security guard named Omar Mateen. At the time, it was the biggest mass shooting in modern American history.

That evening at Pulse was Latin night and most victims were young Latino people doing what we do in gay nightclubs: finding safety away from the prejudice of the outside world and perhaps, for patrons of that evening, from the potential racism of other gay nights. At the time, much confusion existed about the motives of the killer, but the picture has become somewhat clearer. Talking on the phone to police as he carried out his attack, Mateen, who was a Muslim, swore allegiance to the leader of the Islamic State in Iraq and Syria (ISIS) and described himself as a soldier of Islam. He had previously been investigated by the FBI. Some former acquaintances subsequently reported that Mateen hated gay people and his father said he had recently become angry when he saw a male couple kissing in public. In the days that passed, however, various people suggested Mateen was a closeted gay man. Patrons said they had seen him at Pulse within the year before his attack. Others reported interacting with him on apps such as Grindr and Jack'd. One man claimed to have had a sexual relationship with him; another, who had trained as a police officer with him, claimed Mateen had asked him out and had visited a gay bar with him. However, the FBI stated that they had found no evidence that Mateen, who was separated from his second wife, was gay or bisexual. It was later reported that Mateen's ex-wife and her family believed he was gay and that she had heard Mateen's father call him gay. It was also claimed she had been asked by the FBI not to disclose this to the media. Whatever the truth, it is clear that the Orlando attack was both an extremist Islamist terrorist attack and a homophobic hate crime, whether the hatred was born of self-hatred or not.

As a result of the attack, America, for the first time, was forced to confront the reality of deadly homophobia. The outpouring of grief was immense. Here in the UK, the *Daily Mail*, usually keen to go large on anything terror-related, chose not to put the US's biggest terrorist attack since 9/11 on its front page. (Gay) journalist Owen Jones walked off a Sky News newspaper review when he felt (and I agree) that presenter Mark Longhurst and guest Julia Hartley-Brewer repeatedly cast doubt on whether this was a homophobic attack, seeming to suggest that the fact that the club was a gay venue had nothing to do with why it was targeted.

In London, drag performer Son of a Tutu (Ola Jide) arranged a vigil and two minutes' silence in an Old Compton Street defiantly packed with thousands. The Gay Men's Chorus sang; Jeremy Corbyn, Sadiq Khan and Nicky Morgan MP attended; and the crowds chanted, 'We're here, we're queer, we will not live in fear.'

Two days after the attack, the Duke and Duchess of Cambridge signed a book of condolence at the American Embassy in London. The duke, Prince William, told staff that he was about to appear on the cover of *Attitude*. Weeks before, for my last issue as editor, we had taken a mixed group of LGBT+ people – including a trans woman, a non-binary person, two gay people of colour and a Muslim gay man, as well as the mother of young Mark Houghton who died from an unintentional drugs overdose (and to whom this book is dedicated) – to Kensington Palace, where I guided a discussion about growing up LGBT+, bullying and its effect on mental health. Afterwards Prince William posed for the cover, the first time a member of the Royal Family had done so for a gay publication, and gave us a statement, part of which we ran on the cover, that 'No one should be bullied for their sexuality . . . or for any other reason'.

The publication of this issue, intended to be a celebratory and historic event, became something more poignant in light of the Orlando attack. The cover was reported across the world. Much of the media focused on the 'celebrity' aspect. It received less prominent attention than the Duchess of Cambridge's appearance on the cover of *Vogue* a few weeks earlier, something clearly more important than the future King of England, supreme governor of the Church of England and head of the Commonwealth appearing on the cover of a gay publication for the first time in history. The media in general did not explore his reason for doing so in any depth. One gay journalist tweeted 'How does that help me?', missing the point from his privileged position that William will most likely head an organization that represents forty-one countries (out of fifty-three) where homosexuality is still illegal. (There are a further thirty-five non-Commonwealth countries where it is still criminalized.)

In Britain, more trauma followed in 2016, when the horrifying crimes of Stephen Port and Stefano Brizzi came to light. Port, a forty-one-year-old chef living in Barking, East London, was sentenced in November to a whole life term for the overdose with GHB, rape and murder of four young men between June 2014 and September 2015. The story of missed opportunities to catch the man dubbed the 'Grindr serial killer' is astonishing. Port had been sentenced to eight months for perverting the course of justice after he anonymously called the police to alert them to his first victim, twenty-three-year-old Anthony Walgate, whom he had dumped, comatose, outside his flat, giving varied accounts, including telling police he had nothing to do with it but had found him on his doorstep. Police didn't link the deaths of a further three young men whose bodies were found in the same church graveyard in Barking, believing a fake suicide note Port had left near the body of twenty-one-year-old Daniel Whitworth which took responsibility for the death of Port's previous victim, Gabriel Kovari, and even said 'please do not blame the guy I was with last night . . . he knows nothing of what I have done'. It was only when the family of Port's last known victim, twenty-five-year-old Jack Taylor, conducted their own investigation and pestered the police into checking CCTV footage that they saw their brother walking back, with Port, to his flat.

In December 2016, Stefano Brizzi, a forty-nine-year-old Italian national living in London, was found guilty of the murder of fifty-nine-year-old police officer Gordon Semple, whom he had invited over for a 'chemsex' session after making contact on Grindr. Brizzi had dropped out of a £70,000 job with Morgan Stanley after becoming addicted to crystal meth. He strangled Semple, dismembered him and tried to dissolve him in acid. When they searched his flat, police found a downloaded copy of the Satanic Bible on Brizzi's computer and notes apparently written to the devil. After his arrest he told officers, 'I was raised Catholic . . . being gay was evil . . . so I've been into Satan.' He took his own life in prison in February 2017.

Each of these cases is as extreme as it is possible to get and of course do not reflect how gay men live. But nor are they entirely disconnected from the larger chemsex situation. I was told this year by people from several agencies that they are seeing an increase in sometimes extreme violence from men using crystal meth, with individuals most often harming themselves but sometimes others. The police have been accused of homophobia in relation to the Port case, but one gay police officer told me she strongly believed that, while immense mistakes were made, they weren't due to prejudice but, in part, to ignorance of these new drugs and the way they are being used. This in no way excuses incompetence, but it does mirror the experience of hospitals and medics who have seen the chemsex problem explode out of nowhere. Though there is more awareness of the dangers of chemsex among the gay public, with some people now using more discreetly, it's still easy to find people selling drugs or advertising chemsex on apps. Disturbingly, in light of the Port case, the police are now investigating more than fifty-eight further deaths involving GHB. I expect there will be more cases similar to those of Port and Brizzi. These drugs continue to be the most negative and destructive thing that has happened to the gay/bi male community since AIDS.

In spring 2017, there was international outrage when journalists reported the anti-gay crackdown in the southern Russian state of Chechnya, allegedly led by President Akhmad Kadyrov and his son Ramzan. It was said that scores of men suspected of being gay were 'mopped up', kidnapped, tortured, sometimes given back to their families in shame and sometimes killed. Ramzan Kadyrov denied the accusations, saying that Chechnya – a highly conservative Muslim region – did not have any gay citizens. Meanwhile, also in the spring of 2017, it had been reported that Indonesia was becoming more intolerant after two young men were caned in front of crowds and raids of gay saunas and sex parties were carried out. Similarly, in Egypt, considered to be a moderate predominantly Sunni Muslim country, in October 2017 the *Guardian* reported an increased crack-down on gay people after footage of rainbow flags waved at a Cairo concert apparently outraged the country. The government is now considering making homosexuality illegal. Egypt's Supreme Council for Media Regulation later banned any discussion of 'the filthy disease' of homosexuality, the *Guardian* reported, unless any gay person depicted 'shows repentance'.

At London Pride 2017, a group called the Council of Ex-Muslims of Britain (CMEB) marched with placards carrying slogans such as 'Ex-Muslim and proud', 'Allah is gay' and 'Throw Isis off a roof'. There were accusations of Islamophobia from the East London Mosque, to which Pride in London responded by saying, 'We will not tolerate Islamophobia.' CMEB spokesperson Maryam Namazie replied to *Pink News*, 'Why are signs critical of Islam (a belief) and Islamism (a far-right political movement) "anti-Muslim"? . . . We need to stand up to racism and bigotry and at the same time we should be able to criticise religion and the religious right.'

On LBC Radio, former extremist-turned-broadcaster and founder of think tank Quilliam Maajid Nawaz said he intended to join the Pride march after his radio show. Accepting Broadcaster of the Year at the Pink News Awards in October, he said, 'When I saw that 0 per cent of British Muslims surveyed believed that being gay was morally acceptable, when I saw that 52 per cent of British Muslims wanted homosexuality to be criminalized, when I saw that the only ten countries in the world that punished being gay with death were all Muslim-majority, I was ashamed, infuriated, outraged and angry all at the same time. But I knew Muslims who were gay, and so I realized that these results were also due to fear of speaking out.' He praised the Mayor of London, Sadiq Khan, who also attended.

One of the saddest things that has happened since publication of the book occurred on Christmas Day 2016. As the nation was about to go to sleep, bellies full, came the devastating news that George Michael had died. Found in bed on Christmas morning by his partner, Fadi Fawaz, who had apparently spent the night outside asleep in a car, George was pronounced dead at the age of fifty-three.

It wasn't announced until March that George had died of 'natural causes', with fatty liver disease, dilated cardiomyopathy and myocarditis listed as the cause of death. The public seemed to breathe a sigh of relief that it wasn't officially drugs. But this is to overlook what really killed him. Regardless of the fact that the latter two conditions themselves can be caused by excessive use of mephedrone and crack cocaine, it is clear that George Michael died because of long-term addiction and the emotional pain and erratic behaviour that is part and parcel of it. As painful as it is to face it, his multiple car crashes, his time in jail and the less-written-about occasion when he threw himself out of a moving vehicle on the motorway were all part of a tragically familiar downward spiral. As his former partner Kenny Goss said in an interview, 'I think his body just gave up. All these years, it was just weak.'

Some might bristle, as if it is shameful or disrespectful to talk about this, but this itself is part of the problem. Addiction is nothing to be ashamed of. It's not something anyone chooses or has control of, as I have tried to explain in the book. It is not a failure of bad or weak people, but a condition that affects all types of people, from nurses and doctors to vagrants on the street to the most famous and successful, even kindly, huge-hearted musicians who give thousands to charity and help many people – as it was revealed posthumously that George had done. Not to acknowledge how this incredible man was brought down does him and all of us a huge disservice. We cannot address the situation if we do not face it. Even now it appalls and upsets me that he has gone so young. George was essentially no different to the men mentioned in this book. A brief look at his life shows he absorbed the cultural shame about who he was from an early age, even talking about it in interviews.

His story is painful. On the day of his birth in 1963 (four years before men could have homosexual sex legally), George's Uncle Colin, a gay man, took his own life because he could not cope with his sexuality. George sings about it in a song on his 2004 album *Patience*: 'My Mother Had a Brother'. He said in an interview that his uncle's suicide haunted the family and that it was partly because of it that he himself didn't come out till later in life. 'My mother had a fear of me being gay,' he told *Gay Times* in 2007. 'She thought it meant I wouldn't cope with life.'

In an effort to protect George from the same fate, the family, he said, made it clear that being gay was a bad option. 'There was this gay waiter who lived above our family restaurant and I wasn't allowed to go to the top flat when he was in the restaurant . . . in case I caught something. In case I caught gay.'

Something people in recovery from addiction often talk about is a feeling of not wanting to live but not wanting to die either. In George's last single, 'White Light', written after the death of Amy Winehouse, he sings about being glad he is alive but how easy it is to die: 'One more pill, just one more beer, one less star in the atmosphere . . . maybe she just wanted to be free'.

As much as the gay community has celebrated George as an icon of liberation, an unapologetic, proud gay man, the reality is that he died a struggling drug addict at the age of fifty-three. This is catastrophic. I still can't believe it has happened. The death of a famous person is no more important than that of anyone else, but it is, arguably, more painful when we think we know and love a celebrity who really meant something to us culturally. George often spoke of his love for the gay community. I think, drug-free and in his right mind, he would want this to be a wake-up call. It must be.

And I'm glad to say there are reasons to feel hopeful. Despite most of the media not being interested in discussing the specific issues pertaining to LGBT+ people, mental health is now a public issue. There is more awareness among gay organizations that LGBT+ mental health needs to be high on the agenda.

Culturally things are slowly shifting too. In January 2017 cinemagoers were rocked by a film that will impact on how filmmakers tell our stories for years to come. *Moonlight*, about a young black boy growing up in a poor suburb of Miami, is concerned with many things: the experience of people of colour; poverty; Liberty City where the film is set; parenting; mothers; father figures; racism;

but to me, predominantly it is about what this book is about: gay shame.

Based on the playlet *In Moonlight Black Boys Look Blue* by Tarell Alvin McCraney, it's a film that shows the progression of a man's life in three parts. The first, 'Little', sees the child Chiron, his abusive mother addicted to crack, finding an unlikely father figure in the form of a local drug dealer, Juan, who recognizes his difference and supports him. In a heartbreaking moment, 'Little' enquires about the word that the other kids throw at him. 'What's a faggot?' he asks, looking forlornly up at Juan, who tells him it means gay but is a bad word and, even if he is gay, it is not what he is. It is an instant, profound and iconic cinematic moment.

In the next part, 'Chiron', we see the now teenage protagonist shamed after a sexual moment with a teenage friend. The third part of the film, 'Black', shows the adult consequences. Chiron has grown up, hardened, hyper-masculinized and has shut down his ability to express or receive love with anyone at all, let alone another man.

Though it is particular to McCraney's life story, *Moonlight* shines its immense wattage on 'emotional anorexia', when the pain of really showing who you are means you retreat into yourself and withdraw from emotional and/or physical intimacy.

Francis Lee's debut, *God's Own Country*, also brilliantly depicts the pain of emotional shutdown. The phrase 'You cannot love someone until you learn to love yourself' sounds like a meaningless soundbite, but is the crux of recovery. Becoming intimate with another person means facing our core selves and if that's too painful, however much we might want to get close to someone, we will often sabotage the relationship or bolt – until we heal ourselves. *God's Own Country* and *Moonlight* both show this explicitly and – thank God – suggest hope. Healing can happen.

Tarell Alvin McCraney won the Academy Award for Best Original Screenplay and *Moonlight* won Best Picture 2017. 'The Moonlight Effect' as *Entertainment Weekly* called it, means more gay stories will be told. Later, 2017 saw the critically acclaimed *Call Me By Your Name*, and in 2018 comes *Love, Simon* directed by Greg Berlanti, based on the young adult book *Simon vs. the Homo Sapiens Agenda* by Becky Albertelli. I've said we still haven't seen a mainstream gay romantic comedy from Hollywood. *Love, Simon* looks set to be that film.

Elsewhere there are other positives. Superstar RuPaul continues to preach her message of self-love and respect, often tweeting about Alan Downs' book *The Velvet Rage*. Authors such as Patrick Ness write about gay lives in a way similar writers might not have done twenty years ago. The new editor of *Vogue*, Edward Enninful, is a gay man of colour, determined to put diversity at the heart of Britain's most important fashion magazine. In film, Ezra Miller and Cara Delevingne are both breaking the rule that you cannot play lead roles if you are out, in the same way that British pop star Olly Alexander continues to set his own path. There are also more and more confident trans voices joining Paris Lees, such as authors Juno Dawson, C. N. Lester, Charlie Craggs and Rhyannon Styles, race activist and model Munroe Bergdorf and comedian and writer Shon Faye.

The year 2017 was the fiftieth anniversary of the partial decriminalization of homosexuality, which was accompanied by a major series of television and radio programmes including, to my mind the most important, the BBC's *Is It Safe to Be Gay in the UK?*, a vital documentary about hate crime, something I'd not seen on television before. There was also Patrick Gale's moving drama *The Man in the Orange Shirt* and much more. Perhaps, in one go, maybe too much? Dare I say, it might be better to spread content throughout the year? After all, gay people are for life, not just for anniversaries. There was also an exciting Queer British Art exhibition at Tate Britain, as well as the National Theatre's outstanding revival of *Angels in America*. It seemed sad to me, though, that the NT celebrated fifty years since partial decriminalization of homosexuality in England and Wales with a classic American play, something that points to British theatre's general lack of interest in contemporary LGBT lives. The Sheffield Crucible Theatre was outstanding, producing in 2017 both a play about gay parenting, *Of Kith and Kin* by Chris Thompson, and the uplifting musical by Dan Gillespie Sells and Tom MacRae, *Everybody's Talking About Jamie*, celebrating the spirit of a young gender-nonconforming student, with which young LGBT+ people will undoubtedly be obsessed. Its London transfer opens as I write.

One of the most important and positive breakthroughs in the period since the book came out is, finally, a significant reduction in the rate of HIV infections in London, and in England and Wales. As explained in *Straight Jacket*, the rates have been on an upward trajectory for a long time. The latest available figures from 56 Dean Street reveal a 40 per cent reduction in the number of gay men testing HIV positive in 2016, the second year to show a decline. Public Health England also reported a 21 per cent drop nationally in new diagnoses. There has been some controversy over the reason. Many have claimed that PrEP use is wholly responsible, while others have argued that the adoption of San Francisco's 'Getting to Zero' Campaign, which focuses on more testing and on reaching the partners of people newly diagnosed more quickly, has played a bigger part. This is hugely welcome news, but no cause for complacency. The fight for PrEP has galvanized many and its use is now common, with a lot of men buying it themselves as well as Public Health England funding a larger trial, and it is clearly having an effect.

The future, though, still seems unclear. After significant cuts, sexual health services are at breaking point. Dean Street Express, for instance, says it is swamped by people needing their services. Gonorrhea rates across the western world are rising. The threats of 'super gonorrhea' and general antibiotic resistance have yet to permeate the public's consciousness. And while PrEP use is being adopted by significant numbers of white gay and bisexual men, there is lower uptake among people of colour, who are still disproportionately affected by HIV/AIDs within our already disproportionately affected community. When I saw David Stuart for lunch this autumn, he told me about the importance, and Dean Street's intention, of focusing resources on BAME communities.

Another major win is that, despite media grumbling, the NHS is proposing to monitor sexual orientation at the point of contact, which could be a game-changer in understanding how stress and trauma disproportionately affect our health. This is hugely important and makes it more likely that the health inequalities that impact us can be addressed.

Donald Trump's election and Brexit have been seismic shifts in the USA and UK and continue to make the world feel like a more unstable place. Galop – the LGBT+ anti-violence charity – announced that reported homophobic hate crime increased by 147 per cent in the three months after the Brexit vote and continues to rise. Trump shocked America by undermining gains made by Barack Obama and announcing that he was to ban trans people from serving in the US armed forces, something the courts eventually blocked.

As transgender lives become more visible, there has been a backlash and growing antagonism from British media pushing a line that the 'all-powerful' trans lobby is trying to change the gender of all children and that warped doctors are doling out hormone blockers like sweets. Writer and broadcaster Paris Lees told me: 'The situation with trans people today is very similar to that in the eighties with gay people that you describe. There are journalists who, based on zero evidence, portray trans people as dangerous or not who we say we are. Kids, like I was, are hearing that they are wrong, that they are unreal, all the time. I've spoken to many of these families and know that the constant barrage of misinformation on this subject is confusing parents who might want to help their children and may discourage them from seeking potentially life-saving therapies. The media is doing real damage'.

Sadly, perhaps in reaction to all the increased tension with which we live, there seems to be more anger online from us, often towards *us*.

The growing infighting among LGBT people, or that directed towards allies, online and in the real world, is seriously disturbing. The internet is a brutal place generally, but when the fighting is among ourselves it is highly dispiriting. For instance, in December 2016 LGBT students in Portland, Oregon, protested at a talk by

Kimberly Peirce, the lesbian director of the seminal 1999 movie *Boys Don't Cry* about the life of trans man Brandon Teena. Activists accused Peirce of profiting from Teena's death, posting signs such as 'Fuck your transphobia!' and 'Fuck this cis white bitch!'

It is clearly important that marginalized people tell their own stories, but this attack betrays a lack of context and understanding of where we were in 1999.

When American rapper Macklemore released the pro-marriage equality anthem 'Same Love', most of the LGBT community saw it as what it was: a sincere, powerful, pro-equality statement from an ally, who had been inspired to write about the homophobia his uncle experienced. Yet there were many of us who attacked Macklemore online for cashing in, or 'straightsplaining'. This is illogical, an own goal and verging on fascistic. We do not own Macklemore's relationship with his uncle. He's entitled to sing about his feelings about it and I'm glad that he did. He no doubt influenced the thinking of his audiences all over the world.

Similarly, in February 2017 there was online outrage when Labour leader Jeremy Corbyn apparently said people 'choose' to be gay. From the reaction you'd think he had called a press conference to say we should change back. In fact, during a speech at his own LGBT History Month reception, before an LGBT+ audience, he said, 'We're with you, we're in solidarity with you ... Our defence of you is a defence of all of humanity and the right of people to practise the life they want to practise, rather than be criminalized, brutalized and murdered, simply because they chose to be gay, they chose to be lesbian, they were LGBT in any form.'

I don't tell you this to praise Corbyn. I'm grateful he supported us in the 1980s before it was politically expedient to do so, just as I am grateful to Conservative MP Edwina Currie for tabling the Age of Consent vote in 1994. As I said earlier, I don't believe being gay is a choice. But you can argue that deciding to live openly *is* a choice. It is wrong to ferociously attack someone who has supported us for decades over the clumsy use of one word. We have to pick our battles and keep a sense of perspective. If we don't, there will be a backlash.

While you are entitled to dislike their politics, music or films, Jeremy Corbyn, Macklemore and Kimberley Peirce are not the enemy. While we are busy attacking ourselves and our supporters, people who wish to do us real harm are making gains and problems that will severely impact our lives are gathering pace.

Today the world is more unstable than I have ever known it. It could not be clearer that we need change. I hope that the message of this book is pertinent to straight people as well – that addressing our own issues can ripple out and change the world. We need radical thinking because we live in interconnected times, fuelled by ego, greed and paranoia. I am excited that Russell Brand's brilliant book *Recovery* which unashamedly champions the Twelve Step process has been so popular in the mainstream and that people may begin to understand that the way we think individually can affect the world in a bigger way. I know many do not believe it is a problem, but there's no doubt that unless we all get our acts together to stop climate change we'll be struggling just to eat, to get clean water, to survive. The devastation that will accompany the unfolding climate crisis threatens all the gains we have made. Yet we seem to be blind to it.

Ultimately, what has been most inspiring to me since I finished the book, as cheesy as it may sound, is you. Us.

This book naturally focuses on a crisis, but there is tremendous joy and positivity out there. Having travelled the country talking about mental health, I have again met countless numbers of incredible LGBT people doing amazing things with their lives, or simply living them to the full. Whether it's the middle-aged couple I met in a Scottish Waterstones branch (or the store's passionate manager), or the students I met in York and at other universities, or the man I met in Liverpool who told me his inspiring story of resilience through the worst homophobia, or the young people who constantly express wanting to be part of the solution, or those who tell me they have given copies of *Straight Jacket* to friends or have posted about it on social media, there is a growing sense that we can address these problems. Healing is happening.

As I have said, there is no need to suffer in silence. Help is available. It's important to understand that even when things go wrong it does not have to be a disaster. I have seen so many people get knocked down by how they feel but come through or learn to cope with it, and I've seen smiles return to their faces. We may go through difficult times, but there is always help and always the option of pulling ourselves up, as people like us have done for decades. At a recent Change of Scene event, an attendee turned up in full Lurex flapper costume and beads. Never let it be said that we are boring.

I want to leave you with something positive that happened to me recently. It was the kind of reminder we can all do with every now and then. At the end of October I hosted an evening at Foyles bookshop in London for the legendary Armistead Maupin, author of the classic *Tales of the City* series. His new memoir, *Logical Family*, charts his journey from the closet of a racist Republican family through his move to San Francisco, where he started his famous serial about a group of gay, straight and trans misfits coming together. It's a series that changed the lives of a generation. (Warning: spoilers.) Armistead said in our discussion that he stopped at book six, *Sure of You*, in 1989, because he couldn't face seeing his lead character, Michael 'Mouse' Tolliver, dying of AIDS and adding to the cliché that the gay guy never gets his happy ending. So he let Michael go, gently fading him into the San Franciscan sunset. Readers were left at the turn of the decade with the understanding that, though it was unsaid, Michael did not have a future.

Armistead could not have known that the antiretroviral drugs right around the corner would save millions (though there are still massive inequalities in who can get them). One of those saved was Armistead's then partner, Terry Anderson, who, shocked suddenly to be given an extended life he hadn't thought he would have, left Armistead. In the documentary *The Untold Tales of Armistead Maupin*, it's clear that this was devastating to Armistead. He was heartbroken. We've all felt the kind of despair where life seems bleak and hopeless, but, like Terry and then Armistead, none of us knows how dramatically it can change.

A few years later, Armistead met the man of his dreams: a handsome photographer, many years his junior, called Christopher Turner. After seeing him online, Armistead followed him down the street, saying, 'Didn't I see you on Daddy Hunt?' It turned out Chris owned and ran that website. Their friend the writer Neil Gaiman says it's as if they were made for each other. And it seems so. After the Foyles event, I went to dinner with them and our mutual publicist, Alison. It was a privilege and profoundly moving to see Armistead and Chris, more than twelve years a couple and ten years married, cooing over each other like teenagers, as intimate as any pair you could meet. They sat close, helped each other order, eyes sparkling when the other spoke. Armistead calls Chris 'honey'. As someone who grew up being told gay men could not love each other, I found it truly moving. Really. It would melt the heart of the hardest cynic.

What we LGBT+ people have gone through is immense. Some of us have found it easy, others less so. Many thrive, others struggle at times. But as tough as it may seem, no one is too far gone to turn things around. You do not know how your situation can change for the better until it does. Everything is to play for. It's a cliché, but it's true. Please remember that if any of this stuff gets you down.

In 2007 Armistead's fictional gay hero, Mouse, returned in *Michael Tolliver Lives*, confounding all the expectations that an HIV-positive gay man had in 1989. And in real life, Armistead and Chris also got their happy-ever-after ending. Despite all the trouble that is still thrown at us, I do believe it's possible we can all find it too.

Appendix 1

Help

Switchboard (formerly Gay Switchboard)
Help and advice for LGBT people. Call to find details of local services.
www.Switchboard.lgbt
0300 330 0630
10am–11pm every day

Antidote at London Friend
LGBT drug and alcohol service from London Friend.
www.londonfriend.org.uk/get-support/drugsandalcohol
Helpline (offers advice wherever you are in the UK) 020 7833 1674
    10am–6pm Monday to Friday

56 Dean Street, London
Sexual health centre, including substance misuse support in Soho,
    London. For ChemSex support, visit: www.chemsexsupport.com
    www.deanstreetwellbeingprogramme.com

PACE
LGBT mental-health support based in London.
www.pacehealth.org.uk
020 7700 1323
info@pacehealth.org.uk
10am–5pm Monday to Friday

Stonewall
Campaigning and lobbying group.
www.stonewall.org.uk

Nationwide Twelve Step groups

Alcoholics Anonymous UK
Local meetings near you. Some LGBT-specific.
www.alcoholics-anonymous.org.uk
0800 9177 650
help@alcoholics-anonymous.org.uk

Anorexics and Bulimics Anonymous
International site with list of UK meetings.
www.aba12steps.org

Codependents Anonymous
www.coda-uk.org

Crystal Meth Addicts Anonymous
Specific LGBT meetings focused on London. Search for meetings at:
www.crystalmeth.org/cma-meeting/cma-meeting-search.html

Gamblers Anonymous
www.gamblersanonymous.org.uk

Narcotics Anonymous
Local meetings near you. Some LGBT-specific.
www.ukna.org 0300 999 1212

Overeaters Anonymous
Over 200 meetings across the UK.
www.oagb.org.uk
07000 784985

Sex Addicts Anonymous
LGBT-friendly meetings.
saa-recovery.org.uk

Sex and Love Addicts Anonymous
LGBT-friendly and also LGBT-specific meetings.
www.slaauk.org

Underearners Anonymous
For people addicted to undervaluing themselves financially.
www.underearnersanonymous.co.uk

Workaholics Anonymous
International website with list of UK meetings.
www.workaholics-anonymous.org

Regional Help

Brighton & Hove LGBT Switchboard
www.switchboard.org.uk
01273 204050

Leicester LGBT Centre
www.leicesterlgbtcentre.org
0116 254 7412

Birmingham LGBT Centre
www.blgbt.org
0121 643 0821

Albert Kennedy Trust
Support for 16–25-year-old LGBT people made homeless or living in a
    hostile environment, with offices in London and Manchester.
www.akt.org.uk

LGBT Foundation, Manchester
Advice, support and information.
www.lgbt.foundation
0345 30 30 30
@LGBTfdn

Armistead Centre, Liverpool
LGBT-specific sexual-health centre.
www.liverpoolcommunityhealth.nhs.uk/health-services/sexual-health/
    armistead.htm

LGBT Health and Wellbeing in Scotland
www.lgbthealth.org.uk

LGBT Youth Scotland Based in Edinburgh
www.lgbtyouth.org.uk

LGBT Support South Wales
www.lgbtsw.weebly.com/support--groups.html

LGBT Cymru
www.lgbtcymruhelpline.org.uk

Therapy

Remember, unfortunately not all therapists or even therapeutic organizations understand the complex issues that LGBT people face; nor do they always understand addiction and what lies beneath it. Ask any potential therapist if he or she understands childhood trauma and the experience of LGBT people.

British Association for Counselling & Psychotherapy
With 'Find a Therapist' database
www.bacp.co.uk

UK Council for Psychotherapy
With 'Find a Therapist' database
www.ukcp.org.uk

British Psychoanalytical Council
With 'Search for a Therapist' database
www.bpc.org.uk

British Association of Dramatherapists
With 'Find a Dramatherapist' database
https://badth.org.uk

Pink Therapy
With UK directory of LGBTIQ therapists
http://www.pinktherapy.com

UK Therapy Guide
With UK 'Search for a Therapist' database
http://uktherapyguide.com

Counselling Directory
With UK database of counsellors and psychotherapists
www.counselling-directory.org.uk

MIND
No database, but helpful generally on mental-health issues – although the
LGBT section isn't that comprehensive
http://www.mind.org.uk/

HIV and AIDS Support

Terrence Higgins Trust
National sexual-health charity with information on STIs/HIV and where
to test, etc.; also offers support.
www.tht.org.uk

GMFA
The gay men's health charity.
www.gmfa.org.uk

NAM AIDS Map
Sharing knowledge, changing lives.
www.aidsmap.com

National AIDS Trust
Campaigning organization.
www.nat.org.uk

Positive East
HIV support in East London.
www.positiveeast.org.uk
020 7791 2855

Trans-specific Support

Mermaids
Family and individual support for teens and children with gender-identity
issues.
www.mermaidsuk.org.uk

The Beaumont Society
Help and support for the transgender community.
www.beaumontsociety.org.uk

Translondon
Discussion/support group for trans people in London.
translondon.org.uk

Ftm International
Support for the female-to-male community.
ftmi.org

Ftm Network
Support for the female-to-male community.
ftm.org.uk

Transsexual Road Map
tsroadmap.com

Scottish Transgender Alliance
scottishtrans.org

Depend
Support for family and friends of trans people.
depend.org.uk

Clare Project
Based in Brighton for anyone wishing to explore issues around gender.
clareproject.org.uk

Intersexuk.org
Support for intersex people.

Discussion Groups

A Change of Scene
Monthly London-based discussion group of related issues outside of bars
and clubs.
www.facebook.com/AChangeOfScene

Let's Talk About Gay Sex and Drugs
Monthly London-based discussion/performance night.
www.facebook.com/LetsTalkAboutGaySexAndDrugs

Appendix 2
HIV and Safer Sex

Facts about HIV

HIV stands for human immunodeficiency virus. HIV attacks the immune system and, left untreated, leaves the body vulnerable so that it is no longer able to defend itself from infections that it otherwise could fight off. Most people with untreated HIV will eventually go on to develop one or more of a range of life-threatening illnesses, including cancers. When this happens a person is often said to have AIDS, which stands for acquired immune deficiency syndrome, though many professionals now call it 'advanced HIV' or 'late-stage HIV'. People who are diagnosed with an AIDS-defining illness can recover with treatment, but, left untreated, AIDS normally proves fatal.

People who have been infected with HIV are often referred to as being HIV positive.

Although there is currently no cure for HIV infection, the good news is that today there is medication that reduces the amount of HIV virus in an HIV-positive person to extremely low levels and stops the disease progressing, meaning people with HIV can live long and healthy lives – as long as anyone else – if they start the medication soon enough and take it every day.

However, for some the mental and emotional impact of living with HIV is considerable and seriously impacts their wellbeing. Thankfully, most people treat someone with HIV as they would anyone else, but, sadly, there can still be stigma – even from some gay people – and this adds to the stress of being HIV positive.

If you are HIV positive it is of extra importance that you look after both your physical and your mental health.

In the UK, gay and bisexual men (and any other men who have sex with men) are at far greater risk of catching HIV than the general population.

In the general population it is believed that around 1 person in 525 is living with HIV.

In the UK as a whole, 1 gay/bi man in 20 is believed to be HIV positive. This includes both diagnosed and undiagnosed people.

It is believed that in London 1 gay/bi man in 11 is HIV positive, compared to 1 in 28 outside the capital.

One study suggested that on the gay scene in London as many as 1 gay/bi man in 7 has HIV.

It is estimated that about 17 per cent of people in the UK who are HIV positive do not know they have the virus. This means that it will be damaging their immune system without them being aware of it.

This highlights why it is so vital that we all know our HIV status by having regular HIV tests. It may seem scary to face the chance that you may be HIV positive, but **if you are HIV positive it is absolutely better to know it so you can start medication when your doctors advise**. Get your HIV test today!

If you are HIV negative it is important to stay that way. It is also **absolutely vital** that you regularly have HIV tests so that if you do become positive you can start medication as soon as doctors think you should do so in order to stop the damage to your immune system. Public Health England recommend men who have sex with men have an HIV and STI screen at least annually, and every three months if having unprotected sex with new or casual partners.

How do you catch HIV?

In the UK, HIV is usually transmitted sexually, though it can also be spread by sharing needles and injecting equipment or passed from mother to child.

HIV can be transmitted when blood, semen (cum), pre-cum or anal mucus from someone who is HIV positive come in contact with a mucous membrane or damaged tissue or are directly injected into the bloodstream (from a needle or syringe). Mucous membranes are found inside the rectum, vagina, penis and mouth.

HIV cannot be transmitted through saliva (spit) or urine (pee).

The way most gay/bi men catch HIV is from having unprotected anal sex (fucking) without a condom.

Undetectable

In recent years there has been a tremendous advance in the fight against HIV. If an HIV positive person is on effective antiretroviral treatment they will become what is called 'undetectable' which means that no HIV virus can be detected in the blood – though it is still there in small quantities and will increase again if medication is not taken as prescribed.

Recent studies show that if a person's doctor has confirmed that they are undetectable and they have continued taking their treatment and had regular appointments to monitor their viral load then they cannot pass on HIV. In other words, they become uninfectious.

But being undetectable is not a constant state and if a person stops taking their medication then their viral load will go up again.

Reducing the risk of catching HIV

Using a condom when you have anal sex dramatically reduces the risk of catching HIV.

Always use a water-based lube. Lubricant that contains oil damages the condom and may cause tiny holes.

Always change condoms if you are having anal sex with multiple partners.

Reducing partner numbers means you reduce the risk of catching HIV (and other sexually transmitted infections), though it takes only one person to give you HIV.

Oral sex (giving someone a blow job) is considered to be low risk but some people do catch HIV this way. Do not give someone a blow job if you have any cuts or sores in your mouth, or within half an hour of cleaning your teeth or using mouthwash, because this may cause tiny abrasions in your mouth. Not letting him cum in your mouth drastically reduces the risk of catching HIV through oral sex.

If your use of drugs or alcohol is making you take risks, contact the support groups listed on pages 349–53 for help with drink, drugs or sex addiction.

Injecting drugs is dangerous in itself, but also greatly increases the risk of catching HIV and/or hepatitis C through the possibility of sharing infected needles.

You cannot tell if someone is HIV positive from looking at them and many people will not tell you if they are HIV positive because of the possibility of stigma. You cannot take somebody's word for it and **it is your responsibility to protect yourself**.

PEP (post-exposure prophylaxis) is a month-long course of anti-HIV medication which, **if started within 72 hours** of a possible exposure to HIV (unprotected sex with someone who is positive, etc.), will, studies show, stop HIV from taking hold in a person's body. PEP can be obtained from your local sexual-health clinic or from the Accident & Emergency department of your local hospital. The earlier PEP is accessed, the better.

PrEP

This is another recent dramatic development. PrEP (pre-exposure prophylaxis) is anti-HIV medication, which is taken by people who don't have HIV, before and ongoing after any condomless sex, which studies show is highly effective at blocking HIV from taking hold. NHS Scotland provides it but it is not yet available on the NHS in England and Wales outside of limited studies but many activists believe it should be. It can be bought from some private doctors and purchased internationally. PrEP must be taken properly to be affective so it is important that you discuss with your doctor or sexual health clinic how to buy it, take it and so they can monitor you before and after you begin it. The situation is evolving quickly so please check www.iwantprepnow.co.uk and www.tht.org.uk and www.prepster.info

Find your nearest HIV and sexual-health clinic here:

www.tht.org.uk/sexual-health/improving-your-sexual-health/clinics/GUM-clinics

Learn about other sexually transmitted infections here:

www.gmfa.org.uk www.tht.org.uk

Just because you are gay does not mean you will automatically become HIV positive.

HIV is not a judgement, it is a virus. Being unkind or disrespectful to people who are HIV positive is unacceptable. People with HIV deserve love and respect just like everyone else.

Bibliography

Below is a list of books, some that I have mentioned in the book and some that I have not. I have read most but not all of them. There are countless books available on drug and alcohol addiction and many about sex addiction. Twelve Step fellowships produce a range of literature about their specific subjects.

Gay-specific

Cimino, Kenneth, *The Politics of Crystal Meth: Gay Men Share Stories of Addiction and Recovery*, Universal Publishers, 2005

Downs, Alan, *The Velvet Rage: Overcoming the Pain of Growing Up Gay in a Straight Man's World*, Da Capo Lifelong Books, 2006, reissued 2012

Fawcett, David M., *Lust, Men, and Meth: A Gay Man's Guide to Sex and Recovery*, S FL Center for Counseling and Therapy, 2015

Ismay, Richard, *Being Homosexual: Gay Men and Their Development*, Random House, 2009

Kettelhack, Guy, *Easing the Ache: Gay Men Recovering from Compulsive Behaviours*, Hazelden, 2008

Kominars, Sheppard B., *Accepting Ourselves: The Twelve-Step Journey of Recovery from Addiction for Gay Men and Lesbians*, Hazelden Information & Educational Services, 1996

Kort, Dr Joe, *10 Smart Things Gay Men Can Do to Improve Their Lives*, Riverdale Avenue Books, 2013

Kort, Dr Joe, *Gay Affirmative Therapy for the Straight Clinician: The Essential Guide*, W. W. Norton & Company, 2008

Kus, Robert J., *Addiction and Recovery in Gay and Lesbian Persons*, Routledge, 1995

Sanderson, Terry, *How to Be a Happy Homosexual: A Guide for Gay Men*, Gay Men's Press, 1992

Sanderson, Terry, *Making Gay Relationships Work*, The Other Way Press, 1994

Sanderson, Terry, *Assertively Gay: How to Build Gay Self-esteem*, The Other Way Press, 1997

Sanello, Frank, *Tweakers: How Crystal Meth Is Ravaging Gay America*, Alyson Publications, 2005

Shelton, Michael, *Gay Men and Substance Abuse: A Basic Guide for Addicts and Those Who Care for Them*, Hazelden, 2011

Trans support

Bornstein, Kate, *Hello Cruel World: 101 Alternatives to Suicide for Teens, Freaks and Other Outlaws*, Seven Stories Press, 2011

Erickson-Schroth, Laura, *Trans Bodies, Trans Selves: A Resource for the Transgender Community*, OUP (USA), 2014

Teich, Nicholas, *Transgender 101: A Simple Guide to a Complex Issue*, Columbia University Press, 2012

Drugs

Narcotics Anonymous Fellowships, *Narcotics Anonymous* (main text), available from ukna.org

Narcotics Anonymous, *It Works How and Why – The Twelve Steps and Twelve Traditions of Narcotics Anonymous*, 1993

Hari, Johann, *Chasing the Scream: The First and Last Days of the War on Drugs*, Bloomsbury Circus, 2015

Sex addiction

Sex Addicts Anonymous Fellowship, *Sex Addicts Anonymous* (main text), available from www.saa-recovery.org.uk

Sex and Love Addicts Anonymous, *Sex and Love Addicts Anonymous* (main text), available from slaauk.org

Carnes, Patrick, *Contrary to Love: Helping the Sexual Addict*, Hazelden 1994

Carnes, Patrick, *In the Shadows of the Net: Breaking Free from Compulsive Online Sexual Behavior*, Hazelden, 2007

Carnes, Patrick, *Out of the Shadows: Understanding Sexual Addiction*, Hazelden, 2005

Hall, Paula, *Understanding and Treating Sex Addiction*, Routledge, 2012

Jack, Anthony, and Wilson, Gary, *Your Brain on Porn: Internet Pornography and the Emerging Science of Addiction*, Commonwealth Publishing, 2015

Maltz, Wendy, and Maltz, Larry, *The Porn Trap: The Essential Guide to Overcoming Problems Caused By Pornography*, Harper Paperbacks, 2010

Weiss, Robert, *Cruise Control: Understanding Sex Addiction in Gay Men*, Gentle Path Press, 2005, second edition 2013

Weiss, Robert, *Sex Addiction 101: A Basic Guide to Healing from Sex, Porn, and Love Addiction*, Health Communications, 2015

Weiss, Robert, and Schneider, Jennifer P., *Untangling the Web: Breaking Free from Sex, Porn, and the Fantasy in the Internet Age*, Gentle Path Press, 2006

Alcoholism

Alcoholics Anonymous literature available from www.alcoholics-anonymous.org.uk

Carnes, Patrick, *12 steps: A Gentle Path Through the Twelve Steps: The Classic Guide for All People in the Process of Recovery*, Hazelden, 2012

Kus, Robert J., *Gay Men of Alcoholics Anonymous: First-Hand Accounts*, Winterstar Press, 1990

Shame

Bradshaw, John, *Healing the Shame That Binds You*, Health Communications, 1991

Brown, Brené, *I Thought It Was Just Me (but it isn't): Telling the Truth About Perfectionism, Inadequacy, and Power*, J. P. Tarcher/Penguin Putnam, 2008

Brown, Brené, *Daring Greatly: How the Courage to Be Vulnerable Transforms the Way We Live, Love, Parent, and Lead*, Portfolio Penguin, 2013

Codependency

Beattie, Melody, *Codependent No More: How to Stop Controlling Others and Start Caring for Yourself*, Hazelden, 1989

Mellody, Pia, and Miller, Andrea Wells, *Facing Codependence: What Is It, Where It Comes From, How It Sabotages Our Lives*, HarperOne, 2002

Love and relationships

Mellody, Pia, *Facing Love Addiction: Giving Yourself the Power to Change the Way You Love*, HarperOne, 2003

Mellody, Pia, *The Intimacy Factor: The Ground Rules For Overcoming the Obstacles to Truth, Respect and Lasting Love*, HarperCollins, 2003

Body-image and eating disorders

Anorexic and Bulimics Anonymous Fellowship, *Anorexic and Bulimics Anonymous* (main text), available at www.aba12steps.org

Overeaters Anonymous Fellowship, *Overeaters Anonymous* (main text), available at www.oagb.org; other OA books available at www.oagb.org.uk

Morgan, John F. *The Invisible Man: A Self-help Guide for Men with Eating Disorders, Compulsive Exercise and Bigorexia*, Routledge, 2008

Pope, Harrison G., and Phillips, Katharine A., *The Adonis Complex: How to Identify, Treat and Prevent Body Obsession In Men and Boys – The Secret Crisis of Male Body Obsession*, Free Press, 2002

Roseberg, Mark, *Eating My Feelings*, Free Rivers Press, 2013

Tarman, Vera, and Werdell, Philip, *Food Junkies*, Dundurn Group, 2014

Some feel-good books for young people

For everyone

Barker, Meg-John, and Scheele, Julia, *Queer: A Graphic History*, Icon Books, 2016

Dawson, Juno, *This Book is Gay*, Hot Key Books, 2014

Lamé, Amy, *From Prejudice to Pride: A History of LGBTQ+ Movement*, Wayland, 2017

Specifically for guys

Albertalli, Becky, *Simon vs. the Homo Sapiens Agenda*, Penguin, 2015
Lee, Mackenzi, *The Gentleman's Guide to Vice and Virtue*, HarperCollins, 2017
Levithan, David, *Boy Meets Boy*, Harper Collins Children's Books, 2013
Levithan, David, *Two Boys Kissing*, Egmont, 2014
Maupin, Armistead, *Tales of the City* series, Black Swan, 1984–2014
Ness, Patrick, *Release*, Walker Books, 2017 – and other work by Patrick Ness
Silvera, Adam, *More Happy Than Not*, Soho Teen, 2015

For girls

Danforth, Emily M., *The Miseducation of Cameron Post*, Balzer & Bray, 2012
George, Madeleine, *The Difference Between You and Me*, Viking Books for Young Readers, 2012
Hidier, Tanuja Desai, *Born Confused*, Scholastic Press, 2003
Lo, Malinda, *Ash*, Hodder Children's Books, 2010
Sanchez, Alex, *Boyfriends with Girlfriends*, Simon & Schuster, 2011

Trans

Bertie, Alex, *Trans Mission: My Quest to a Beard*, Wren & Rook, 2017
Craggs, Charlie, *To My Trans Sisters*, Jessica Kingsley Publishers, 2017
Mock, Janet, *Redefining Realness: My Path to Womanhood, Identity, Love & So Much More*, Atria Books, 2015
Styles, Rhyannon, *The New Girl: A Trans Girl Tells It Like It Is*, Headline, 2017
Dawson, Juno, *The Gender Games: The Problem With Men and Women, From Someone Who Has Been Both*, Two Roads, 2017
Lester, C. N., *Trans Like Me: A Journey for All of Us*, Virago, 2017

Plays and novels

Cleugh, Grae, *Fucking Games*, London: Royal Court/Methuen, 2001

Crowley, Mart, *The Boys in the Band*, New York: Samuel French, 1968

Fierstein, Harvey, *Torch Song Trilogy*, New York: Signet Books, 1979

Holleran, Andrew, *Dancer from the Dance*, New York: HarperCollins, 1978

Kaye Campbell, Alexei, *The Pride*, London: Nick Hern Books, 2008

Patrick, Robert, *Pouf Positive*, from the collection of short plays *Untold Decades*, Stonewall Inn Editions, New York: St Martin's Press, 1988

Todd, Matthew, *Blowing Whistles*, London: Josef Weinberger Plays, 2005

Other books of interest

Alcoholics Anonymous, *Twelve Steps and Twelve Traditions*, available at www.aa.org

Benshoff, Harry M., *Monsters in the Closet: Homosexuality and the Horror Film*, Manchester University Press, 2004

Cameron, Julia, *The Artist's Way: A Course In Discovering and Recovering Your Creative Self*, Pan, 1995

Gerhardt, Sue, *Why Love Matters: How Affection Shapes a Baby's Brain*, Routledge, 2004

Hay, Louise L., *You Can Heal Your Life*, Hay House, 1984

Hay, Louise L., *You Can Heal Your Life: Affirmation Kit*, Hay House, 2005

Kramer, Larry, *The American People*, Vol. 1, Farrar, Straus and Giroux, 2015

Levine, Peter A., *Waking the Tiger: Healing Trauma – The Innate Capacity to Transform Overwhelming Experiences*, Berkeley, North Atlantic Books, 1997

Miller, Alice, *The Drama of the Gifted Child*, Basic Books/Virago, 1979

Shilts, Randy, *And the Band Played On: Politics, People, and the AIDS Epidemic*, Souvenir Press, 1987

Smallwood, David, *Who Says I'm An Addict?: A Book for Anyone Who Is Partial to Food, Sex, Booze or Drugs*, Hay House, 2014

Thompson, Rosemary A., *Nurturing Future Generations: Promoting Resilience in Children and Adolescents through Social, Emotional, and Cognitive Skills*, Routledge, 2006

Tolle, Eckhart, *The Power of Now*, Yellow Kite, 2001

Papers, studies and articles

Clements-Nolle, K., Marx, R., and Katz, M., 'HIV prevalence, risk behaviors, health care use, and mental health status of transgender persons: implications for public health intervention', *American Journal of Public Health*, 2001, 91(6): 915–21

Clements-Nolle, K., Marx, R., and Katz, M., 'Attempted suicide amongst transgender persons: the influence of gender-based discrimination and victimization', *Journal of Homosexuality*, 2006, 51(3): 53–69

Feldman, Ruth, *et al.*, 'Conflict resolution in the parent-child, marital and peer contexts, and children's aggression in the peer group: a process-oriented cultural perspective', *Developmental Psychology*, 2010, 46(2): 310–25

Feusner, J. D. *et al.*, 'What causes BDD: research findings and a proposed model', *Psychiatric Annals*, 2010, 40(7): 349–55

Hatzenbuehler, M. L., Keyes, K. M., and McLaughlin, K. A., 'The protective effects of social/contextual factors on psychiatric morbidity in LGB populations', *International Journal of Epidemiology*, 2011, 40(4): 1071–80

Hetrick, E. S., and Martin, A. D., 'Developmental issues and their resolution for gay and lesbian adolescents', *Journal of Homosexuality*, January 1987, 14(1–2): 25–43

Hopkins, Alex, 'Gay saunas: how many more will die?', *Beige*, 30 October 2012

King, Michael, *et al.*, 'A systematic review of mental disorder, suicide, and deliberate self harm in lesbian, gay and bisexual people', *BMC Psychiatry*, August 2008, 8(70); DOI: 10.1186/1471-244X-8-70

King, Michael, *et al.* 'Mental health and quality of life of gay men and lesbians in England and Wales: Controlled, cross-sectional study', *British Journal of Psychiatry*, December 2003, 183(6), 552–58; DOI: 10.1192/03-207

Kross, Ethan, et al., 'Facebook use predicts declines in subjective well-being in young adults', University of Michigan, 2013

Lamis, D. A., *et al.*, 'Body investment, depression and alcohol use as risk factors for suicide proneness in college students', *Crisis*, 2010, 31(3): 118–27

LGBT Foundation Manchester, *Part of the Picture: LGB people's drug and alcohol use in England 2009–14*, Lesbian and Gay Foundation and University of Lancaster, 2014

Mathy, R. M., 'Transgender identity and suicidality in a nonclinical sample', *Journal of Psychology & Human Sexuality*, 2003, 14(4): 47–65

Mays, V. M., and Cochran, S. D., 'Mental health correlates of perceived discrimination among lesbian, gay, and bisexual adults in the United States', *American Journal of Public Health*, 2001, 91(11): 1869–76

National AIDS Trust, *Boys Who Like Boys: a Study of Where Young MSM Learn about Sex, Relationships and HIV*, National AIDS Trust, 2015

PACE, *Risk & Resilience in LGBT+ People in England: New Report*, PACE, 2015

Plöderl, Martin, *et al.*, 'Suicide risk and sexual orientation: a critical review', *Archives of Sexual Behavior*, 26 February 2013, 42(7): 15–27

Public Health England, *Promoting the health and wellbeing of gay, bisexual and other men who have sex with men*, PHE Publications, June 2014

Shields, J. P., *et al.*, 'Impact of victimization on risk of suicide among lesbian, gay, and bisexual high school students in San Francisco', *Journal of Adolescent Health*, April 2012, 50(4): 418–20

Sigma Research, *What Constitutes the Best Sex Life for Gay and Bisexual Men? Implications for HIV Prevention*, BMC Public Health, 2013

Stonewall, *The School Report: the Experience of Gay Young People in Britain's Schools in 2012*, Stonewall, 2012

Stonewall, *The Teachers' Report 2014: Homophobic Bullying in Britain's Schools*, Stonewall, 2014

Todd, Matthew, 'How to Be Gay and Happy', *Attitude*, August 2010

Todd, Matthew, 'The Invisible Children', *Attitude*, March 2012

Acknowledgements

I am extraordinarily grateful to the many, many people who contributed to this book, especially those who were so honest and open about their most personal, private experiences in the hope that it might help other people. This was an act of community in itself, which has inspired me massively. I want to say a special thank-you to the parents who lost children, who gave me their time in the most difficult of circumstances. Meeting them profoundly moved me and gave me an unwavering conviction that all of this needed to be written about. I hope their experiences can help shine a light to a kinder, saner future.

Thank you to my publisher Brenda Kimber for her lengthy support and enthusiasm, and for championing this book (and for the Oprah book!), Alison 'best in the business' Barrow, Doug Young, Katrina Whone and all at Transworld for supporting this book, and to Sophie Missing for all her invaluable input and positivity. Most importantly, thank you to Brenda Updegraff for her outstanding editing, support, empathy, patience and for helping me see what needed to be said more clearly. This book was not an easy one for any of us to work on and I couldn't have done it without you. Thank you so much.

I owe a debt of gratitude to Justin Sanders, Vince Nicholls and Mike Buckley at Attitude Media, who generously allowed me substantial time out of the office when I needed it, even when it was inconvenient, and who always encouraged me to get it done(!). And special thanks to Andrew Fraser, Adam Mattera and then Cliff Joannou for enthusiasm and rising to the challenge of being thrown in at the deep end. Thank you to the staff of *Attitude*, old and new.

I'm so grateful for the support of Daniel Fulvio, *Attitude* Deputy Editor at the time when I first started writing about these issues, and for reading the first draft and giving me honest feedback, and to his lovely boyfriend, Martin Moriarty, for dinner, kindness and pep talks, which were all very much appreciated. (And to Lucky, my favourite hairy friend.) Thank you to Polly Vernon and Tracy McVeigh at the *Observer* for publicizing the 'Issues' issue, without which this wouldn't ever have been written. Thank you to all those who supported me or helped in many different ways, including Alexander Smith, Lee Jenkins, David Stuart, Pat Cash, Johann Hari, Tony Hallam, Max Gogarty, Will Fairman, Ian Drummond, Allan Stenhouse, Ben Summerskill, Ruth Hunt and Stonewall, Yusef Azad at the National AIDS Trust, Leigh Chislett and Dr Alan McOwan at 56 Dean Street, Paul Martin OBE and Andrew Gilliver and all at the LGBT Foundation, Tim Franks, PACE, to David and all at LGBT Birmingham, Sarah Graham, Monty Moncrieff at London Friend, Toni Hogg and all at Antidote, Paul Antrobus, Tony Gregory, Charlie Condou, Jeremy Goldstein, Dorothy Byrne, Neil Crombie, Joe Evans, Ian Marber, Fat Tony, Ste Softley, Patrick Doyle and everyone I spoke to for research.

For reading drafts and giving honest feedback: Matt Mueller, Cameron Laux, Wayne Dhesi, Tom Guy, Allan Stenhouse – thank you, I appreciate it.

Thank you to therapists David Smallwood for helping me understand the problem and for your time, care and kindness, and Paul Croal and Sheryl Close for supporting me across the years.

Extra special sparkly thanks to Hugh Berry and the Wanderers for their life-support system.

Special thanks also go to Paul Flynn, Matt Cain and Paris Lees for author-to-author advice, and for never call-diverting. (Almost never.) Extra-special gold-plated thanks to Simon Marks for showing me what change can look like.

I also want to express my love and thanks to my brother, sister-in-law and, especially, to my mum and dad. Recovery has taught me that no one's perfect; we are all a product of what came before us; we all make mistakes and do the best we can. Thank you for putting up with me. It can't have been easy having all this stuff laid out in public and I am grateful for your support of my career, now more so than ever. There's nothing to forgive from my side, but I am sorry for any of the times I have been a pain in the neck. You have been the most amazing parents, brother and sister-in-law and I love you all. Love too to the laughing gnome and his sister.

Thank you to the readers of *Attitude* who shared their stories with me and told me where we were going right and wrong, especially to those who wrote in about the 'Issues' issue and made me realize there was something in this.

Thank you to the member of the McQueen family who looked me in the eye and told me I was doing the right thing.

To my home group, for making it all doable.

To all the people of all different kinds who have been part of my recovery and helped me understand I was not alone.

Lastly, to my agent, Jon Elek, a (straight) man who listened to me with an open mind, intelligence and integrity, who got it when others did not. There's no way I could have written this without your relentless patience and support. From the bottom of my heart, thank you, thank you, thank you. I am so lucky to have you as my agent.

To Dr Simon Hazelwood for unwittingly starting it all off.

Finally, to Tim, for saving my life. The house is still burning, sister.

Text Acknowledgements

The author and publishers are grateful for permission to reproduce excerpts from the following:

Man Alive: 'Consenting Adults – Part 1: The Men', copyright © BBC 1967. Excerpts from *Healing the Shame That Binds You: Expanded and Updated Edition* by John Bradshaw, © 1988, 2005; reprinted with the permission of The Permissions Company, Inc., on behalf of Health Communications, Inc. Excerpt from *Chicago – The Musical* reproduced courtesy of the authors; music by John Kander and lyrics by Fred Ebb, book by Fred Ebb and Bob Fosse; © 1973, 1974 and 1975 by Kander-Ebb, Inc. Excerpt from 'How World of Warcraft helped me come out as transgender' by Laura Kate Dale, 2014, © Guardian News & Media Ltd 2016; reproduced by permission of GNM Ltd. Excerpt from 'Hercules And Love Affair's Andy Butler and John Grant: making music mined in the soul', 2014, © Guardian News & Media Ltd 2016; reproduced by permission of GNM Ltd. Excerpt from 'Hate crime is an everyday reality for gay people, expert warns', 2015, © The Telegraph; reproduced by permission of Dr Stevie-Jade Hardy. Extract from *The Invisible Man: A Self-help Guide for Men with Eating Disorders, Compulsive Exercise and Bigorexia* by John F. Morgan, © 2008; reproduced by permission of Routledge, an imprint of Taylor & Francis Group. Excerpt from 'Sugar is "addictive and the most dangerous drug of the times"', 2013, © The Telegraph; reproduced by permission of Telegraph Media Group Ltd. Excerpt from 'I've had 100 ops . . . I knew I'd die if I didn't get help', 2005, © The Sun; reproduced by permission of The Sun/News Syndication. Extract from *This Is Me* by Ian Thorpe, © 2012, 2014; reproduced by permission of Simon & Schuster UK Ltd. Excerpt from 'Rugby League star Keegan Hirst becomes first Brit player to come out as gay', 2015, © The Sunday Mirror; reproduced by permission of Mirrorpix. Excerpt from 'Healing Hands', words and music by Elton John and Bernie Taupin, © 1989 Rouge Booze Incorporated/HST Publishing Limited; Universal Music Publishing Limited; all rights reserved; international copyright secured; used by permission of Music Sales Limited. Excerpt from 'Thank U', words by Alanis Morissette, music by Alanis Morissette and Glan Ballard, © 1998, 1974 Music/Universal Music Corporation; Universal/MCA Music Limited; all rights reserved; international copyright secured; used by permission of Music Sales Limited. Extract from *Where the Wild Things Are*, © Sendak Estate 2015; reproduced by permission of Random House Children's, a division of Penguin Random House UK.

Index

About the Author

Matthew Todd was editor of *Attitude* between 2008 and 2016. His final issue featured Prince William, the first time a member of the Royal Family had ever posed for the cover of a gay magazine, and won him Scoop of the Year at the British Society of Magazine Editor Awards 2016. Matthew had previously won Editor of the Year 2011 (Men's Magazine Category) and 2015 (Men's Brand). In 2011 Stonewall named him Journalist of the Year and shortlisted him for Journalist of the Decade in 2015.

A sometime stand-up comedian, Matthew's play *Blowing Whistles* has been performed in London, the US and Sydney and received four-star reviews from the *Evening Standard*, *Sunday Express*, *Spectator*, *Time Out* and Whatsonstage.com, where Michael Coveney described it as 'the brightest gay play in ages' and the West End Whingers as 'the best gay play since *Beautiful Thing*'. He appears regularly on TV and radio, and in 2017 wrote and presented a short film for BBC *Newsnight*. In 2017 *Straight Jacket* was voted LGBT Book of the Year by readers of *Boyz* magazine and shortlised for the Polari Prize and Matthew was awarded the Freedom of the City of London for services to the LGBT community. He lives in London.